The Atlas of ATLANTIS
and other lost civilizations

The Atlas of

ATLANTIS

and other lost civilizations

Discover the history and wisdom of Atlantis, Lemuria, Mu and other ancient civilizations

JOEL LEVY

A GODSFIELD BOOK
www.godsfield.co.uk

For Miki, Mark, Nick, Matt, Larry and Maugan

First published in Great Britain in 2007
by Godsfield Press,
a division of
Octopus Publishing Group Ltd
2–4 Heron Quays,
London E14 4JP

Distributed in the United States and Canada by
Sterling Publishing Co., Inc.
387 Park Avenue South, New York, NY 10016–8810

ISBN-13: 978-1-84181-315-8
ISBN-10: 1-84181-315-X

A CIP catalogue record for this book
is available from the British Library

Printed and bound in China

2 4 6 8 10 9 7 5 3 1

CONTENTS

INTRODUCTION   6

Part 1
PLATO'S ATLANTIS   12

Part 2
THE MEDITERRANEAN WORLD   26

Part 3
THE AMERICAS –
ATLANTIS AND THE NEW WORLD   46

Part 4
THE ATLANTIC OCEAN   60

Part 5
THE PACIFIC –
ATLANTIS, MU AND LEMURIA   78

Part 6
THE WEST INDIES   100

Part 7
ANTARCTICA   112

Part 8
THE INDIAN OCEAN   118

Part 9
LEGENDARY LANDS OF THE CELTS   130

Part 10
OTHER LOST WORLDS   140

Part 11
ATLANTIS AND THE NEW AGE   160

BIBLIOGRAPHY   166

INDEX   168

ACKNOWLEDGEMENTS   176

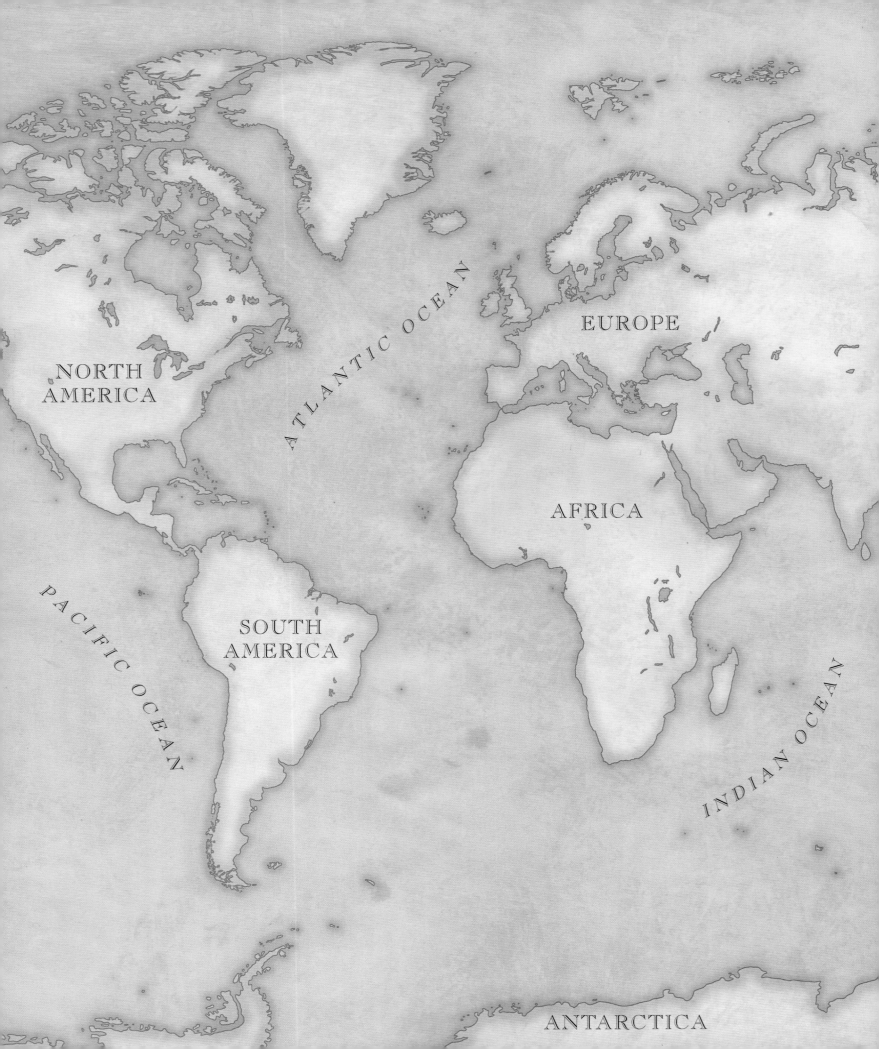

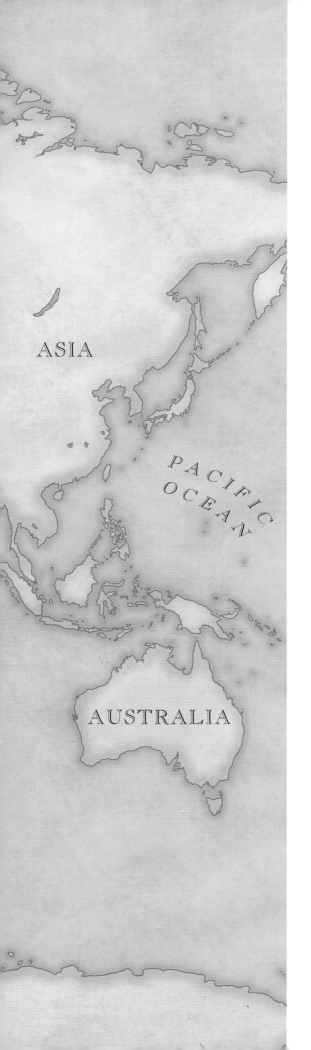

ASIA

PACIFIC OCEAN

AUSTRALIA

INTRODUCTION

Atlantis exists in the borderlands between history and fiction, fact and folklore. To find it, one needs a complex and unique combination of geography, history, mysticism, anthropology, mythology, philosophy, archeology and biography. But the search itself is rewarding and fascinating – in many ways more revealing than the actual discovery of Atlantis could ever be.

Read this book and join that search. Explore every corner of the Earth, from the Poles to the tropical rainforests, from the depths of the oceans to the interior of the planet, and encounter cultures, people and ideas from every period of history. Span the arc of human imagination, from the darkest recesses of evil to the grandest visions of light. By the time you have finished you will have learned about the epic march of human history and the grand sweep of spiritual evolution, and will have opened a treasure trove of arcane trivia. You may even form your own ideas about where and how to seek Atlantis.

The eternal city

Estimates of the number of books written on Atlantis run into hundreds and even thousands. And Atlantis is just one of dozens of lost lands and mythical places thrown up by cultures throughout history and around the world. That you are reading this book suggests that you share with these legions of writers a personal interest in Atlantis. But just where did the idea of Atlantis come from? How has it changed over the years, and what does it mean today? Why is the notion of lost lands in general, and Atlantis in particular, so beguiling?

As Part 1 describes in detail, the first mention of Atlantis comes in the writings of Plato, an ancient Greek philosopher and statesman who lived in the 5th and 4th centuries BCE. In two works known as the *Dialogue of Timaeus* and the *Dialogue of Critias*, Plato describes an island continent upon which flourished a very prosperous kingdom that became the centre of a powerful empire before being destroyed in a colossal natural disaster caused by the gods as punishment for its hubris. Plato tells at length how the story of Atlantis was preserved and came down to him, and describes the founding, history, geography and constitution of Atlantis. To the educated elite of the Classical world, Plato's Atlantis was well known, although opinions vary as to whether it was considered to be a fiction or a description of a real place.

Opinions are still divided today, although many Atlantologists (people who study Atlantis) and the general public often have a

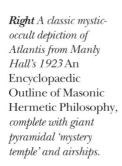

Right A classic mystic-occult depiction of Atlantis from Manly Hall's 1923 An Encyclopaedic Outline of Masonic Hermetic Philosophy, complete with giant pyramidal 'mystery temple' and airships.

very different picture of Atlantis from the one Plato painted in prose nearly two and half thousand years ago. Today's Atlantis is a complex composite of different versions propounded through the ages – from Plato's original, through the wild theories of mystics, visionaries and seers in the 19th and 20th centuries, to the purely fictional versions of more recent sci-fi/fantasy writers, filmmakers and artists. A typical modern description of Atlantis might include pyramids, crystals, telepathy and flying vehicles, none of which feature in Plato's

version. He describes a tropical country bounded by mountains, with a fertile plain criss-crossed with irrigation works, in the middle of which sat a glorious capital city of concentric canals, centred on a fortified hill (or Acropolis) of palaces and temples. While undoubtedly magnificent, Plato's Atlantis was more like an exaggerated version of cities and states with which he would have been familiar, but with bronze rather than iron as the main metal – in other words, a highly advanced Bronze Age civilization. He even gives a specific date for its peak: 9500 BCE.

The problem for Atlantologists is that conventional history recognizes no evidence for a Bronze Age civilization of any kind from that period, let alone an advanced one on the scale of Atlantis. In the conventional chronology, 9500 BCE is deep in the Stone Age, a period of prehistory when humankind was, at best, taking its first steps in agriculture and had not yet mastered metallurgy, writing, monumental construction or even the art of living in towns or cities. So there is a serious disjunction between Plato's claims and what archeology tells us.

Below An evocative depiction of the archetypal flood survival motif, in Hermann Hendrich's End of Atlantis*; the Atlantis story should be seen in the context of the near-universal deluge myth.*

THE SOURCE

Nonetheless millions of people over the millennia have remained convinced that Plato did not simply make up the lost land of Atlantis. Partly this is due to the nature of his description – its matter-of-fact tenor and the level of detail he provides are convincing. But there is a deeper reason for the persistent popularity of Atlantis as a concept, and this is linked to the way in which it has changed from (in Plato's conception) one of several contesting but roughly equivalent states, to the much grander role accorded to it by modern Atlantology. This is due to the intriguing similarity beteen the myths of many of the world's cultures, particularly ones regarding origins, culture heroes (figures who establish civilizations or teach the tenets of civilization), floods and other natural disasters.

The best-known examples of this cross-cultural continuity are flood myths. In the West, the most familiar flood myth is the tale of Noah's Ark and the biblical Deluge, but Noah's story mirrors others, such as those of Utnapishtim from the ancient Babylonian *Epic of Gilgamesh*, the ancient Greek Deucalion, Matsya from the Hindu Puranas, and Viracocha of the Incas, to name but a few. Alongside these are myths that tell of culture heroes from far away (often across the ocean), and of how the secrets of agriculture, writing, building and other technologies came to be learned. To laymen and experts alike, the commonality of such stories suggests a single shared source, and by extension a shared history: in other words, the possibility that widely separated cultures might owe their origins to a common source. This concept is known as 'diffusionism', because it implies that civilization – or at least the technologies that constitute civilization – arose in one place and diffused around the world, rather than arising separately from different centres of innovation, which is the conventional, mainstream view.

The evolution of Atlantology

Diffusionism is of central importance to the story of Atlantis, because it led to the promotion of Atlantis from a historical footnote to a far more exalted role as the Mother of Civilizations – the Ur-civilization at the start of human history and the crucible of humankind's greatest achievements.

Below *This 1664 map of Atlantis by Athanasius Kircher is among the best-known depictions of the geography of Atlantis. Note that north is at the bottom of the map.*

haphazard use of emerging discoveries in disciplines such as archeology, anthropology and linguistics. Donnelly and others marshalled this evidence to 'prove' that all the major civilizations of world history owed their existence to Atlantis, and had been founded either by Atlantean colonists or by refugees fleeing from the cataclysmic destruction of the continent.

Hot on the heels of the Proto-scientific phase came a second, equally influential phase, which might be termed Mystical Atlantology. Inspired by the writings of Donnelly and others (and doubtless encouraged by their best-selling status), a number of mystics, seers and visionaries produced their own interpretations of Atlantis, often using occult means (such as astral travel or channelling the spirits of the dead) to gain their information. Mystical Atlantology added many significant elements to the modern conception of Atlantis, such as telepathy, crystal power and flying vehicles.

FURTHER DEVELOPMENTS

By the late 20th century, however, advances in the sciences – especially geology – had seriously undermined the claims of previous generations of Atlantologists, by apparently proving that no lost continents could ever have existed in the Atlantic or elsewhere. But Atlantis refused to die, instead giving rise to a new phase – Revisionist Atlantology. This suggested that Plato should not be taken literally, but was referring to a prehistoric super-civilization unknown to present-day historians, the discovery of which would be one of the great archeological finds of all time.

Revisionist Atlantologists have since sought Atlantis in almost every corner of the globe, and today it is virtually impossible for an ancient civilization of any significance to be discovered without someone in the media suggesting a link to Atlantis. Most Revisionist Atlantologists do not make grand diffusionist claims for their candidates, but some of the most eye-catching examples of recent years, such as the theories of Graham Hancock (as later described in Part 7), are in the diffusionist tradition.

It was the 19th-century writings of Ignatius Donnelly, as detailed in Part 4, expounding his diffusionist theory, that really put Atlantis on the modern intellectual map. With Donnelly came the first major step in the evolution of Atlantology, which had more or less stagnated since the Classical Era. His work ushered in many similar diffusionist theories, such as those regarding the lost continents of Mu and Lemuria, in what might be called the Proto-scientific phase of Atlantology. This was characterized by its liberal, but uncritical and

ATLANTIS AS A TOPICAL ISSUE

Modern-day affection for Atlantis and other lost lands can be seen as part of a long tradition of hankering after a Golden Age. The ancient Greeks viewed their age as a sadly diminished echo of blessed former eras, while the biblical tale of Eden, the Fall and the expulsion from Paradise is central to Judaeo-Christian traditions. In the story of Atlantis, Plato created (or reported?) a new myth, but one that has been taken to heart over the millennia because it illustrates powerfully this ancient tradition. The central narrative of Atlantis – a world of bountiful blessings and primitive but noble values, which becomes corrupted through materialism and hubris – perfectly articulated the concerns that exercised the ancient Greeks. Today, this narrative seems more relevant than ever. A rising level of eco-awareness and a growing fear that technological-industrial civilization is going to bring environmental collapse down on our heads, is matched with increasing mistrust of the values and hubris of modern consumer-capitalist society and 'globalism'. In this context Atlantis serves as a powerful metaphor for the future, even as, for the ancient Greeks, it encapsulated the past.

HOW THIS BOOK WORKS

This book covers all four phases of the evolution of Atlantology, from the original Classical conception, through the Proto-scientific and Mystical phases to the most up-to-date Revisionist theories. As befits an atlas, it is arranged primarily along geographical lines, so that each of the first nine sections refers to a specific region, the lost lands associated with it, and the related theories, personalities, debates and histories.

Part 1 explores Plato's account of Atlantis and his life and world, while Part 2 details the most important theories about Atlantis in the Mediterranean, most of which fall under the Revisionist approach. Part 3 looks at the Americas, investigating theories that link Atlantis and other lost lands to the New World. Part 4 explores the Atlantic region, introducing in particular the influential Proto-scientific Atlantology of Ignatius Donnelly. Part 5 concentrates on the Pacific region and on Lemuria and Mu, 'sister' lost continents to Atlantis, while Part 6 focuses on the work of Edgar Cayce and others who link Atlantis to the West Indies. Part 7 looks at Graham Hancock's development of ideas

Above Artist Andrew C. Stewart's Atlantis Submerged *depicts a drowned world accessible only to the denizens of the deep but awaiting potential discovery by advanced submersible technology.*

about an Antarctic super-civilization, while Part 8 investigates Indian Ocean sites that have been linked to prehistoric civilizations on land exposed during the last Ice Age, but subsequently deluged.

Part 9 shifts the focus back to the Atlantic coast of Europe, specifically its intersection with the geography of fairyland, covering several legendary places from the Celtic world. Part 10 covers lost worlds that either do not fit any of the other regional categorizations or do not relate directly to Atlantis. Finally, Part 11 examines the Atlantis phenomenon in the context of New Age thought, and assesses the spiritual and environmental lessons that have been drawn from it.

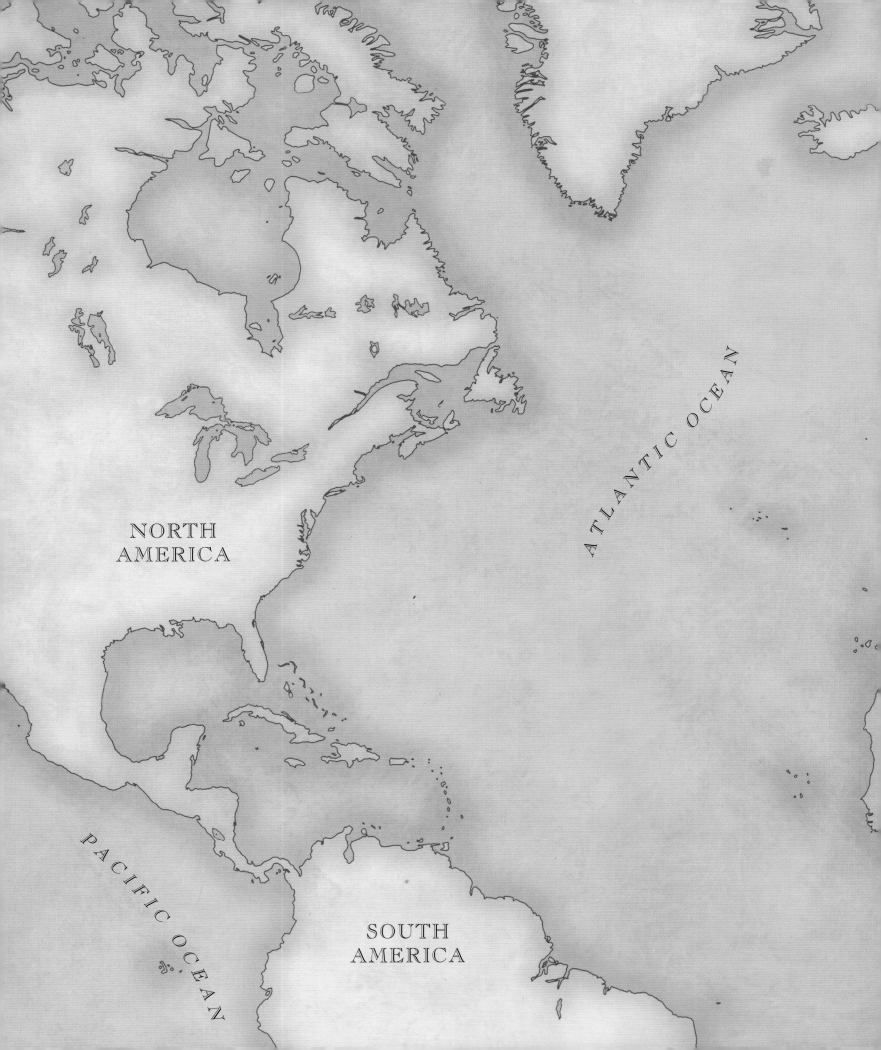

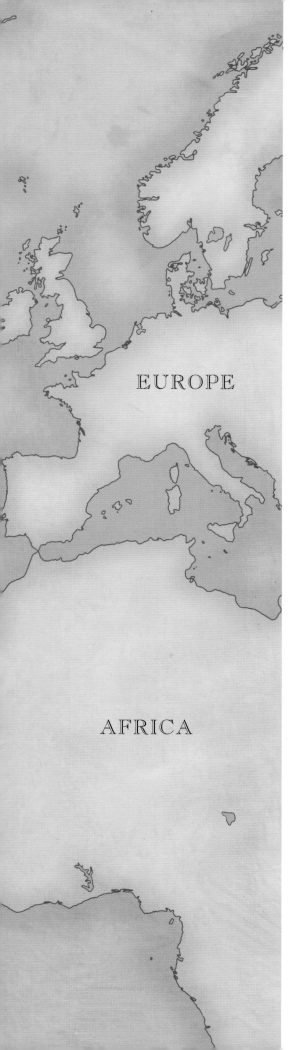

PART 1

PLATO'S ATLANTIS

'In this island of Atlantis there was a great and wonderful empire.' So begins the description of the legendary island continent in Plato's *Dialogue of Timaeus*, one of the primary sources of subsequent knowledge about Atlantis. In this and his *Dialogue of Critias*, Plato explains the geography, politics and history of Atlantis and its relationship to the Mediterranean world, both in his own era and some 9,000 years before.

Plato seems to place his lost continent squarely in the Atlantic, the ocean that derived its name from the mighty kingdom. This section examines his original story of Atlantis, including the process by which he claimed to have learned of it, the details he divulged, why it came to be destroyed, and the lessons and morals that he drew from the fabulous island kingdom.

Atlantis and Egypt

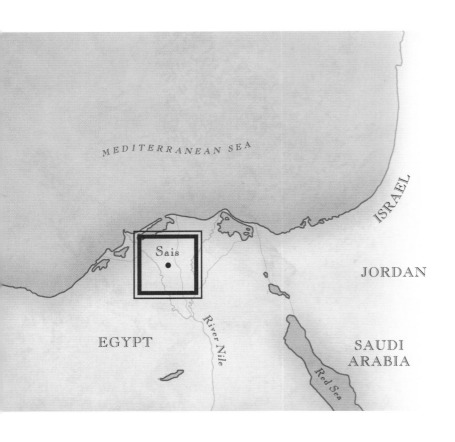

MEDITERRANEAN SEA

ISRAEL

Sais

JORDAN

EGYPT

River Nile

SAUDI ARABIA

Red Sea

Ancient Egypt plays a central role in the Atlantis myth for several reasons. According to Plato, it was Egypt that preserved the knowledge of Atlantis when all other nations had forgotten it, while according to later scholars, Egypt itself was the foremost inheritor of the Atlantean legacy.

In Plato's dialogue *Timaeus*, he describes in detail how he came into possession of the knowledge of Atlantis. He makes it clear that he acquired the story via his great-grandfather Critias, who in turn heard it from his grandfather (also called Critias), who learned it from his father Dropides, who heard it from his cousin Solon.

Solon (640–560 BCE) himself had learned the story during his travels in Egypt in about 590 BCE, when he visited the Nile delta city of Sais, capital of the 26th pharaonic dynasty and a major centre of religion and learning. There Solon had met the high priest Psonchis, and heard tell of the great nation the Egyptians called Etelenty, the history of which they had preserved for an incredible 9,000 years.

Psonchis chided Solon and the Athenians for being 'nothing but children' when it came to knowledge of history, and explained that this was partly because regular natural disasters had destroyed the records kept by his Greek ancestors. Egypt, Psonchis boasted, was spared such calamities by virtue of its geography, and so the ancient knowledge had been preserved, written down by scribes

and carved into a pillar in the temple, which Solon himself observed and which Psonchis translated for him.

THE WISE MAN OF ATHENS

Solon was a figure of major importance in the early history of Athens – a warrior, poet, statesman and lawmaker, he was known as one of the Seven Wise Men of Athens. Returning from his visit to Egypt, Solon began an epic verse called *Atlantikos*, although he never completed the poem. It is often assumed that the unfinished manuscript (or perhaps a copy of it) must have come into the possession of Plato, which would explain how he knew about Atlantis in such detail.

THE PYRAMID CONNECTION

As the myth of Atlantis has developed in more recent times and authors such as Ignatius Donnelly (see pages 62–65) began to look for archeological, linguistic and scientific evidence of the prior existence of Atlantis, Egypt began to assume a quite different role in the tale. In *Timaeus*, Psonchis makes it clear that Egypt was not yet a nation

when Atlantis ruled the known world and that the kingdom of the pharaohs only began 500–1,000 years after the fall of Atlantis – that is, *c*.8500 BCE (although conventional historical scholarship suggests this is wildly improbable and that unified nations first arose in Egypt around 3500 BCE).

Later theories, formulated in the 19th and 20th centuries, proposed that Egypt itself owed its existence to Atlantis. According to this line of argument, Egypt was founded either by Atlantean colonists while Atlantis still existed or by refugees from the fall of the once-mighty civilization. They brought with them much of their knowledge, wisdom and science, including the arts of writing, architecture, monumental masonry, medicine, and so on, as well as their religion and culture. Although much of this knowledge was eventually lost, enough survived to enable the Egyptians to build the pyramids, the Sphinx and many other great feats of architecture, and to enjoy a level of linguistic, medical, scientific and cultural sophistication that might otherwise be hard to explain.

The main evidence for this controversial theory (largely dismissed by conventional

Egyptologists when it was first proposed and derided by modern historians) comprised the similarities between Egyptian and other civilizations, including ones that were separated by the Atlantic Ocean, which in the conventional reading had never had any contact with one another. Donnelly and other subsequent Atlantean scholars pointed to the construction of pyramids in cultures as far apart as Egypt, Central America (the Aztecs and Maya), South America (the Incas and earlier civilizations), the Canaries and even the Pacific Islands. Parallels were drawn between Egyptian hieroglyphs and Mayan glyphs, while the Egyptian gods were linked to similar pantheons in Mayan, Aztec and other religions.

If widely separated civilizations have common elements, the natural conclusion is that these civilizations have common roots, and this is where Atlantis comes in. The theory is that the Atlantean colonists/refugees bequeathed their gods, writings and skills to the 'daughter civilizations' that they founded, and that although these subsequently evolved into the different forms we know today, the similarities between them reveal their common ancestry.

Right *Justus van Gent's* Solon (c.1476, *although there is some debate about whether this is actually a depiction of Aristotle). The Dutch master followed the conventions of the day in depicting the ancient poet, statesman and lawgiver in contemporary dress.*

THE CHAIN OF DESCENT OF ATLANTEAN LORE

Ancient Egyptians, *c.*9000 BCE, are conquered by Atlantis, but liberated by Athens

⬇

Egyptian priests and scholars record the events on papyri; later the information is transferred to columns in the Temple of Neith in Sais

⬇

Solon visits Sais, *c.*590 BCE, talks to Psonchis and begins his epic poem *Atlantikos*

⬇

Solon's relative Critias II (591–501 BCE) learns the tale

⬇

Critias III (born 511 BCE) learns the tale from his grandfather Critias II; then tells it to Socrates

⬇

Socrates (469–399 BCE) tells it to his student Plato (*c.*427–347 BCE), and/or Plato reads the manuscript of Solon's unfinished *Atlantikos*. Plato writes his *Dialogue of Timaeus* and *Dialogue of Critias c.*360 BCE

The city of Atlantis

Today's widespread concept of Atlantis, found in thousands of books, novels, articles and films, precious and inspiring to millions of people, can be traced back almost entirely to one man's description – the account provided by Plato in his Dialogue of Critias.

In Plato's account Atlantis is the name of both the island-continent and its capital city, and the two are usually used interchangeably. The city of Atlantis was a model ancient metropolis, wonderfully appointed with every marvel that Bronze Age civilization could offer.

Like ancient Athens, Atlantis was built around a mighty Acropolis – a citadel on a hill, consisting of a complex of palaces, temples, gardens and baths. When Poseidon took possession of the land, he chose the low mount as a suitable dwelling place for his concubine Cleitas and carved out three concentric rings of canals around it. The hill had a flattish top about 1 km (½ mile) across, and was furnished with two springs that Poseidon had caused to rise: one of warm water and one of cold, so that Cleitas and her five pairs of twins by Poseidon should have hot and cold running water. Later this was developed into the central Acropolis, while the concentric rings of land that surrounded it were subsequently built up to become the city of Atlantis.

At the absolute centre of the Acropolis was the 'holy of holies' – a shrine sacred to Cleitas and Poseidon. No one was allowed to enter, but offerings were made to the shrine in recognition of the fact that this was the place where the original ten kings of Atlantis first experienced what Plato calls 'the light' – presumably encountering their divine progenitor and receiving the laws of the land.

① THE TEMPLE OF POSEIDON

Next to the shrine was the Temple of Poseidon, which was about 200 x 100 m (660 x 330 ft), and was described by Plato as being of 'a strange barbaric appearance'. The whole of the outside was covered in silver, except for the pinnacles, which were gilded. The ceiling of the temple was made of ivory inlaid with gold, silver and orichalcum (thought to be some sort of copper-gold alloy, or an entirely unknown element, second in value only to gold), while all the other interior surfaces were also covered in orichalcum. The centrepiece of the temple was an elaborate statue of Poseidon himself, driving a chariot pulled by six winged horses and surrounded by a hundred Nereids (sea nymphs) riding on dolphins. The statue was so tall that Poseidon's head grazed the ceiling, and all of the figures were made of gold. More golden statues surrounded the outside of the temple, depicting the original kings, their wives and descendants, while the tributes of vassal nations added to the magnificence of the ornamentation.

② BATHS AND GARDENS

Surrounding the Temple of Poseidon were magnificent palaces, and alongside these cunning use had been made of the hot and cold springs that Poseidon had caused to flow. These bubbled up from fountains set in a shady courtyard inside a large building equipped with cisterns, baths and swimming pools for hot and cold bathing, which could be used even in winter. There were separate bath-houses for royalty, for citizens and for women only, and even baths for cattle and horses. The run-off from the baths and springs was used to feed beautiful pleasure gardens, known as the Groves of Poseidon, and was also conveyed to the outer circles of the city by an ingenious system of aqueducts, to create a water-supply system of the sort not seen again until the height of Roman civilization 10,000 years later.

③ THE PILLAR OF POSEIDON

In the Temple of Poseidon, in a position that Plato describes as the centre of the island (although presumably this does not mean geographically, since the Acropolis mount is elsewhere described as being towards the south), was a pillar of orichalcum, on one side of which were inscribed the laws of Atlantis as laid down by Poseidon. These constituted his covenant with the people of Atlantis, much as the Hebrews had their Ten Commandments. The laws governed relations between the ten kings and their peoples, and safeguarded the rights of each. Plato makes it clear that, so long as they were adhered to, these laws would allow for an equitable and enlightened system of government that could lead to a sort of paradise on Earth. On the other side of the pillar were inscribed terrible curses on those who disobeyed the laws.

④ THE BULL CULT OF ATLANTIS

Plato also describes an extraordinary bull cult centred on the Temple of Poseidon. Apparently bulls were allowed to roam the temple, and the ten kings, when they gathered together at five- and six-year intervals, would engage in a sacred bull hunt. They had to catch a bull without the use of weapons other than staves and nooses. When they had succeeded, they would cut its throat and let the blood pour over the Pillar, before using the rest of the bull as a burnt offering.

'The centrepiece of the temple was an elaborate statue of Poseidon himself, driving a chariot pulled by six winged horses.'

Plato

The central figure in the genesis of Atlantis is Plato, but who was he and why did he write about the lost continent? From what is known of him, is it possible to tell whether he might have invented Atlantis as a fable and, if so, what his motives may have been?

Probably the pre-eminent philosopher in Western thought, Plato has been so influential that modern philosopher A.N. Whitehead has described all subsequent philosophy as 'a series of footnotes to Plato'. He was also a poet, warrior, traveller, slave and teacher in his time. Born in Athens in 428 or 427 BCE to a family that claimed descent from the ancient Athenian kings, he lived through a period when the once-mighty city-state endured many vicissitudes of war, defeat, conquest and tyranny. As a young man, Plato became a disciple and close friend of Socrates, the ground-breaking and inquisitive philosopher who would later be sentenced to death to appease mob sentiment. Socrates' teachings and his unfortunate end both had a profound impact on Plato.

Appalled by the way Athens had treated his mentor and disgusted by what he felt the city-state had become, Plato travelled to other Greek states and Mediterranean civilizations, including Egypt. On his return to Athens he served in the army and was decorated, and began to write philosophical treatises. Later he lived in Greek colonies in Italy and Sicily, studying, teaching and getting involved in politics. At one point Plato was captured by his enemies and enslaved, but escaped. He set up an academy, or school of philosophy, in Athens, before returning to Sicily as an advisor to the king of Syracuse. Eventually he retired to Athens to write his last three books, two of which were the dialogues *Timaeus* and *Critias*.

ATLANTIS IN CONTEXT

Plato wrote on an amazing variety of subjects, covering everything from metaphysics to ethics, education to religion, aesthetics to mathematics. In relation to Atlantis, his most relevant interests were those to do with politics and his ideas about the perfect state and the perfect form of government. The trial and execution of Socrates had marked him deeply, instilling a suspicion (if not loathing) of the danger of mob rule and what could happen if the uneducated and unvirtuous were allowed too much say in affairs. In his seminal work *The Republic*, and

Left A Roman bust of the philosopher Plato, after a Greek original. A bust such as this might have graced the home of a wealthy person with pretensions to a philosophical education, for the work of Plato – including the story of Atlantis – was well known to educated Romans.

in several later works including *Timaeus* and *Critias*, he set out his ideas for the perfect state, which can best be described as a sort of enlightened despotism, led by a benevolent philosopher-king, whose sound mental training and moral virtues would ensure justice and prosperity.

Classical scholars usually argue, therefore, that Plato wrote about Atlantis because he wanted to give an illustration of an ideal state and how the practice of his ideas would affect its historical fate. What many people do not realize is that the ideal state he wrote about was not Atlantis, but Athens. In *Timaeus* it is explained that Atlantis had become an overbearing imperial power and was attempting to subjugate the last independent lands of the known world; and that only

Athens, the most virtuous state, stood against it. Atlantis is presented as a contrasting example of the way in which a state can start off with many blessings and virtues, (for instance the natural mineral and agricultural bounty of the continent, and the political system of carefully divided tenfold kingship of the Atlanteans, their commitment to the rule of law and their respect for the rights of their citizens) but go sadly astray (see pages 22–23).

Above The Parthenon in Athens was completed less than a decade before the birth of Plato. The Parthenon sat atop the Athenian Acropolis, an obvious potential source of inspiration for Plato's description of the Atlantean Acropolis.

'*What many people do not realize is that the ideal state Plato wrote about was not Atlantis, but Athens.*'

The Atlantean city and surrounds

In Plato's account Atlantis is the name of both the island-continent and its capital city, and the two are usually used interchangeabley, as when referring to Rome the city and Rome the ancient empire. The city of Atlantis was a model ancient metropolis, wonderfully appointed with every marvel that Bronze Age civilization could offer.

Plato's characters explain that Atlantis was a rich and bountiful land of mountains and plains, with a great capital towards the southern end of the island. The continent was roughly oblong in shape, with high mountains near the coast and a broad, flat plain in the interior. It was about 550 km (340 miles) long in one direction and 370 km (230 miles) wide in the other. The land was higher in the north and sloped away to the south. Much of the original landscaping of the island continent had been created by the god Poseidon, who had taken it as his personal fiefdom in the mists of prehistory and subsequently divided it up between his descendants.

> *'The Atlanteans were great builders, constructing many temples, palaces, harbours and docks.'*

① RULERS OF ATLANTIS

Atlantis was divided into ten portions so that each of Poseidon's sons should have a princedom of their own. The eldest son Atlas, was overlord of the whole continent; hence its name. The ten princes met at the Temple of Poseidon (see page 16) at intervals of five and six years, alternately, to air any grievances and pass judgements.

② CANALS

The Acropolis was surrounded by its three concentric rings of canals, carved out by Poseidon to guard Cleitas. Later their descendants built bridges over the canals for roads, and dug channels for naval access. The outer canal and the strip of land between it and the next one were three *stadia* wide – roughly 0.5 km (⅓ mile).

⑤ IRRIGATION

The entire central plain was irrigated by huge ditches – one ran for nearly 200 km (125 miles) around the whole centre of the continent, while subsidiary ditches criss-crossed the land.

⑥ TRANSPORT

The canals were used to transport wood, food and other goods from the towns and villages in the mountains to those on the plains and, in particular, to the capital and the ships that plied the great canal linked to the sea.

⑦ MASTER BUILDERS

The Atlanteans were great builders, constructing many temples, palaces, harbours and docks. Each ring of land in the city was encircled by a huge wall, set with towers and gates where the bridges and tunnels passed through. The outer wall was covered in brass, the middle one in tin, while the third glowed a coppery-red because it was covered in orichalcum (see page 16).

⑧ AQUEDUCTS

Aqueducts carried water to the outer circles of the city, where there were more temples, gardens and civic buildings, including *gymnasia* and *stadia*. In particular, a great racecourse 180 m (600 ft) wide ran round the entire length of the central circle of the city. White, black and red stone was dug from quarries within the city, and the buildings of the capital were constructed from a mixture of the three types.

⑨ GREATER ATLANTIS

Beyond the central zones and canals, the city spread out within another great wall, which encircled the whole region, beginning and ending where the canal met the sea. Here was a great harbour and extensive docks. 'Greater Atlantis City' was thus about 15–20 km (9–12 miles) in diameter. Given that Plato described it as 'densely crowded with habitations', it must have been a mighty metropolis with a large population.

⑩ ATLANTEAN ARMY

The central plain was divided into administrative units of 10 *stadia* (roughly 2 km/1¼ miles) square, 60,000 in all. Each unit was responsible for raising a levy of various types of troops and one-sixth of a war-chariot team, so that the total Atlantean army included 10,000 chariots and a vast multitude of foot soldiers.

③ MINERAL WEALTH

The continent was blessed with mineral wealth, and the mountains were dotted with mines where the Atlanteans dug for ore, especially the legendary mineral orichalcum. Within the Acropolis' Temple of Poseidon was a mighty pillar made entirely of orichalcum on which were carved the laws of the land.

④ NATURAL BOUNTY

Atlantis was thickly wooded and teemed with both domestic and wild animals, including many elephants. The soil was very fertile and a huge abundance and variety of plants grew there, from fruits and nuts to pulses and vegetables. The irrigation system enabled the citizens to grow two crops a year. The Atlanteans thus ate a rich and varied diet.

The destruction of Atlantis

Most cultures have myths of a Golden Age when humankind was happy and carefree, but which came to an end with a calamitous Fall. Atlantis exemplifies this eternal drama, combining it with elements of the flood myth.

Plato's first mention of Atlantis is in his dialogue *Timaeus*, in which the character of Critias gives a rather terse account of the continent's cataclysmic demise: 'there occurred violent earthquakes and floods; and in a single day and night of misfortune ... the island of Atlantis ... disappeared in the depths of the sea'. Critias goes on to explain that the lost land lay just below the surface of the ocean, creating an impassable mud-shoal just beyond the Pillars of Hercules, blocking the passage from the Mediterranean into the Atlantic Ocean. He also points out that the Atlanteans were not the only victims of this catastrophe – the Athenian army, which had just conquered Atlantis and thus liberated the subject peoples of the Mediterranean from oppression, was also lost in the disaster, even at the moment of their greatest glory.

THE WRATH OF ZEUS

In his subsequent dialogue *Critias*, Plato gives a lot more detail, both about Atlantis and why it came to be destroyed. Initially Atlantis enjoyed a Golden Age of plenty, with just rule by worthy kings, during which all Atlanteans were virtuous and noble. But it fell from grace when 'human nature got the upper hand' and the Atlanteans became corrupted by their power and glory. Plato writes that, even though to the unsophisticated eye 'they appeared glorious and blessed', in truth 'they were full of avarice and unrighteous power'.

Zeus, the lord of the gods, who is represented by Plato as a just and righteous god (although this is not the case in most Greek myth), observed what had become of

Left A common motif in flood stories is the dispatch of a bird to search for dry land. In the story of Noah's Ark the bird is a dove, but in the Babylonian version – the story of Utnapishtim – the bird is a raven, here shown picking through the bodies of the flood's victims as it searches for land.

the Atlanteans and resolved to punish them – apparently for their own good! Supposedly he felt that appropriate punishment would 'chasten and improve' them. The *Critias* dialogue breaks off before explaining exactly what Zeus did next, but it is clear from the earlier work that the end result was a cataclysm of earthquakes and tsunamis that submerged the entire island continent.

OTHER FALL AND FLOOD MYTHS

If the story of the fall of Atlantis seems familiar, it is because it closely resembles myths possessed by most cultures and religions of the world: myths of the Fall and the flood. Perhaps the most obvious examples in Western culture are the expulsion of Adam and Eve from the Garden of Eden and the story of Noah's Ark. The Atlantis story mirrors both of these – man falls from a state of innocence and so loses his

place in a god-given paradise of plenty, and then is punished by God for his sins by a great deluge that destroys nations. Similar flood legends are found from India to the Amazon. The Greeks themselves had the legend of Deucalion, who receives divine warning to build an ark and so survives a great deluge visited upon sinful humankind by the wrathful gods.

So it is tempting to see Plato's story of Atlantis as drawing on these pre-existing myths, many of which he would have known, and there is no doubt that the destruction of Atlantis is supposed to be a moral fable, even if it also a true account of historical events. Later interpretations of the Atlantis story try to remove the divine agent of destruction and blame it instead on the scientific or occult hubris of the Atlanteans themselves, who are said to have triggered the cataclysm through their own technology or by magic.

Above A medieval engraving of the tale of Deucalion. Deucalion was the ancient Greek equivalent of Noah, although his ark carried only himself and his wife Pyrrha. When they reached dry land they repopulated the Earth by tossing stones over their shoulders that were transformed into people.

Plato's Atlantis – the evidence

A civilization as mighty and powerful as Atlantis and with colonies in many lands should surely have left some hard evidence that it once existed. Equally, an island continent should have left geological traces. The most compelling proof of the authenticity of Plato's account of Atlantis would be archeological evidence in the form of buildings, cities, coins, artwork, inscriptions, arms and armour and other artefacts. Meanwhile geological evidence should show some physical traces of an island continent in the Atlantic.

The most suggestive evidence that Plato's Atlantis never existed is that there is no physical evidence. There are no remains, no inscriptions, no artefacts – in fact, there is nothing to suggest there was any form of civilization whatsoever at the time Plato says Atlantis existed. He clearly describes a high Bronze Age culture, of the sort that did not arise until 3000 BCE at the earliest, more than 6,000 years after the date Plato gives for the destruction of Atlantis. In the Atlantis story, Plato also describes Athens as a similar culture, but there is no evidence that the Greeks reached this level of sophistication until around 1600 BCE.

In Plato's account the Atlanteans are also said to have established colonies in the continent to the west of Atlantis (presumably America) and on the east of the Atlantic, as well as having conquered most of the western Mediterranean. So even if Atlantis itself was sunk beneath the waves with the loss of any archeological evidence, there should be remains left in lands that survived – yet nothing like this has been found. Remember, however, that absence of evidence is not evidence of absence. In other words, just because no evidence of Atlantis has been found does not prove it never existed.

UNDER THE SEA

According to Plato, the large land-mass that was Atlantis was submerged just below the waves, so surely it should be easy to identify. In reality there is no sunken land-mass that matches his description. In Victorian times it was argued that islands such as the Canaries and the Azores were the last remnants of Atlantis – high peaks in the mountains of the original continent, which remained above water after the rest had sunk to the ocean floor. But advances in the understanding of geology and plate tectonics (the processes by which the surface of the Earth is shaped) have shown that this is not possible.

It is now known that the surface of the planet is made up of plates – giant slabs of rock that slide around on top of a molten layer beneath. Most of the plates are on the ocean floor. Running down the middle of the

Below An aerial view of Graciosa Island, one of the Canary Islands in the Atlantic. In the 19th century it was believed that islands like these might be the mountain peaks of sunken Atlantis, projecting above the waves.

Atlantic, for instance, there is a boundary between two plates where new rock is being formed and the ocean floor is spreading out from here (the boundary is marked by the Mid-Atlantic Ridge, a system of undersea mountain ranges, faults and ridges that, when it was first discovered by Victorian oceanographers, was interpreted by some as the remnants of Atlantis. This ocean-floor material is made of a different rock from the continental land-masses, which makes it impossible for the lighter, less dense continental lands to sink into it. The Azores and the Canaries were created by local hotspots of magma welling up through the ocean floor to create volcanoes, which grew until they projected far above the sea bottom. In other words, they are not relics of a lost land-mass, but separate geological entities of independent origin.

PLATO AND DIFFERENT TYPES OF TRUTH

The archeological and geological evidence certainly suggests that Plato made Atlantis up (probably to serve a philosophical point), yet Critias, one of the characters in the dialogues, insists that the tale is true. Does this mean Plato is saying that it is literally true? Atlantean scholar Stephen Hodge points out that Plato might have recognized different types of truth: 'For Plato, even myths may at times be true, even though they refer to palpably fictitious events.' Therefore, by embodying a philosophical or ethical truth, a myth can be true even when it is not literally true. Perhaps this is what was really going on in Plato's account of Atlantis, and perhaps this is how we should look at the story today.

***Above** The imposing peaks of the Azores suggested to many Atlantologists that Plato's story was feasible and that remnants of the Atlantean land-mass must lie below the surrounding ocean.*

EUROPE

Tartessos

Carthage

Helike

Troy

Tan

Thera

Crete

M E D I T E R R A N E A N   S E A

AFRICA

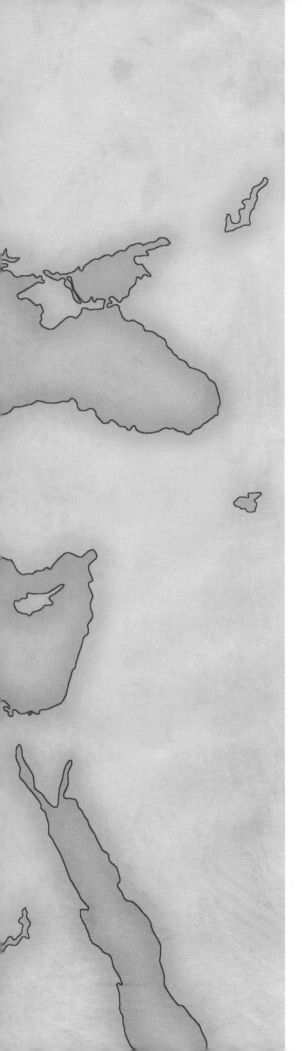

PART 2

THE MEDITERRANEAN WORLD

In the light of the implausibility of Plato's account of Atlantis being literally true, many scholars have tried to salvage Atlantis with a new synthesis stating that Plato drew on legends of a real place, but made mistakes in the way the story was translated or transmitted, or was confused about dates and measurements.

Given that Plato and his alleged sources were very much part of the Mediterranean world, many historians, writers and theorists have naturally sought the 'true' origins or inspiration of Atlantis within the Mediterranean itself. Locations as varied as eastern Spain, North Africa, the Aegean and western Turkey have been plausibly suggested. This section looks in detail at these locations. It covers the ancient disaster that befell the Greek city of Helike, which may have inspired Plato, and looks at a range of other ancient lost cities, states and civilizations of the Mediterranean, each of which is claimed by its exponents to be the 'true Atlantis'.

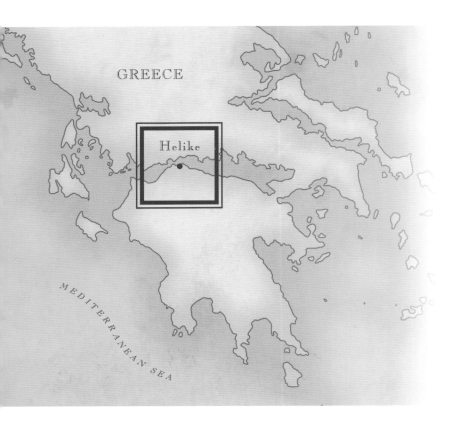

GREECE

Helike

MEDITERRANEAN SEA

Helike – the lost city

Whereas most Atlantologists look for the 'true Atlantis' in the mists of prehistory, one intriguing suggestion is that Plato drew his inspiration not from ancient history, but on events during his own lifetime, and that the real Atlantis was the lost city-state of Helike.

Helike was at one time the leading Greek city-state in Classical Greece, a prosperous and dynamic political, military and economic force that led the coalition of city-states known as the Achaean League. It founded colonies around the eastern Mediterranean and was renowned and revered as a centre for the worship of Poseidon. Helike lay on the Gulf of Corinth in Achaea, on the north coast of the Peloponnese peninsula.

One night in 373 BCE Helike was wiped off the face of the Earth by a tremendous cataclysm, as a massive earthquake and lethal tsunami combined to sink it beneath the waves. The political map of Greece was changed at a stroke, and the territory previously commanded by Helike was now seized by its neighbours.

PLATO AND HELIKE

The destruction of Helike happened when Plato was about 54, and he must have known about it. He would also have realized this was just one of a series of devastating earthquakes to afflict Greece over the previous 50 years, several of which had

had enormous military and political repercussions through their destruction of armies and cities. Around 17 years later he came to write his *Dialogue of Timaeus* and *Dialogue of Critias* and record the legend of Atlantis.

HELIKE AND ATLANTIS

There are several parallels between Helike and Atlantis that lend credence to the suggestion that this city-state was the true inspiration for Plato's ideas:

- Both were powerful city-states that had founded colonies.
- Both worshipped Poseidon as their principal god and had important sanctuaries to the sea-deity in the centre of their respective capitals.
- Both were destroyed in a matter of hours by the terrible combined cataclysm of earthquake and flood.
- Both disappeared completely beneath the engulfing waves.

 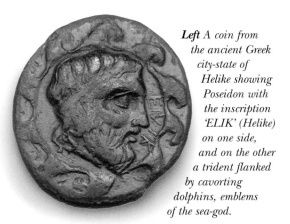

Left A coin from the ancient Greek city-state of Helike showing Poseidon with the inscription 'ELIK' (Helike) on one side, and on the other a trident flanked by cavorting dolphins, emblems of the sea-god.

Right A rare bronze sculpture from ancient Greece, from around 460–450 BCE, shows Poseidon, tutelary deity of both ancient Helike and its possibly fictional progeny Atlantis.

• In both cases this fate was attributed to divine punishment for their citizens' sins – after the destruction of Helike it was widely rumoured that Poseidon had punished the city for its arrogance in refusing to support temples to him that had been established in its colonies, or alternatively, for having defiled the sanctuary dedicated to him.

Given these similarities, it seems plausible that if Plato wanted to invent a fictitious civilization to illustrate his political philosophy, and wanted to use it as the basis for a fable about the rise and fall of a state and its cataclysmic destruction, his thoughts would inevitably turn towards Helike – an Atlantis-like event that occurred within his own lifetime and on his own doorstep.

FINDING THE LOST CITY

For thousands of years the location of Helike was one of the great secrets concerning the ancient world. In Roman times tourists would sail over it to look down on its broken streets and shattered statuary. For instance, in 174 CE the traveller Pausanias reported visiting the site of Helike and looking down at the walls of the ancient city. Eventually, however, it was buried in silt and lost. Since the 19th century, archeologists had sought for it in vain in the waters off Achaea, until, comparatively recently, sea-floor imaging conclusively showed there was no sunken city offshore in the relevant area. Instead it seems likely that, rather than sliding into the sea after the earthquake and tsunami, as had previously been assumed, Helike was actually submerged beneath an inland lagoon. The lagoon could have been formed when the earthquake caused subsidence, creating a dip that was filled with water by the

onrushing tsunami. Over the centuries the lagoon silted up, leaving Helike buried underground, several kilometres *inland*.

Sure enough, extensive drilling of boreholes and excavations have revealed that this is exactly what happened, and Helike has now been rediscovered just a little way inland. Intriguingly, archeologists have also discovered Helike's early Bronze Age progenitor, a prehistoric town that seems to have suffered a similar fate, but some 2,000 years earlier. Might legends of this catastrophe have survived until Plato's day, and played a part in inspiring the legend of Atlantis?

'For thousands of years the location of Helike was one of the great secrets concerning the ancient world.'

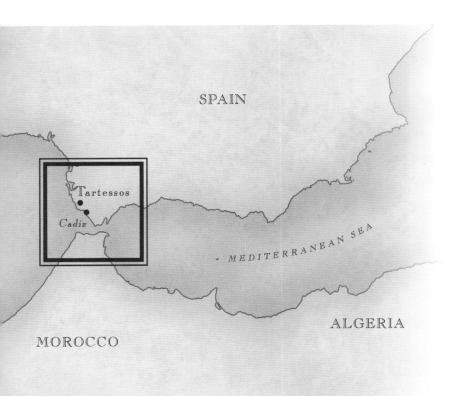

SPAIN

Tartessos

Cadiz

MEDITERRANEAN SEA

ALGERIA

MOROCCO

Tartessos – a Bronze Age city-state

Far beyond the boundaries of Greek experience, at the very edge of the known world, the semi-legendary Bronze Age city-state of Tartessos was famed for its wealth and trading might. Recent discoveries suggest that a century-old theory linking it to Atlantis could be right.

DATING ERRORS

Theories about Tartessos being Atlantis exemplify a major feature of Revisionist Atlantology, namely the very selective interpretation of Plato and the assumption that his account contains errors of translation and transcription. The most important

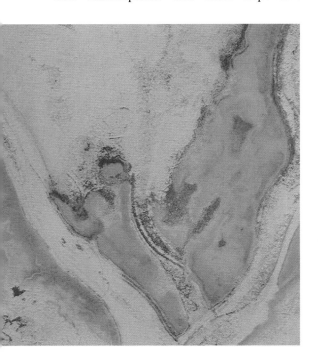

Left This satellite photo supposedly shows the remains of two temples, their location marked by the two slightly darker circular patches in the centre left.

assumption is that Plato got his dates wrong by a factor of ten, so that Atlantis existed not 9,000 but 900 years before Classical Greece, which would place it squarely within the Bronze Age, a period that matches both Plato's descriptions of Atlantis and Athens and the dating of a number of candidate cities, states or civilizations touted as the 'true Atlantis', including the Bronze Age city-state of Tartessos.

BEYOND THE PILLARS OF HERCULES

Tartessos is something of a historical enigma, known today through references by ancient authors (including the biblical scribes Isaiah and Ezekiel), but not via any direct archeological evidence. It was a powerful Bronze Age city-state on the plains of the

Iberian peninsula near modern-day Cadiz, just beyond the Straits of Gibraltar (also known as the Pillars of Hercules). Cadiz itself was originally called Gades, and was a city founded by the Phoenician trading empire specifically to trade with nearby Tartessos. It was the Phoenicians who first introduced Tartessos to the historical record when they made contact with them *c.*1000 BCE, although the city-state may have been founded hundreds of years earlier.

Ancient sources speak of the fabulous wealth of Tartessos, which derived from its extensive silver mines and its supremacy in the tin trade, probably by means of its control of the trading routes with south-western Britain, source of the tin. Tin was essential for the manufacture of bronze. Tartessos is often identified with Tarshish, the city to which Jonah is travelling in the Bible story. Tarshish is said to be rich in minerals and is located at 'the ends of the Earth' – an apt description for a city on the edge of what constituted the known world for the cultures of the eastern Mediterranean. Tarshish was also a trading ally of the Levantine kings Solomon and Hiram of Tyre.

Right *The Lady of Elx or Elche. Found in 1897, the bust subsequently spent time in the Louvre and Madrid's Museo del Prado before arriving at its current home, the National Archeological Museum of Spain.*

THE LADY OF ELX

It has been suggested that the Lady of Elx (or Elche) – a strange statue discovered in the Tartessos region, of unknown origin and uncertain date – is a rare artefact of the Tartessos civilization, and possibly even of Atlantis. The Lady is a large stone bust of what appears to be a woman – although some people argue that it is actually a male figure – with an elaborate headdress of a style that does not match any known culture, although it is usually said to be Romano-Iberian. An aperture in the back of the bust suggests that it may have been part of a funerary urn (an item used to store the ashes of a cremated person). Unfortunately for Atlantis/Tartessos enthusiasts, the conventional dating of the bust is to the 4th century BCE, considerably later than both Atlantis and Tartessos.

The city-state suddenly disappeared from the historical record in the 6th century BCE. It was generally assumed that it had been wiped out by the Carthaginians, the trading empire set up by Phoenician colonists in the western Mediterranean, in order to remove a competitor and safeguard their stranglehold on trade in the region.

TARTESSOS AND ATLANTIS

Tartessos was first identified with Atlantis in the 1920s by scholars Richard Hennig and Adolf Schulten, and more recently by Dr Rainer Kühne, owing to a number of suggestive correspondences with Plato's account. Plato describes one of the ten kingdoms of Atlantis as the kingdom of Gadeiros, and places it near Iberia. A common suggestion is that Plato's sources wrongly interpreted an Egyptian word as 'island', when in fact the Egyptians (unfamiliar with islands) may have meant 'shore' or 'coast', meaning that Atlantis was not an island after all, but simply on the coast of an existing land-mass. In this reading, the Atlantean kingdom of Gadeiros becomes the Iberian coastal kingdom of Gades and Tartessos is Atlantis.

Like Atlantis, Tartessos was rich in mineral wealth and was the centre of a trading empire. It was in roughly the right location, beyond the Pillars of Hercules, and was sited in a great plain surrounded by mountains. Also like Atlantis, it vanished remarkably quickly. Intriguingly, new evidence suggests that the true agent of its destruction were massive flash floods, so perhaps – like Atlantis – Tartessos perished beneath the waters.

TARTESSOS REDISCOVERED

Satellite photos of the plain near Cadiz, appear to show some of the features of Atlantis, including concentric rings of canals and structures that match the proportions of the temples that Plato describes. This is the claim of German scientist Dr Rainer Kühne, who in 2004 told the BBC: 'We have in the photos concentric rings just as Plato described'. Kühne's attribution builds on the work of Atlantologist Werner Wickboldt, who claims 'This is the only place that seems to fit [Plato's] description'. Kühne also argues that Plato's description of Athens clearly matches Bronze Age Athens, dating the story to the correct time for Tartessos to be Atlantis. Some Atlantologists, however, believe that Tartessos was not Atlantis itself, but a trading partner, possibly set up by Atlantean colonists.

The Sea Peoples

Atlantis is not the only ancient mystery of the Mediterranean region. A similar degree of uncertainty and speculation surrounds the enigmatic Sea Peoples, a force of marauders and conquerors who suddenly appeared during the Bronze Age. But could these mysteries be connected?

Egyptian inscriptions (of the type said to have preserved the history of Atlantis) record that in around 1200 BCE Pharaoh Merenptah, and later Pharaoh Rameses III, defended Egypt against an attack by the Haunebu, a mysterious coalition of nations or tribes that had not been previously recorded in the annals of any civilization. These nations also appear in many ancient letters written between the rulers of the empires and city-states of the period. They have since become known as the Sea Peoples, and they left a trail of destruction throughout the Late Bronze Age world, attacking from the sea and razing cities to the ground.

The archeological and historical record also reveals that, at almost exactly the same time, several major civilizations of the Mediterranean and Near East collapsed. Inevitably the appearance of the Sea Peoples has been linked to this wave of collapse and destruction. For instance, in the early 12th century BCE, Ammurapi, king of Ugarit, received a letter from the Hittite king Suppiluliuma II, warning him to beware of an aggressive nation 'who live on boats'. Within a short time of receiving this message, Ugarit was utterly destroyed and vanished from history.

WERE THE SEA PEOPLES ATLANTEANS?

The ancient records paint a picture of the Sea Peoples that has led several scholars to draw links between them and Atlantis. For example, Dr Kühne points out a number of parallels between the two groups:

* The Sea Peoples are described as a confederation of nations. Plato describes how Atlantis was divided into ten kingdoms that acted as a confederation.
* The Sea Peoples are reported to have come from islands. Atlantis was an island.
* The general picture of the Sea Peoples is that they swept in from the west to visit destruction and conquest on lands and territories at the eastern end of the Mediterranean. Plato describes how Atlantis conquered the western Mediterranean and then launched invasions against the eastern lands, and was very nearly successful in subjugating most of the known world.
* The Egyptian inscriptions say that the Sea Peoples were in league with the Libyans. Atlantis was said to have conquered Libya, so it would be expected that its armies would have been accompanied by those of its vassal nations.
* The inscriptions of Rameses III speak of battling huge numbers of troops. Plato describes how Atlantis could call up armies of hundreds of thousands.
* It is obvious that the Sea Peoples were adept sailors. The Atlanteans were

Left One of the Amarna letters, clay tablets inscribed in cuneiform, which were copies of diplomatic correspondence between the Egyptian pharaoh and other rulers of the mid-14th century BCE. It is in letters similar to these, which passed back and forth between the Late Bronze Age superpowers, that traces of the Sea Peoples can be found.

renowned for their command of the seas and their naval technology.

- The Rameses inscriptions speak of the Sea Peoples' towns and villages drowning under a deluge – could this be the same deluge that destroyed Atlantis?

According to Kühne, the true home of the Sea Peoples/Atlanteans may have been the city-state of Tartessos in Iberia (see pages 30–31), although since this existed until *c.*600 BCE, this theory needs to explain a six-century gap between the time of the Sea Peoples and the 'fall' of their homeland.

THE CASE AGAINST

Apart from the dating issues (which require a reinterpretation of Plato's dating to enable Atlantis and the Sea Peoples to have co-existed), the more serious argument against the Atlantean link is that most scholars think the Sea Peoples probably came from Greece or Italy, and that they may well have been migrating tribes of Mycenaean Greeks, a civilization already well known to historians. A great deal of the archeological and linguistic evidence supports this claim, but doesn't support the Atlantis theory.

Below An Egyptian relief from the Temple of Rameses III in Madinat Habu, in Thebes, dating from around the 12th century BCE – the period associated with the mysterious Sea Peoples. It shows Egyptian soldiers battling with ship-borne opponents.

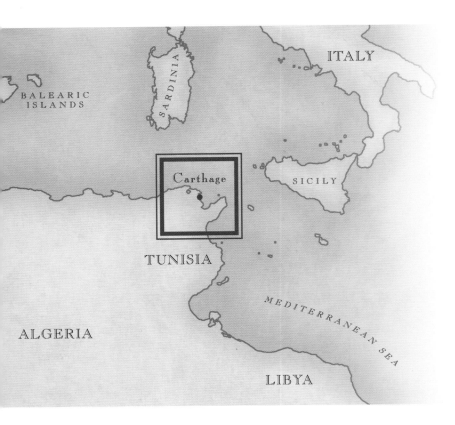

Carthage – the shining city

Capital of a trading empire and for centuries the greatest power in the western Mediterranean, Carthage seems in many ways a natural model for Atlantis. The city was among the greatest of the era, with a broadly concentric design and a system of canals and docks for its mighty trading fleet. Could it have inspired Plato?

Carthage is most familiar to history as Rome's great rival: her sworn antagonist through the three Punic Wars; homeland of Hannibal, who marched his elephants across the Alps; and the city that was eventually razed to the ground by the victorious and vindictive Romans in 146 BCE. But for many centuries before the rise of Rome, Carthage was a major trading power, and by Plato's time it had become an empire with an aggressive expansionist policy, colonizing or conquering almost all of the western Mediterranean and setting its sights further afield.

THE SHINING CITY

Carthage was founded in 814 BCE by the Phoenician Queen Elissar, known to the Romans as Dido. The Phoenicians were a Semitic people from the Levant, centred around the city of Tyre, who specialized in trade and shipping and set up colonies and trading posts all round the Mediterranean and even on the Atlantic coast of Europe. At first Carthage was a vassal colony, but eventually it became the centre of Phoenician power, growing into one of the largest cities in the ancient world, and possibly one of the largest in pre-industrial European history. It commanded trade routes from Britain to the Canaries – perhaps even as far as Zimbabwe – and was known as the Shining City.

CARTHAGE AND ATLANTIS

There are many parallels between Carthage and Plato's Atlantis. Both were expansionist trading empires. Like Atlantis, Carthage ruled the western Mediterranean as far as the borders of Egypt and southern Italy. In

Left A reconstruction of the military harbour of ancient Carthage, showing impressive engineering, vast docks and wide canals, and a concentric plan.

particular, Plato's description of Atlantis resembles the city of Carthage. Carthage was centred on an Acropolis built on a low hill with a temple on it, had enormous city walls in concentric rings, an extensive canal system linked to massive harbours for its navy and mercantile fleet and a broad, flat hinterland criss-crossed with irrigation canals. Overall it had a roughly circular plan.

Plato, who had spent many years in Sicily where the Carthaginians had a history of exploitative and despotic overlordship, may well have meant his portrait of Atlantis to be a barbed reference to the bullying Phoenician empire. Perhaps he drew on his knowledge of Carthage itself to provide the model for Atlantis. This means accepting, however, that Plato invented Atlantis as a pure fabrication, rather than writing about a real place or embroidering legends of a genuine prehistoric civilization.

MINI-ATLANTIS

Another theory is that Carthage itself took Atlantis as a model, and was founded and designed in imitation or homage, as a kind of Atlantis in miniature. This is part of a larger theory about Atlantis, which is that Plato's story was substantially true, and that Atlantean colonists and refugees from its destruction spread out across the world and founded most of the known civilizations, including the Phoenician culture. When the Phoenicians came to found Carthage, they used the memories and secret knowledge of Atlantis preserved by their kings and high priests to guide their design of the new city. Perhaps it is therefore appropriate that Carthage went on to become almost a second Atlantis as the centre of a mighty empire that met with eventual downfall and total destruction.

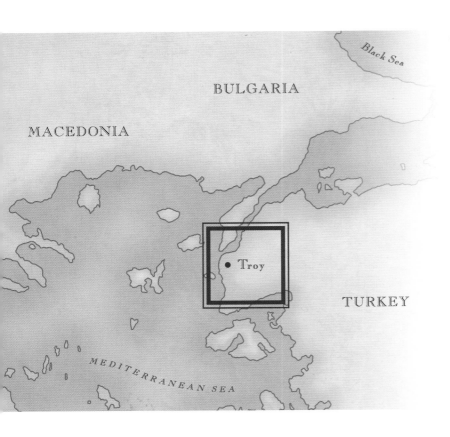

BULGARIA

MACEDONIA

Black Sea

• Troy

TURKEY

MEDITERRANEAN SEA

Troy – city of heroes

Like Atlantis, Troy is famous even today, thanks to Helen of Troy and its appearance in ancient Greek literature and to its semi-legendary, semi-mythical history. Like Atlantis, its location and even its existence were a mystery. But the similarities do not end there, for there are many parallels between the two city-states. Could the solution of one mystery also have solved the other?

Troy is familiar to most people through its central role in the 8th-century BCE Homeric epics *The Iliad* and *The Odyssey*, which tell the story of the war between the Greeks and the Trojans and of the eventual conquest and destruction of Troy. It is now believed that Homer (assuming he existed) composed his epics by writing down oral traditions that were ancient even in his day, and which probably dated back to Bronze Age Mycenae, *c.*1200 BCE.

Troy and Atlantis have been linked many times over the millennia. Plato's student, Aristotle (384–322 BCE), connected the two, while the geographer Strabo (63 BCE–24 CE) pointed to similarities between the tales. The most influential modern proponent of the theory that Troy and Atlantis may be one and the same is the geoarcheologist Eberhard Zangger.

ZANGGER'S THEORY

What if Plato's source on Atlantis really was Solon, who genuinely got the story from an Egyptian priest, but neither of them realized that what they were hearing was none other than the legend of Troy, recast in unfamiliar

terms by the exotic Egyptians? This, in a nutshell, is the basis of Zangger's theory, which he backs up with a range of explanations and parallels.

There are many apparent disjunctions between Atlantis and Troy that suggest that

Above An archive photograph from Heinrich Schliemann's pioneering excavations (1870–1882) of what he claimed was Troy.

cannot be the same. Atlantis was much earlier and in a totally different location from Troy – or was it? Zangger adheres to a theory suggested by other experts that the Egyptians used a lunar rather than solar calendar and were actually referring to months instead of years in their dating of Atlantis. Rather than being 9,000 years earlier, it was 9,000 months, putting Atlantis in roughly the right period for Bronze Age Troy (and also corroborating Dr Kühne's theory about Plato's description of ancient Athens matching Bronze Age Athens; see pages 30–31).

There are also plausible explanations as to how the Egyptian account could point to a Trojan location for Atlantis. Atlantis is supposed to be an island – beyond the Pillars of Hercules and a hard-to-navigate strait – which is 'greater than' Libya and Asia Minor. As we've already seen, however, the Egyptians may have used 'island' to refer to anywhere on the coast or by the shore. There were several locations described as the Pillars of Hercules in ancient times, including the entrance to the Black Sea, while Troy is indeed situated just beyond the hard-to-navigate Bosporus Straits. Zangger proposes that 'greater than' meant 'more important than' and was actually a comment on the political clout of the Trojan state, which (like Atlantis) was the centre of an important trading empire and a major influence on the Bronze Age world.

There are other important similarities between Troy and Atlantis. Like Atlantis, Troy was a city in the middle of a fertile plain, built around a citadel on a low hill and protected with mighty, metal-covered walls. Most obviously, it was engaged in a major war with the Greek states, just as Plato describes for Atlantis. There is even archeological evidence that major earthquakes and tsunamis hit the area in roughly the same period, destroying large parts of the city.

DARK AGE GREECE
In the dialogue *Timaeus*, before Atlantis is introduced, Plato has the Egyptian priest Psonchis explain why the Greeks have no records of Atlantis: the reason is that, thanks to repeated natural disasters, the once-advanced Greek civilization fell into an illiterate Dark Age when a sophisticated society of warriors and intellectuals gave way to a simple one of shepherds and farmers – a Dark Age from which it was only recovering in Solon's time. This closely matches what really did happen as the Mycenaean civilization of Bronze Age Greece collapsed after a series of natural disasters (and, Zangger argues, internecine wars), losing the art of writing and retreating to a simpler model of society, just as Psonchis outlined.

MISSING LINKS
Zangger is so convinced of his theory that he wants to excavate the Trojan site at Hissarlik in Turkey for evidence. Not everyone agrees with him, however. Most Trojan experts dismiss his theory, while ancient-language scholar Dietrich Mannsperger says that Zangger's plans to excavate make as much sense as wanting to excavate Plato's (clearly fictitious) Republic. Certainly there are still many details that do not add up. To offer just two examples, Plato says that elephants were plentiful on his island continent, and that tropical conditions made it possible to grow two crops a year – neither of which was true of Troy.

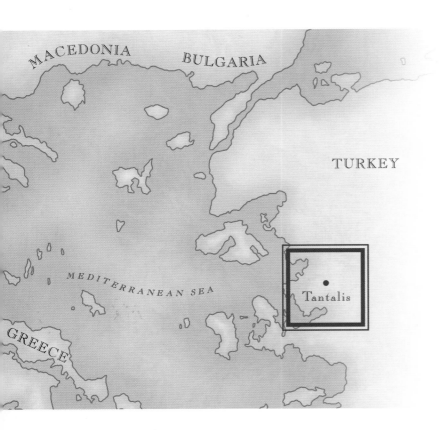

Tantalis – Atlantis in ancient Lydia

Tracing the mythological roots of the Atlantis story may be the true path to uncovering its real origins. One attempt to do so draws parallels between the Titan Atlas and another mythical figure, Tantalus, and locates Atlantis in Tantalis, a kingdom in Lydia, an ancient region of western Asia Minor (modern Turkey).

The Tantalis theory is the brainchild of historian Peter James, who outlined it in his ambitiously subtitled 1995 book *The Sunken Kingdom: the Atlantis Mystery Solved*. James wondered if some of the details of how Solon acquired the tale of Atlantis might have come down to Plato in a distorted or garbled manner. As he points out, 'Solon travelled elsewhere, notably to the kingdom of Lydia in western Anatolia (Turkey). There, at the court of King Croesus – proverbial for his riches, but historical nonetheless – Solon is said to have swapped stories not only with the king, but with the great fable-writer Aesop.'

The significance of the Lydian link is that Atlas, a central figure in the Atlantis story for whom the continent and its capital were named, also has important links with this area of Anatolia. Atlas was the Titan whose task it was to support the heavens, and who is popularly depicted bearing a globe. Although in Greek myth he was banished to the West to carry out this employment, his roots (James claims) were in Anatolia, and it was from this region that the Greeks had acquired the myth in the first place.

THE LYDIAN CONNECTION

In Lydia itself, Atlas was cognate with another mythological figure, Tantalus. Like Atlas, Tantalus had divine parentage; and like Atlas (who, along with the other Titans, eventually tangled with the Olympian gods), Tantalus fell foul of Zeus and was condemned to an eternity of punishment. Today we are familiar with Homer's version of the myth, in which Tantalus is mired in Tartarus, the most dreadful part of Hades, where he suffers the eternal torments of hunger and thirst while luscious figs or grapes and refreshing water are always just beyond his grasp. From this we get the modern verb 'to tantalize'.

The Lydians, however, had a different version of the myth, in which Tantalus' punishment was that he had to support the weight of a huge rock to which he was chained. In other words, he was an Anatolian Atlas. Like Plato's Atlas, Tantalus was also said to have ruled over a kingdom in the mortal world – the city-state of Tantalis. When he fell foul of Zeus, the storm god was said to have smote the city with lightning bolts, shattering the earth and drowning the

NIOBE ON MOUNT SIPYLUS

Gazing out over the site of the lost city of Tantalis is an awesome figure shaped by ancient hands from a naturally occurring rock formation. Local tradition holds it to be Niobe, a daughter of Tantalus, whose children were slain by the gods in punishment for boasting of her fecundity and who fled to Mount Sipylus, where she turned to stone as she wept. The porous limestone of the rock accumulates water, which drips out to make it look as though she is weeping.

city beneath a lake. The parallels with Atlantis are clear. According to James, this is the story that Solon picked up in Lydia, which grew through exaggeration into the story of Atlantis, relocated to the West because of its associations with Atlas.

ATLANTIS UNDER THE LAKE

The ancient city of Tantalis (like Atlantis) was believed to have been rich in mineral wealth and powerful in the region through trade and force of arms. It was located below Mount Sipylus, near modern-day Izmir, and James links it to the ancient Lydian kingdom of Zippsala, mentioned in diplomatic correspondence of the 15th century BCE. Zippsala is believed to have been an upstart vassal kingdom that challenged the authority of the Hittites, the dominant power in Asia Minor at the time, and the name provides a clear link with Sipylus, helping to confirm, James argues, that there was indeed a Late Bronze Age kingdom where the Classical sources claimed. Crucially, Tantalis was believed by ancient writers to lie beneath a lake that, in times past, was much larger than today. James believes that the legend of the fall of Atlantis refers to the actual fate of Tantalis. Sited in a major earthquake zone, it may have plunged beneath the waters of the lake in a catastrophic deluge, just as Plato describes. Excitingly, its remains could lie there still, awaiting excavation.

To accept James' theory necessitates making many allowances and admitting that the 'true Atlantis' bore scant resemblance to the island continent described by Plato. There is also a serious lack of hard archeological evidence to back up his claims.

Above A Renaissance depiction of the Titan Atlas, bowed beneath the weight of the globe as part of his punishment for being on the losing side in a war with the Olympian gods.

'The significance of the Lydian link is that Atlas, a central figure in the Atlantis story for whom the continent and its capital were named, also has important links with this area of Anatolia.'

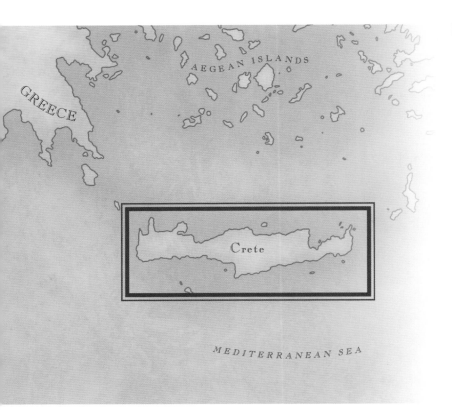

GREECE

AEGEAN ISLANDS

Crete

MEDITERRANEAN SEA

The Minoans and the island of Crete

The genesis and centre of the Bronze Age in the Aegean was the Minoan civilization based in Crete. Like Atlantis, it flourished amid great magnificence, only to collapse after suffering the ravages of various natural disasters and war.

Today visitors to Crete are astounded by the vibrancy and beauty of Minoan art, a cultural achievement that speaks volumes about the sophistication of the culture that developed on the island from around 2600 BCE. It was here that the Bronze Age in the Aegean area began, and the Minoan civilization, named for the mythical King Minos, founded a trading empire based on trade in tin and copper (the ingredients of bronze), as well as luxury goods such as saffron and ivory. Advances in agriculture on Crete and the growing reach of Minoan influence, led to growth in population and wealth and the construction of a series of great buildings, the most important of which was at Knossos. Today these are known as palaces, but in fact their true function is unclear – they may have combined the roles of temple, court, market and warehouse.

The Minoans established colonies on the surrounding islands and the Greek mainland, and their dominance extended as far as the northern shores of the Black Sea, where most of their grain was grown. Despite several setbacks and times of apparent instability, possibly caused by earthquakes and famines, the Minoans flourished until around 1500 BCE. This is believed to be the date of a mighty eruption on the nearby island of Thera (modern-day Santorini), although this is the subject of heated debate (see pages 42–43). For whatever reason, the Minoans went into decline and were conquered by the Mycenaean Greeks of the mainland just a few decades later, *c.*1450 BCE.

BASIC ERRORS

Minoan civilization is a popular candidate for the 'true Atlantis', based on the assumption that either the Egyptians or the

Left Knossos was the greatest of the Minoan palaces and was believed to be the centre of a bull cult.

Greeks who transmitted the story to Plato made some basic errors in the dating, location and dimensions of Atlantis. The Egyptians, with their parochial world view, may well have considered Crete to be in the 'far west', leading to Plato's misconception about the location of Atlantis; and if the dates and measurements were wrong by a factor of ten (see page 30), Crete becomes a much better fit. Scholars such as Rodney Castleden argue that confusion may have arisen either through mistakes in the Egyptian writing system used by the ancient record-keepers, or because they used the Minoan-derived Mycenaean script Linear B. And when Plato wrote that Atlantis was 'greater than' Libya and Asia, he may have mistranscribed the word *meson* ('between') as *mezon* ('greater'). For the Egyptians, Crete was indeed *between* Libya and Asia.

THE MINOAN CIVILIZATION AS ATLANTIS

Supporting the case for Crete as Atlantis, there are numerous parallels between Minoan civilization and Plato's Atlantis:

- Both were great trading empires, backed by powerful navies that founded colonies and sought to expand their spheres of influence.
- The distribution of the palace sites on Crete suggests that it may have been a confederation of sub-kingdoms, just like Atlantis.
- The principal temple of the Minoans in the palace at Knossos may have been dedicated to Poseidon, just like the main temple in Atlantis.
- The Minoans were famous for their bull cult, in which ritual bull hunts in the palaces played a central role. Plato says that a ritual bull hunt in the main palace was the central feature of Atlantean religion.
- At one time the Greeks believed that the Pillars of Hercules were two headlands on Crete itself.
- The Egyptians called the Minoans the *Kheftiu*, which means People of the Pillar, giving another link to the pillar motif.
- Both the Minoan civilization and Atlantis fought the Greeks, and were eventually conquered by them.

- Thanks to the eruption on Thera, the Minoans may have suffered a cataclysm of earthquakes and floods, which led to their downfall, just like that of Atlantis.
- Plato's reference to elephants may have been based on the fact that the Egyptians traded a lot of ivory with the Minoans. Minoan agricultural prowess may have given rise to his claims about the Atlanteans harvesting two crops a year.

Impressive as this list of parallels is, there are some obvious flaws in the theory. Crete has obviously not sunk beneath the waves. The Greeks were familiar with the Minoan civilization and had myths of their own about it, so it is not clear why they would confuse or elaborate stories about Crete into wild tales of Atlantis. And, for all the similarities, there are plenty of differences between Atlantis and the Minoan civilization – if one ignores these to make the link fit, why credit Plato's tale at all?

Below A Minoan fresco showing young men bull-leaping.

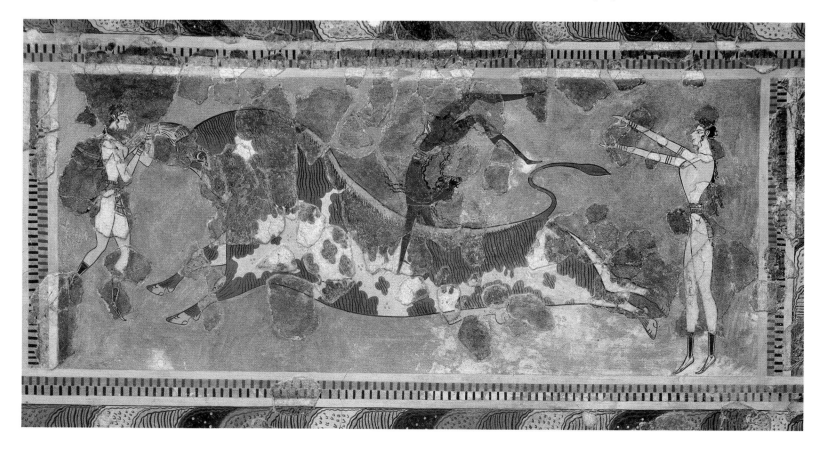

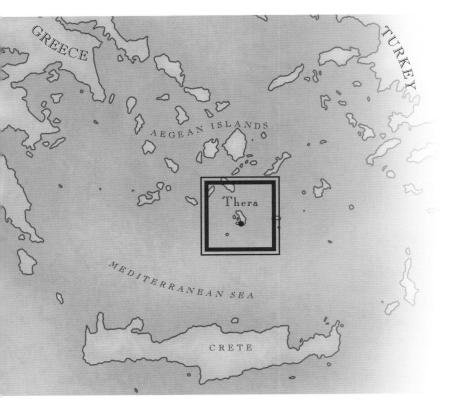

The eruption of Thera

A cataclysm on the scale Plato describes must have left its mark on history and geography, and should therefore be simple to track down. The most obvious parallel from conventional history is the tremendous eruption on Thera – perhaps the most violent volcanic explosion in the history of civilization.

Modern-day Santorini is the name given to a small archipelago of islands that constitute the remains of what was once a large caldera (volcanic crater ring). It was a prosperous and sophisticated centre of Minoan civilization until it blew up in spectacular fashion during the Middle Bronze Age, leaving only fragments of land still projecting from the sea – the largest of which was known as Thera. Four times as much material was thrown into the atmosphere as occurred during the famous explosion of Krakatau in 1883, and the eruption is now believed to have had a Volcanic Explosivity Index rating of 7. Only one other eruption in the last 10,000 years was of this magnitude (Tambora, in 1815), and some vulcanologists believe that Thera was bigger. The tsunamis generated by the eruption would have been up to 150 m (500 ft) high, according to some estimates.

THERA AND ATLANTIS
The coincidence between an advanced Bronze Age civilization and a tremendous cataclysm involving earthquakes and floods has naturally led to Thera being identified

with Atlantis, most prominently by the Greek seismologist Angelos Galanopoulos in the 1960s. He and others argued that Atlantis developed from confused memories of the Thera event, which wiped out the Minoan colony there and would have visited terrible damage on Crete. Archeological sources suggest that the eruption happened around 1500 BCE, which is when the Minoan civilization began to collapse.

Right Amphorae still in the shop where they were being offered for sale, buried beneath the ash from the eruption of Thera until uncovered by archeologists nearly 3,500 years later.

Thera itself may have resembled Plato's description of Atlantis – broadly circular in plan, with a central built-up area surrounded by a ring of water. The disjunction between dates, location and measurements can be explained as before (see pages 30 and 37). When the Egyptians suddenly lost touch with what had been a major trading partner, they must have made the link with the disaster that would have affected everyone in

the eastern Mediterranean region, and thus the legend was born.

CONTRADICTORY EVIDENCE

Unfortunately, the story is much less straightforward than it seems, largely because of uncertainty over the actual date of the eruption. While archeological evidence – from contemporary records and the apparent dates of artefacts from archeological layers assumed to be concurrent with the eruption – seems to suggest a date around 1500 BCE, the geological and biological evidence from radiocarbon dating, sediment cores, tree rings and so on, suggests a much earlier date, probably around 1640 BCE. Unless the dating system for the whole Minoan civilization is wrong, this means that the Minoans survived and flourished for around 150 years after the eruption.

The evidence from Thera itself also suggests that earth tremors and smoke would have given the Therans months or even years of warning, and the absence of bodies in archeological sites on the island suggests that they successfully evacuated in time.

Although the northern coast of Crete would have been devastated by the tsunami and the Minoan fleet was probably reduced to matchsticks, most of Crete would have survived unharmed as the ash plume from the volcano went in another direction. It is also worth pointing out that Plato's account says nothing about a volcano. Taken together with all the other inconsistencies between Plato's Atlantis and what we know about Thera, Galanopoulos' theory looks tenuous at best. As with so many other Mediterranean candidates for the 'true Atlantis', it is necessary to ask one important question: If, in order to make the theory fit, you dismiss large chunks of Plato's account as mistakes, elaborations or later inventions, why accept any of it as true?

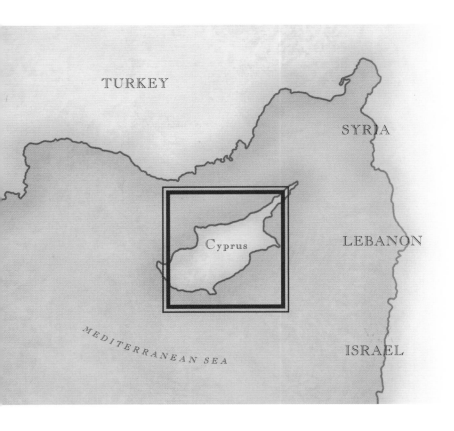

TURKEY

SYRIA

Cyprus

LEBANON

MEDITERRANEAN SEA

ISRAEL

Cyprus – last remnant of Atlantis?

Sea-floor mapping of the eastern Mediterranean has prompted the development of a new theory, siting Atlantis just off the coast of Cyprus, and it is claimed that sophisticated sonar scans have detected the actual Acropolis and walls of the lost city.

Beneath the waters of the Mediterranean, between Cyprus and Syria on the Asian mainland, the sea floor rises to a broad, relatively shallow shelf called the Cyprus Arc. According to Iranian-American Atlantologist Robert Sarmast, the Cyprus Arc was above sea level 12,000 years ago and, together with the areas of Cyprus that still lie above the waves, was the fabled land of Atlantis.

Today the Cyprus Arc lies about 1–1.6 km (up to 1 mile) below the waves, but in the past the Mediterranean has been much lower than it is today. Tectonic shifts have closed up the Straits of Gibraltar and cut it off from the Atlantic, and since the input of water via rainfall and rivers is significantly lower than the rate of loss through evaporation, this has caused the entire basin to dry up, to a depth of at least 3–5 km (2–3 miles), exposing the Cyprus Arc. Sarmast argues that this last happened relatively recently, and that the resulting land-mass closely matches Plato's description, including a large plain facing south, ringed by high mountains to the north.

Indeed, he insists that he and his team have matched no fewer than 50 elements of Plato's account with the Cyprus Arc. Most spectacularly, he claims that the data shows a sea mount in the midst of the Atlantean plain that exactly matches the dimensions Plato gives for the Acropolis hill, and that detailed side-scan sonar shows unmistakably artificial wall-like structures around the base of the hill. These, Sarmast insists, are obviously the fabled concentric walls of Atlantis. 'Can any sane person claim that all of this is mere coincidence?' he asks rhetorically.

WHO IS ROBERT SARMAST?

Sarmast is an Iranian-American ex-architect who packed in his job to become an explorer. After several years spent studying Atlantis, he unearthed old Russian bathymetric (ocean-depth measurement) data about the eastern Mediterranean and identified the Cyprus Arc as a likely region. Sarmast is no stranger to hyperbole, announcing that because of his discovery, 'The whole world is going to shift to this island [Cyprus]. It will be the greatest archeological discovery in history. It will change religion, it will change politics, science. The ramifications are almost endless. Cyprus will be the talk of the world for the next 500 years.'

Below The Iranian-American Atlantologist Robert Sarmast, who claims that 'Cyprus will be the talk of the world for the next 500 years' once his discovery of Atlantis is acknowledged.

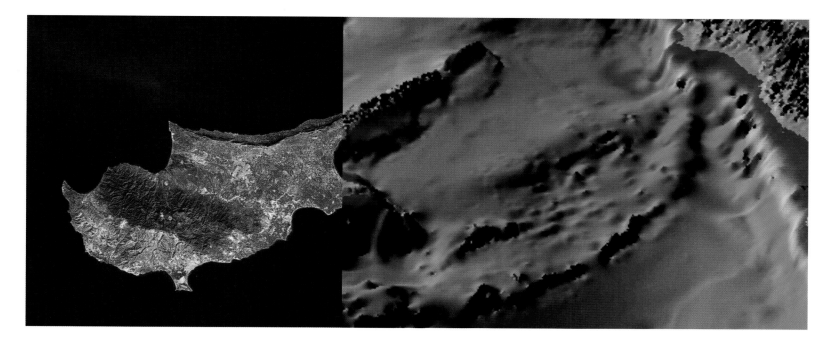

According to Sarmast's theory, the Cyprus Arc is the obvious location for Atlantis. As Plato describes, it lies between two continents (Africa and Europe), and its broad fertile plains and easy access to surrounding areas would have given it obvious advantages for agriculture and trade. Placed in the centre of the Mediterranean world, it could have spread its civilization to Egypt, the Near and Middle East and Greece and Asia Minor. However, the low-lying nature of the land-mass meant that it was doomed, for when a massive earthquake *c.*9500 BCE broke the Gibraltar 'plug' that kept the waters of the Atlantic at bay, they blasted into the empty basin in a vast waterfall more than 1 km (½ mile) high, and raced through the partially empty Mediterranean in a giant tsunami that drowned Atlantis, just as Plato describes.

FLAWS IN THE THEORY

The most obvious problem with Sarmast's theory is that Plato seems to place Atlantis squarely in the Atlantic Ocean, but Sarmast points out that: a) he may have misinterpreted his Greek/Egyptian sources; b) the ancients only had a shaky grasp of geography and may have meant quite different things by terms such as 'Pillars of Hercules' and 'the ocean' to the way these are understood today. Is it reasonable, though, to insist on the

significance of matching some aspects of Plato's description while discounting others?

Apart from this, there are more serious objections to Sarmast's claims. Conventional geology tells us that the Mediterranean basin last dried up and then reflooded during the Miocene, about five million years ago. The drying left massive salt deposits behind, which suggests that the Cyprus Arc would have been a salty wasteland, not fertile farmland. Refilling of the basin after the reopening of the Gibraltar Straits would have taken much longer than a day and night, as described by Plato (see opposite column). Not everyone is convinced that the apparent structures located by Sarmast are indeed man-made (they might be natural formations) and, despite his bombast, they do not really appear to match Plato's description. In other words, even if they are man-made, they may not have anything to do with Atlantis.

Sarmast plans to answer these objections with a new expedition to the area. He insists that cores of the Cyprus Arc seabed will reveal pollen spores and other evidence that it was above the waves *c.*12,000 years ago, and that closer examination of the area around the 'Acropolis' will reveal 'A lot of megalithic structures, temples, bridges, tunnels and canals and a lot of artefacts; there is a whole city down there.'

Above This composite picture shows the main body of Cyprus to the left, and the topography of the sea bottom between Cyprus and the Levantine coast to the right – this is the shallow shelf known as the Cyprus Arc.

'*According to Robert Sarmast, the Cyprus Arc was above sea level 12,000 years ago and, together with the areas of Cyprus that still lie above the waves, this was the fabled land of Atlantis.*'

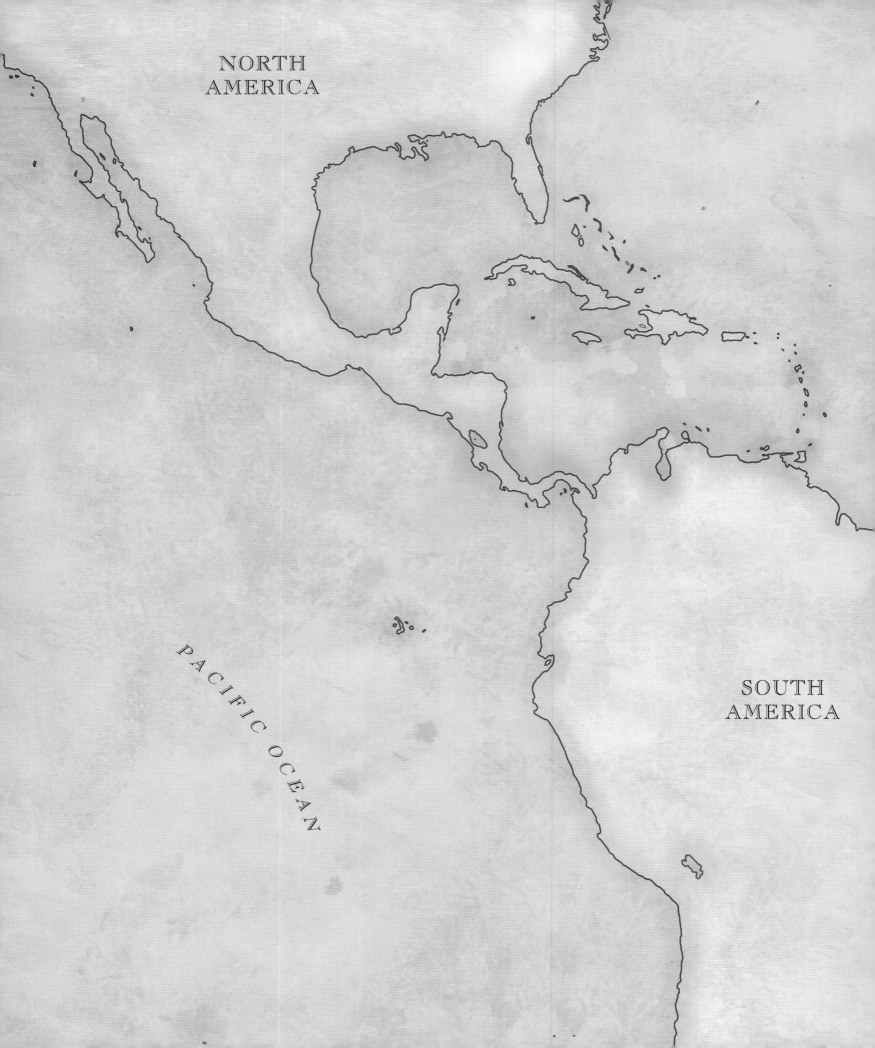

PART 3

THE AMERICAS – ATLANTIS AND THE NEW WORLD

In *Timaeus* Plato refers to Atlantis as sitting in the Atlantic Ocean between Europe and the 'opposite continent', reflecting the widespread ancient Greek belief that on the other side of Oceanus – the mighty ocean that was believed to surround the Mediterranean world of Europe, Africa and Asia – lay a vast encircling continent.

Almost as soon as it was realized that the Americas constituted a New World, educated people familiar with the legend of Atlantis began to link the two. The evidence of the impressive but doomed civilizations of the Incas, the Aztecs and their predecessors, the Maya, strengthened the connection. For many it became a matter of fact that Plato's Atlantis was, in fact, the new land of America. This section examines the most important of the theories connecting Atlantis with the Aztecs, Maya, Incas and the high plains of Bolivia, but begins by looking at the evidence that other ancient writers also knew about lands to the west of the Atlantic.

A New World to the west

Plato was not the only ancient writer to refer to lands across the western ocean. In fact one of the most prominent features of the geography of Western imagination has been the presence of mythical or legendary western territories. How do these places relate to Atlantis? Could they be evidence that other writers also knew of the lost continent?

Although well acquainted with the lands in and around the Mediterranean, and generally aware of the geography of the Middle East thanks to their dealings with the Persians, the ancient Greeks had only vague notions of what lay beyond the Pillars of Hercules, out in the Atlantic and beyond. This was partly because of the limits of seafaring technology at the time, and partly because the Phoenicians (and later the Carthaginians) actively blocked any Greek attempts to venture beyond their Mediterranean world (see page 30).

The ancient Greek geographer and cartographer Hecataeus (*c.*550–476 BCE) was roughly contemporary with Plato. His world map summarizes the ancient Greek world view, showing the known world with the Mediterranean in the centre encircled by a great ocean known as Oceanus (an extremely similar map is shown on the facing page). It was also generally believed that there was an 'opposite continent' (not represented on Hecataeus' map), perhaps encircling Oceanus itself, and it was to this that Plato referred. However, it may be reading too much into the belief to say that the ancient Greeks knew about the Americas.

Right A 1555 map of Florida and the Antilles, the West Indian islands named for the fabled land of Antillia, believed by some Atlantologists to be the western remnants of the continent of Atlantis itself.

ISLANDS IN THE WEST

As well as the encircling opposite continent, lands and particularly islands in the west were a common feature of ancient myth, legend and folklore. Greek folklore, for instance, spoke of the Garden of the Hesperides – nymphs who tended a beautiful orchard of magical apples. The Garden was placed in the far west, in some versions in a land beyond the western sea. The far west was also the favoured destination for the souls of the dead or for departed heroes. The Isles of the Blessed (or the Fortunate Isles), which feature in both Classical and Celtic legend, were said to be islands on the far side of Oceanus, while the Elysian Fields – the area of the ancient Greek afterlife equivalent to

Paradise, where heroes and the virtuous spent eternity in bliss – were sometimes also placed on lands or islands in the far west.

ANTILLIA

Ancient writers also wrote about more specific lands across the western ocean. Aristotle recorded that the Carthaginians knew of an island in the Atlantic Ocean known as Antilia (or Antillia), which has been taken by many later scholars to be a corruption of the word Atlantis, although this is probably not the case. Antillia was later mentioned by the Graeco-Roman writer Plutarch (*c*.46–127 CE), who described it as two islands and equated them with the Isles of the Blessed. According to Plutarch, who claimed to be recording facts passed on by 'Atlantic sailors' (Phoenicians?), the Antilles were 1,900 km (1,200 miles) west of Africa and enjoyed the temperate climate and geography required for agriculture (recalling Plato's description of Atlantis).

Antillia or the Antilles reappeared in Portuguese and Irish legend and even figured on medieval maps of the Atlantic, so that Columbus planned to stop off there on his voyage of discovery in 1492. On these maps Antillia was shown as being about the size of Portugal, although according to some Portuguese traditions it was actually one of the Azores. When the actual islands of the Caribbean were discovered, they were collectively termed the Antilles as a result of these early beliefs. For many Atlantologists, the Antilles are simply relics of Atlantis that survived the Deluge, and ancient and pre-Colombian traditions regarding them prove that there was traffic between the Old and New World, and by extension between Atlanteans and the Old World, well before Columbus sailed the ocean blue.

***Below** An 1867 woodcut showing the world according to the 5th-century BCE traveller Herodotus, which illustrates the ancient Greek world view.*

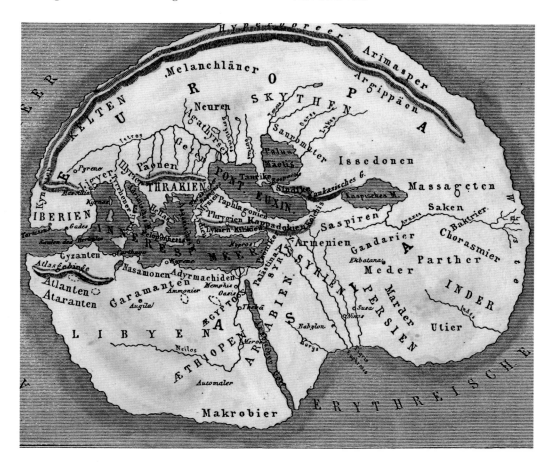

FRAGMENTS OF ATLANTIS

According to a 5th-century CE commentary on *Timaeus* by the Greek philosopher Proclus, an ancient geographer called Marcellus who may have lived *c*.100 BCE described a series of islands in the Outer Ocean (that is, Oceanus), including seven small ones and three large ones, one of which was dedicated to Poseidon. Marcellus' descriptions seem to match quite well with the Caribbean islands – for instance, one of the large islands appears to match the dimensions of Cuba. Was the large island that Marcellus described actually Atlantis, which also 'belonged' to Poseidon? Or did he somehow know about the geography of the Caribbean? Marcellus apparently attributed his information to other ancient historians, and Atlantologists speculate that he had access to lore derived from Atlantean refugees or colonists, and that the islands he described were surviving fragments of the larger lost continent.

The Aztecs

The Aztecs were a sophisticated, advanced civilization that ruled much of present-day Mexico until the Spanish arrived in 1519. Soon after the Spanish conquest the Aztec culture was compared with Atlantis, an association that continues to this day.

The Aztecs were the last in a very long line of sophisticated Meso-American civilizations, the first of which date back to 1000 BCE. Originally vassals of earlier empires, the Aztecs later rose to power in and around the Valley of Mexico in the 15th century CE and, through war and intimidation, established their dominance over much of central Mexico. They reached the height of their power in around 1500 CE, shortly before the Spanish arrived with guns, steel, horses and germs, to bring the Aztecs' world crashing down around their ears.

The achievements of the Aztecs included: a sophisticated road and postal system; feats of engineering and construction, including the raising of mighty pyramids; writing, poetry, literature and the arts; mandatory education for all adolescents; advanced agriculture, astronomy and mathematics; and much else. But they also had a darker side, epitomized by their cult of death and rapacity for human sacrifice. According to the Aztecs themselves, when the Great Pyramid in Tenochtitlan was rededicated after enlargement in 1487 CE, 84,000 prisoners were sacrificed in four days (although contemporary scholars say this was probably a gross exaggeration).

AZTLAN, THE WHITE ISLAND

In 1551, 30 years after the Spanish conquest, Spanish priest Francisco López de Gómara wrote a sort of 'official history' called *Hispania Victrix*, which first drew attention to possible links between the Aztecs and Atlantis and helped to promote the idea that the Americas were synonymous with Plato's lost land. Atlantologists point to several pieces of evidence that back up this early assertion. One of the most influential is the story of the Aztecs' origins, which they traced

Right *A view of Mexico City, c.1673, before Lake Texcoco was drained and built over as it is today. Built on the ruins of the Aztec capital of Tenochtitlan, this early version of Mexico City shows obvious similarities with Plato's city of Atlantis.*

QUETZLCÓATL

One of the primary Aztec gods was Quetzlcóatl, the feathered serpent. Quetzlcóatl was a culture hero who, in some versions of his myth, was described as a white-skinned, blue-eyed, blond, bearded man from the east who taught the ancient Americans the secrets of civilization, including writing, agriculture and so on. To many Atlantologists – especially those of a racist cast, who believed that indigenous American cultures could only have reached their levels of sophistication with Old World help – this was clearly a mythologized memory of the arrival and influence of Atlantean refugees or colonists.

Above The Central American god Quetzlcoatl could take both human and animal form, manifesting as a feathered serpent.

back to a legendary homeland called Aztlan, variously translated as the Isle of Cranes or the White Island. The place name Aztlan offers an obvious etymological link to Atlantis, while according to some Atlantologists parallel myths in Egypt refer to a 'White Island' in the west that was the original home of culture heroes (mythical figures who brought knowledge of civilization and technology).

The Aztec foundation myth said that the Mexica, as they called themselves, and six other tribes of Nahua peoples (Nahuatl was the language of the Aztecs) emerged from primordial caves and settled on the island of Aztlan. Later they migrated to their new homeland on Lake Texcoco, where they built their capital city Tenochtitlan (subsequently levelled by the conquistador Hernán Cortés (1485–1547), who founded Mexico City in its stead).

Accounts of why they left Aztlan vary. Atlantologists sometimes claim that Aztec sources say they were forced to move by

a flood, although this interpretation is controversial at best; the more conventional story is that they were directed to do so by a god, or to escape rule by tyrants.

PYRAMIDS AND CANALS

For Atlantologists, the Aztlan story is obvious proof of an Atlantean link, but in truth this link is tenuous. It is generally accepted that if Aztlan was a real place, it was probably an island in a lake or marsh somewhere to the north of Mexico City. There are, however, other suggestive links between the Aztecs and Atlantis. The Aztec capital Tenochtitlan was a mighty city centred around temples and palaces, built in the middle of a lake with canals and causeways connecting the different parts – in other words, at least superficially similar to the capital city of Atlantis. Perhaps the layout was inspired by some Atlantean link. The Aztecs, like other American cultures, had pyramids similar to those found in Egypt and Mesopotamia – possible proof of common origins?

'The Aztec capital Tenochtitlan was a mighty city centred around temples and palaces, built in the middle of a lake with canals and causeways.'

The Maya

Lost cities lurk beneath the thick vegetation of the Central American rainforest, with only the tallest pyramids poking their tops above the jungle canopy. Here lived the Maya, whose ancient and impenetrable texts may reveal the legends of Atlantis.

The Maya were an influential pre-Colombian Meso-American civilization, based mainly in and around the Yucatán peninsula and modern-day Guatemala, Belize, Honduras and El Salvador. It peaked during the Classic phase of 250–900 CE (before suffering a catastrophic collapse due to ecological degradation and climate change), but still existed as a patchwork of city-states by the time of the Spanish conquest. Mayan peoples still make up much of the region's population today, speaking the same languages as their ancient ancestors.

The Maya had the most advanced writing system of any American civilization and, for an essentially Stone Age civilization, were incredibly sophisticated in terms of their architecture, agriculture, mathematics and especially astronomy. They built massive temple and palace complexes, including step pyramids that inevitably suggested links to ancient Egypt. Their religion and possibly their whole culture seems to have been based on a cyclical interpretation of time and history, which could be read and predicted through astronomy, astrology and mathematics.

CRACKING THE CODEX

Literacy and writing were reserved for the Mayan elite and were soon lost in the face of Spanish suppression, which included burning

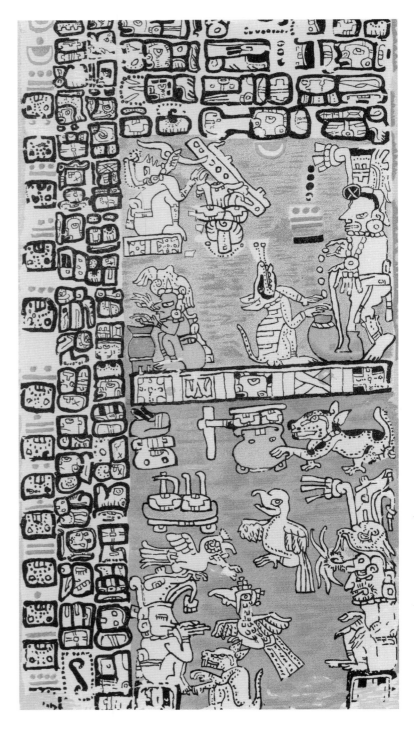

Right *Part of the* Troano Codex, *showing the complex mix of pictograms, logograms and illustration that characterized Mayan writing. It was this Codex that led Brasseur to his spurious translation concerning the legend of Mu.*

as many Mayan books (known as codices) as possible, on the basis that they were the work of the Devil. Since the Mayan heartland was poor, inaccessible and little known to the outside world, knowledge of the amazing monumental remains of this civilization was mostly lost until the mid-19th century.

Among the early scholars to take an interest in the Mayan civilization was French clergyman Abbé Charles-Étienne Brasseur de Bourbourg (1814–74). Travelling as a missionary in Central America, he saw first-hand evidence of the once-mighty civilization and also drew on the work of other scholars and ethnographers, including the 16th-century Spanish priest Diego de Landa, bishop of Yucatán. De Landa was responsible for the mass destruction of Mayan literature, but also preserved his interpretation of their 'alphabet'. Brasseur used this as the basis for translating a Mayan book he had come across, known as the *Troano Codex*. Apparently the *Codex* revealed a Mayan legend about a great land named Mu, which drowned in a cataclysm. Unfortunately de Landa's initial interpretation of the Mayan system of writing was erroneous (it did not use an alphabet but a combination of pictograms and syllable phonetics), and therefore so was Brasseur's.

QUEEN MÓO OF ATLANTIS

Although Mu is usually identified as a lost continent in the Pacific (see pages 90–93), Brasseur's work inspired a quite different reading by another pioneer of Mayan studies, the amateur archeologist Augustus le Plongeon (1826–1908). Le Plongeon had a richly varied career as a shipwreck survivor, teacher, Gold Rush land surveyor, medical huckster and photographer. His travels and excavations in South America convinced him that the Egyptians and all of the world's other civilizations were derived from progenitors in the Americas, particularly the Maya, whom he believed predated them all.

Using Brasseur's work and his own studies (he spoke at least one Mayan language and had many indigenous contacts and informants), le Plongeon combined translations of the glyphs (inscriptions) that he had uncovered on temples and palaces with his own interpretation of the *Troano Codex* to give an outlandish story concerning a Queen Móo and her dynastic struggles. This ancient queen had supposedly fled Central America, cradle of world civilization, for the remnants of Atlantis (also known as Mu), which itself had earlier been settled by the Maya before perishing in a cataclysm. From here she had gone to Egypt, where she became the basis for the goddess Isis. In other words, le Plongeon had invented an involved chronology tying together the Maya, Mu/Atlantis and ancient Egypt, in that order.

ELEPHANTS AND ERRORS

Although he had initially won respect for his pioneering fieldwork, le Plongeon's wild theories – apparently based on hunches, over-interpretation and his own idiosyncratic translations – left him marginalized and ridiculed. It was also increasingly obvious that Egypt and other Old World civilizations predated the Maya, and it subsequently became apparent that Brasseur's and le Plongeon's theories about Mayan writing were off the mark. Nonetheless, le Plongeon's writings continue to be influential, and Atlantologists often point to parallels between the Maya and other civilizations, such as pyramids and supposed Mayan glyphs of elephants (which, according to Plato, were a particular feature of Atlantis, but are not found in the Americas), as proof of a common ancestry and links to Atlantis.

Below Some of these Mayan petroglyphs (rock-carved characters) vaguely resemble elephants, not found in the Americas since prehistoric times but mentioned by Plato as abundant in Atlantis.

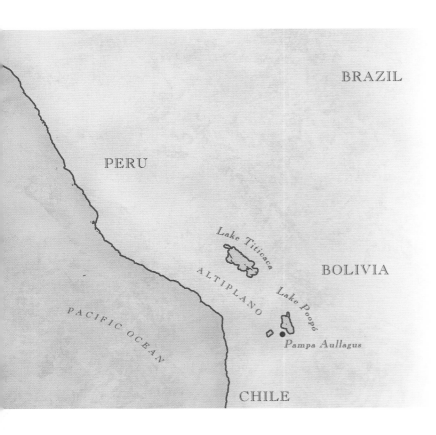

BRAZIL

PERU

Lake Titicaca

ALTIPLANO

BOLIVIA

Lake Poopó

PACIFIC OCEAN

Pampa Aullagus

CHILE

The Incas and Atlantis

The third great civilization of pre-Colombian America was the empire of the Incas, which stretched almost the entire length of the Andes. At its heart lay a high plain that, incredibly, seems to match Plato's description of Atlantis, and upon which evidence of potentially Atlantean technology has been uncovered.

The Incas were originally a small tribe from near Cuzco in modern-day Peru, who expanded their power and influence over the space of just a few generations from the mid-15th century CE and were still at the height of their power when the Spanish invaded Peru in 1532. Their culture was marked by sophisticated systems of agriculture, communications, education, bureaucracy, medicine, astronomy and monumental masonry. Their empire was a confederation of many different nations, tribes and languages, upon which they tried to impose overarching, unifying principles, such as core religious practices and the widespread use of their language, Quechua.

ATLANTIS ON THE ALTIPLANO

To the south of the heart of the Inca empire, lies a huge plateau high in the Andes – the Altiplano. After the Tibetan plateau, this is the largest high plain on Earth. It has an average height of 3,300 m (11,000 ft) and is ringed with high mountains and volcanoes. In prehistoric times it was mostly filled with a vast inland sea, of which two main remnants exist today – Lake Titicaca and Lake Poopó.

In 1978 Scottish surveyor and aerial-photography analyst Jim Allen realized that the Altiplano seemed to match closely the description given by Plato of the plain on which the capital city of Atlantis sat. According to Plato, this plain was rectangular, enclosed by mountains, with a small mount at its centre, close to the sea. Allen used a particular translation of Plato, which also specified that the plain was elevated high above sea level and was midway down the 'long' side of the continent. These descriptions closely fit the Altiplano, and Allen even got Plato's specific measurements of 3,000 x 2,000 *stadia* to match by slightly reinterpreting the size of this ancient unit. Over the course of several expeditions Allen located what he believed to be the small mount that had formed the heart of Atlantis city – a hill called Pampa Aullagus, not far from Lake Poopó, which is what Allen believes Plato meant when he said that Atlantis city was close to the 'sea'. He argues that it was a sudden inundation by the waters of Lake Poopó, combined with earthquakes (common in the region), that destroyed the city (see pages 58–59).

In summary, Allen believes that South America is the still-extant continent of Atlantis, positioned more or less exactly where Plato described it; that the plateau of the Altiplano is probably the only place in the world that actually matches Plato's description of the central plain of Atlantis; that the capital city of Atlantis was situated near the shores of Lake Poopó; and that its ruins probably lie beneath salty silt in and around the lake.

SUPPORTING EVIDENCE

To back up his theory, Allen points to a range of evidence, including:
* *Atl* and *antis* are both Amerindian words meaning respectively 'water' and 'copper'. According to Plato, both of these were important features of Atlantis, while they are also characteristic of the Altiplano and the pre-Colombian cultures that we know existed there. (However, it should be pointed out that *Atl* is a Nahuatl or Aztec word, and thus from a completely different part of the Americas.)
* Orichalcum – possibly an alloy of copper and gold – was common in Atlantis.

The Incas and other local cultures made extensive use of an alloy of copper and gold.

- The mountains around the central plain of Atlantis were said to be rich in precious minerals. The mountains around the Altiplano have produced vast quantities of gold, silver and other ores.

- The cultures of the Altiplano, from the Incas back in time to their ancient ancestors, display many similarities with Old World civilizations, such as pyramid-building, monumental masonry, head-flattening (an alarming but harmless practice in which boards are strapped to infants' skulls to shape them) and many others. This suggests a common ancestry.

- One of the tutelary deities of the Altiplano region was Tunapa, god of the waters – a possible parallel for Poseidon. A Quechua parallel of Tunapa/Poseidon was Viracocha, a culture hero associated with a great, civilization-destroying flood in the Lake Titicaca region, and who was sometimes depicted as a blond or red-headed, blue-eyed traveller from afar, like the Aztec/Maya Quetzlcóatl, to whom he is similar. Is this evidence that civilization was spread across the Americas and elsewhere by refugees from Atlantis on the Altiplano?

Above *The village of Quillacas on the Bolivian Altiplano, an important site on what Jim Allen calls the Atlantis Trail.*

'*In 1978 Jim Allen realized that the Altiplano seemed to match closely the description given by Plato of the plain on which the capital city of Atlantis sat.*'

The canals of the Altiplano

The first clue that alerted Jim Allen to the Atlantean potential of the Altiplano also proved to be the most significant piece of evidence for his theory – the presence of a network of huge canals, just as Plato describes.

The Altiplano is home to the ancient city-state of Tiwanaku, which predates the Inca by a thousand years or more and was a strong influence on cultures in the region. Atlantologist Stephen Hodge points out that even if Allen is right about the canals being man-made, it might be more logical to trace them to the Tiwanakans, who were known to be masters of irrigation and hydrology.

On the other hand, Atlantologist Herbie Brennan claims that Tiwanaku was constructed in the shape of a massive port, despite being high above sea level, and that this may be evidence that it is actually 8,000 years old (or more) and that the Altiplano was at sea level when it was constructed. He suggests that Tiwanaku may have been a maritime trading partner of Atlantis, or at least that it proves advanced civilizations could have existed within the timeframe Plato described.

① LAKE POOPÓ

The lakes of the Altiplano are large but shallow, which means they can grow and shrink tremendously, depending on rainfall. Allen was partly attracted to Pampa Aullagus as a convincing site for the city of Atlantis because of its location – in the centre of the plain yet only around 7.5 km (5 miles) from the water, just as Plato describes. Here, however, we see Lake Poopó swollen until it virtually encompasses the city.

② WATER WORKS

When Jim Allen initially surveyed satellite photos of the Bolivian Altiplano, one of the first things that caught his eye was what appeared to be a giant canal in the desert to the west of Lake Poopó. Over the course of the next 25 years Allen made several trips to Bolivia to investigate the mystery of these canals for himself. He claims that the canals are clearly visible in the landscape, and that – contrary to the opinion of many experts – they are not simply dry river beds that follow the course of geological faults, but man-made constructions that provide evidence of hydrological engineering on an astonishing scale.

③ MEASURING UP

Allen claims that the giant canal he located with the satellite imagery conforms exactly to the dimensions ascribed to it in the *Critias* dialogue. Plato described it as being a *stadia* (180 m/600 ft) in width, and Allen measured the width from the top of one embankment to the other as 180 m (600 ft). He subsequently went on to discover myriad other canals, including a huge network criss-crossing the Altiplano that conforms to the proportions of the grid Plato described criss-crossing the Atlantean plain.

④ RINGS OF LAND AND WATER

In particular, Allen's proposed site for the Atlantean Acropolis, Pampa Aullagus, appears from aerial photography and field investigation to be surrounded by concentric rings in the landscape – rings that were, Allen claims, once filled with water to create a series of concentric canals exactly as Plato describes. Not everyone finds Allen's evidence and interpretation of the aerial photos convincing, but the landscape has been much altered by earthquakes, land subsidence and drastic changes in the level of Lake Poopó, which could well have obscured exact details of this putative Atlantis.

⑤ THE SUNKEN CITY

Today this mount is known as Pampa Aullagus and Allen explains that in the local Aymara dialect, Aullagus can be interpreted to mean 'drain' or 'sunken', or even 'place that is no more'. He also describes how, visiting the site today, it is still possible to see variegated stones of red, white and black, the same colours of stone that Plato describes as giving the city of Atlantis such a striking appearance.

'Pampa Aullagus appears from aerial photography to be surrounded by concentric rings in the landscape.'

The destruction of Altiplano Atlantis

Unlike Plato's Atlantis, South America is still above the waves, and the Altiplano itself is thousands of metres above sea level. How can Jim Allen reconcile this with his theory, and is there any evidence of what happened to Altiplano Atlantis and its inhabitants?

Allen argues that Plato's account was garbled by the passage of aeons of time, or has been overinterpreted to mean that the whole continent of Atlantis sunk, when in fact only the capital city perished, thanks to a combination of floods, earthquakes and tsunamis. The Altiplano is an almost completely enclosed bowl, into which scores of rivers drain, but from which it is hard for water to escape. Torrential rain can lead to flash floods, while Lake Poopó itself, owing to its shallowness, is notorious for massive fluctuations in extent. It might therefore be possible that a massive storm or series of storms caused Lake Poopó to inundate the Atlantean city around Pampa Aullagus.

The Andes are a highly active geological zone, and earthquakes are common. Pampa Aullagus itself clearly shows massive subsidence where an earthquake has shattered one of its flanks. Perhaps flooding was accompanied by such a quake or series of quakes, which helped to collapse the city beneath the encroaching waters. To add a third possible agent of doom, Allen also points out that tilting of the Altiplano has left the southern, Lake Poopó end lower than the Lake Titicaca end. He theorizes that if this tilting was caused by a single, catastrophic earthquake, vast quantities of water from the latter lake would suddenly have been tipped into the southern end of the Altiplano, in the form of a giant tsunami that would have wiped out everything in its path, just moments after a devastating earthquake. Plato's description of the doom of Atlantis would have been amply fulfilled, as the city simultaneously subsided and drowned.

Right *Lake Poopó is shallow and its area fluctuates in response to rainfall and evaporation. Previous shorelines can be seen in the photo as lighter and darker shaded areas ringing the current shoreline.*

DATING THE DESTRUCTION

Fossil shorelines around the existing lakes of the Altiplano and around the rim of the whole plateau preserve the record of ancient water levels. From these Allen has been able to deduce that while the whole area would have been under the massive palaeo-lake known as Lake Tauca at the date given by Plato for the existence of Atlantis (*c.*9000 BCE), during the period 1500–1200 BCE Lake Poopó would have been at just the right height to fill the concentric 'moats' around Pampa Aullagus. And 1200 BCE is the revised date for the destruction of Atlantis favoured by many scholars, on the basis that the ancient Egyptians would have used a lunar calendar (see page 37); it also fits in with known historical phenomena, such as the advent of the Sea Peoples (see pages 32–33).

WHAT HAPPENED NEXT?

According to Allen and many others, there is a mass of evidence of pre-Colombian transatlantic contact between the Old and New Worlds. Allen suggests that the River Plate estuary and Tartessos in Spain were at either end of the thriving transatlantic trade route between the Atlantean empire in South America and the Bronze Age Mediterranean world. The fabulous wealth of the gold, silver, copper and tin mines of Bolivia made Atlantis rich and powerful, while – in seeking to control and protect the trade network – Atlanteans may have colonized the European/African side, just as Plato describes. Allen thinks that the legendary trading expeditions of Solomon and Hiram to Tarshish (see page 30) were not to Tartessos, but actually to the Plate estuary.

Above A view from Lake Poopó of the mountains surrounding the Altiplano. These mountains mean that the Altiplano fits Plato's description of a great plain ringed by mountains.

Allen's theory is that with such trade networks in place, and with their advanced maritime technology and naval power, a natural route for Atlantean refugees would have been across the Atlantic, pitching up in the Mediterranean as the Sea Peoples (see pages 32–33). Meanwhile other groups went out across the Americas, founding the Meso-American civilizations and giving rise to foundation myths such as those of the Aztecs.

EUROPE

PART 4

THE ATLANTIC OCEAN

After Plato, the person considered to be the most important writer and theorist on Atlantis is the 19th-century American Ignatius Donnelly, author of *Atlantis: The Antediluvian World*. In this seminal book he examines the case for Atlantis being exactly where Plato said it was – in the Atlantic Ocean.

This section examines Donnelly's massively influential work and his extraordinary life; it also looks in detail at two Atlantic Ocean island chains – the Azores and the Canary Islands – that have frequently been linked with Atlantis, both by Donnelly and his successors and by previous speculators on the subject. In addition, it examines two intriguing recent suggestions that place Atlantis either on a sunken 'palaeo-island' just in front of the Straits of Gibraltar or in Ireland.

Ignatius Donnelly and Atlantis

Although Plato is the ultimate source (and possibly the sole creator) of the Atlantis myth, it is generally accepted that Atlantology - the modern fascination with and study of Atlantis - is almost entirely the legacy of American politician, journalist and amateur historian Ignatius Donnelly.

Left The Egyptian Pharaoh Akhenaten (1364–1374 BCE) making an offering to the sun-god Aton. Sun worship was common to civilizations on both sides of the Atlantic. Donnelly put this down to the influence of Atlantis.

In 1882 Donnelly published *Atlantis: the Antediluvian World* ('antediluvian' means 'before the flood'). It was an international best-seller and propagated ideas about Atlantis that still form the core beliefs of most Atlantis enthusiasts. Subsequent Atlantologists, from Madame Blavatsky and Augustus le Plongeon to Edgar Cayce and Rudolf Steiner, owe much to Donnelly's vision.

Donnelly argued that the matter-of-fact style Plato employed showed that he was recording real history, not a moral or philosophical fable:

Neither is there any evidence on the face of this history [that is, the Dialogues] that Plato sought to convey in it a moral or political lesson, in the guise of a fable … There is no ideal republic delineated here. It is a straightforward, reasonable history of a people ruled over by their kings …

Atlantis had indeed existed in the middle of the Atlantic, as claimed by Plato, and had indeed perished in a sudden deluge.

DONNELLY'S CLAIMS

But Donnelly also went much further than Plato. Building on new theories about the Maya and their possible origins, which were emerging from the new archeology of Central and South America, and blending these with the exciting discoveries from Old World archeology regarding the Egyptians and other ancient civilizations, Donnelly argued that all these civilizations – indeed all the ancient civilizations on Earth – had their origins in Atlantis (with Egypt as the oldest of these Atlantean 'colonies' or daughter civilizations). Atlantis was the original source of everything from metallurgy and agriculture to pyramid-building, writing and other technologies. Ancient languages and their modern descendants could be traced back to Atlantis, as could the sun-worshipping religions of the Maya and the Egyptians. The mythical and divine figures of religions hailing from the Nile Valley to Scandinavia and India could all be traced back to real kings, queens and heroes of Atlantis, and the world's manifold Flood myths were race memories of the destruction of Atlantis.

ATLANTIS IN THE ATLANTIC

Since Plato had been quite definite about the location of Atlantis, Donnelly assumed it must lie beneath the Atlantic waves. Seizing upon the latest (and, at the time, only poorly understood) data from ocean-floor sounding expeditions, he triumphantly pointed to the newly discovered Mid-Atlantic Ridge, and in particular a broader part of the Ridge in the middle of the North Atlantic called the Dolphin Ridge. The only parts of this ridge that project above the waves today are the Azores, a chain of volcanic islands that Donnelly claimed were the last remnants of Atlantis. The rest of the continent had sunk beneath the waves, but had once formed a land bridge right across the Atlantic (which Donnelly described as a 'connecting plateau'), or at least had provided a stepping stone for easy access from Europe and Africa to the Americas. This, said Donnelly, accounted for many parallels between Old and New World flora and fauna (in fact he was either wrong about the parallels or they could be explained by continental drift).

Above A Mayan temple at Chichen Itza. Donnelly pointed to the construction of pyramids on both sides of the Atlantic as proof that pyramid building had started in Atlantis.

'*Atlantis was the original source of everything from metallurgy and agriculture to pyramid-building and writing.*'

Ignatius Donnelly

A maverick hero to his admirers and the 'Prince of Cranks' to his detractors, Ignatius Donnelly lived a remarkable life marked, above all, by an unshakeable belief in his own genius. He was a best-selling author, controversial politician and even a candidate for the American vice-presidency. Intellectual boldness (or hubris) led him to try his hand, by turns, at law, journalism, city planning, publishing, politics, history, archeology, geology, Shakespearian scholarship, cryptography and science fiction.

Born on 3 November 1831, in the city of Philadelphia, of Irish heritage, the young Ignatius Donnelly was a precocious literary talent, who went on to study law and was admitted to the Bar in 1852. Intending to make something of himself and to spread the seeds of his genius, he moved to Minnesota, published a newspaper and tried to set up a utopian community called Nininger City, a co-operative farm that he envisaged growing into a second Chicago. Unfortunately the Panic of 1857 (a real-estate crash) cut off funding for the project and Donnelly was left as the utopian city's only resident.

Right A plan of the projected city of Nininger, on the banks of the Mississippi, an agrarian utopia dreamed up by the young Ignatius Donnelly. Unfortunately financial constraints meant that reality never came close to matching these grandiose ambitions.

LAW AND LIBRARIES

Through his journalism Donnelly became involved in politics, being elected lieutenant-governor of the new state of Minnesota in 1859 and serving as a Republican congressman from 1863 to 1869. However, his extremely progressive politics (he was anti-slavery and supported women's suffrage) upset some people, and when it was discovered that he had spent most of his time in Washington in the Library of Congress, researching Atlantis, he was kicked out.

BEST-SELLERS

Donnelly's *Atlantis: the Antediluvian World* made his name. He followed it up with *Ragnarok, the Age of Fire and Gravel* (1883), about his theory that a massive comet impact had wiped out prehistoric high civilization and left its mark on the world's myths; and later with several works on Shakespeare, in particular *The Great Cryptogram: Francis Bacon's Cipher in Shakespeare's Plays* (1888), in

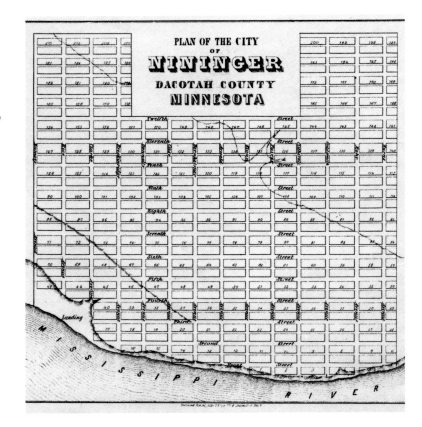

which he laid out the still-influential theory that Shakespeare's plays were actually written by Sir Francis Bacon and contained a code to that effect. He became a regular on the lecture circuit, explaining his controversial but appealing theories to packed houses around the country.

LATER CAREER

Donnelly went on to pen a science-fiction novel, *Caesar's Column* (1890) and various other books. He also made periodic attempts to restart his political career, running unsuccessfully for Congress, successfully for the Minnesota State Legislature and even, in 1892, for vice president on the ticket of the People's or Populist Party, one of the periodic unsuccessful attempts to introduce a third party into American national politics. He was not elected and also failed in a bid to become governor of his adopted state. He died, appropriately for such a visionary, on 1 January 1901, the first day of the new century.

DONNELLY'S REPUTATION

Today Donnelly is best known for his Atlantis theories, but even in his own day he was a controversial and larger-than-life character. He had many detractors, who referred to him derisively as the Sage of Nininger (his failed utopian city), the Prince of Cranks (because of his fringe historical/scientific theories, which were universally panned by contemporary and subsequent mainstream experts) and the Apostle of Discontent (because of his rabble-rousing politics and tireless championing of the 'little man' against big business and the elite).

More recently, Donnelly has been termed the Great American Failure, because despite his relentlessly high opinion of himself and his contribution to society, he sadly failed at almost everything he tried: utopian community-building, bidding for high office, and proving controversial theories in the face of establishment scorn. The truth is, however, that as well as being a bold, self-educated scholar and a man ahead of his time in political terms, he succeeded in exciting widespread national and international interest in the issues dearest to him.

'Today Donnelly is best known for his Atlantis theories, but even in his own day he was a controversial and larger-than-life character.'

Above Ignatius Donnelly in 1898, just a few years before his death. At this time he was touring the country, lecturing to packed houses about his controversial but popular theories.

Atlantean myth and religion

Donnelly believed that all of the major cultures had drawn their religions and mythologies from a single progenitor, the mighty Ur-civilization of Atlantis, and that the evidence for this claim was to be found scattered throughout the myths and symbols of ancient civilizations.

SOLAR GODS AND SYMBOLS

Parts II and IV of Donnelly's seminal *Atlantis: the Antediluvian World* concern the myths, religions and symbols of what he argues are the daughter civilizations of Atlantis (or 'colonies', as he terms them). Donnelly uses this evidence to reconstruct the myths, religions and symbols of ancient Atlantis. Specifically, he says that the Atlanteans were sun-worshippers, with a solar god as the main (or perhaps sole) member of their pantheon. Chief among their symbols was the solar cross, still known to us today as this symbol (see opposite).

THE ORIGIN OF MYTHS

Donnelly was also a strong believer in euhemerism, the theory that mythological accounts reflect actual events and/or people – in other words, that real historical happenings and personages become transformed over time into myths and mythical figures. He traces back flood myths, which he finds to be nearly ubiquitous across the world, to the destruction of Atlantis. He traces back creation myths, myths of first humans, myths of how culture, civilization and technology were acquired, and myths of gods in general to the impact of the Atlanteans on the people they influenced and the lands they colonized.

① ARABIA

Donnelly claimed that the pre-Islamic peoples of Arabia traced their ancestry back to the Adites or sons of Ad. 'Ad' he links linguistically to Ad-lantis, with Ad presumably referring to Atlas, first high king of Atlantis, and by extension to all Atlanteans.

② INDIA

Donnelly focused on the Indo-Europeans (a grouping in India and elsewhere that had only recently been identified by linguistic pioneers, who had realized that Sanskrit was related to and seemed to predate languages such as Greek and Aramaic). He claimed that their ancestors/progenitors, the ancient Aryans, descended directly from Atlantis. As evidence he pointed to the names given to the 'first man' by various Indo-European cultures. The Hindus, he claimed, called the first man Ad-ima.

③ PERSIA

Donnelly said that the Persians called the first man Ad-amah. Here again was the linguistic link to 'Ad'.

④ MESOPOTAMIA

Donnelly claimed: 'we thus find the sons of Ad at the base of all the most ancient races of men, to wit, the Hebrews, the Arabians, the Chaldeans [one of the peoples of Mesopotamia], the Hindoos, the Persians, the Egyptians, the Ethiopians, the Mexicans, and the Central Americans; testimony that all these races traced their beginning back to a dimly remembered Ad-lantis.'

⑤ CENTRAL AMERICA AND PERU

Sun-worship was the central tenet of the Maya, Incas and Aztecs, Donnelly pointed out, linking this to the sun-worship of the ancient Egyptians, Babylonians and Phoenicians. The Incas' great festival of the sun was called Ray-mi, a name he linked to Ra and Rama.

⑥ SCANDINAVIA

Donnelly drew parallels between Wotan (Odin), the prime god of the Norse pantheon, and a Votun who apparently featured in the religion and myths of a Central American people called the Chiapenese, whose myths also seemed to record pre-Columbian travels in Africa.

⑦ PHOENICIANS AND HEBREWS

In the Bible the first man is, of course, Adam. According to Donnelly, the supreme god of the Phoenicians was called Adon, and was related to the Greek god Adonis, and to the Hindu group of gods called the Aditya. Again the 'Ad' link is evident.

⑨ GREECE

Donnelly spent a whole chapter explaining that the gods of ancient Greece were originally the kings of Atlantis. He focused in particular on the prevalence of the number 12, saying that there were 12 Olympian gods, 12 signs of the Zodiac, 12 gods in Babylonian myth and 12 Norse gods. This, he claimed, was because there had been 12 kings of Atlantis (although this seems to ignore the fact that Plato clearly states there were *ten* kings).

Ankh

Solar Cross

THE SIGN OF THE CROSS

The cross is an ancient and ubiquitous symbol that predates Christianity and is often associated with the sun. Donnelly pointed out that crosses could be found all over the ancient Middle and Near East, in Egypt (especially as the ankh, a symbol representing the life-force: a cross with a handle or loop at the top), in T-shaped and ringed crosses found in Palenque, Teotihuacan and elsewhere in Central America, and in pre-Christian Ireland, all of which he believed were Atlantean colonies.

⑧ EGYPT

The main focus of Egyptian worship was the sun god Ra, which Donnelly linked to the original Atlantean sun-worshipping cult (also pointing out the similarity to the name of the Hindu sun god Rama). He also claimed that Thoth was said to have been a 'foreign god', who invented the alphabet and introduced it to Egypt; Thoth's original name, Donnelly claimed, was At-hothes, providing the linguistic link to At-lantis.

⑩ LAND OF THE GODS

Because of its role as the birthplace of civilization, and the happiness and prosperity enjoyed there before the cataclysm, Donnelly argued that Atlantis was the original model or location for such mythical sites as the Garden of Eden, the Gardens of the Hesperides, the Elysian Fields, the Gardens of Alcinous (a fabulous paradise on an island described by Homer), Olympus (home of the Greek gods) and Asgard (home of the Norse gods).

Atlantean language, architecture and technology

A key plank in Donnelly's platform was that the technologies of civilization, which include language, building methods and other less obvious manifestations, derived from one original source, and that cross-cultural similarities proved this.

THE ALPHABET

The 19th century was an exciting time for linguists, or more specifically archeo-linguists, as a number of ancient scripts and languages were decoded, enabling historians to read about ancient civilizations in their own words. It was also a time when the science of linguistic taxonomy was developed – the method by which languages could be grouped into families based on their similarities and links, which in turn provided information about the historical relationships between the groups who spoke those languages. However, these disciplines were in their infancy and early mistakes were made, such as the incorrect interpretation of the Mayan alphabet, based on the work of Bishop Landa, which led Augustus le Plongeon astray.

Donnelly, too, made heavy reliance on Landa, using him as the basis for a table that he constructed comparing Mayan with Old World alphabets, such as Greek and Sanskrit. Donnelly focused on the alphabet because he regarded it as 'one of the most marvellous inventions for the advancement of mankind ... Without it our present civilization could scarcely have been possible.' He traced the various European alphabets back to the Egyptians and Phoenicians, and pointed to traditions among both these peoples that 'the art of writing' was not invented by people, but by the gods. To him this meant

Right An Assyrian bronze sculpture of the 10th–6th century BCE. Donnelly claimed that the technology of alloying copper and tin to make bronze had been invented by the Atlanteans, and was passed on to 'daughter' civilizations such as the Assyrians.

only one thing: 'The gods were, doubtless, their highly civilized ancestors – the people of Atlantis…'

To help prove this contention, Donnelly used his table to draw correspondences between the shapes of letters in Mayan, Sanskrit, Greek, Hebrew and other languages. For instance, the letter that Landa had identified as an 'H' roughly resembled a vertical rectangle with lines across it. To Donnelly this clearly resembled the archaic Phoenician symbol:

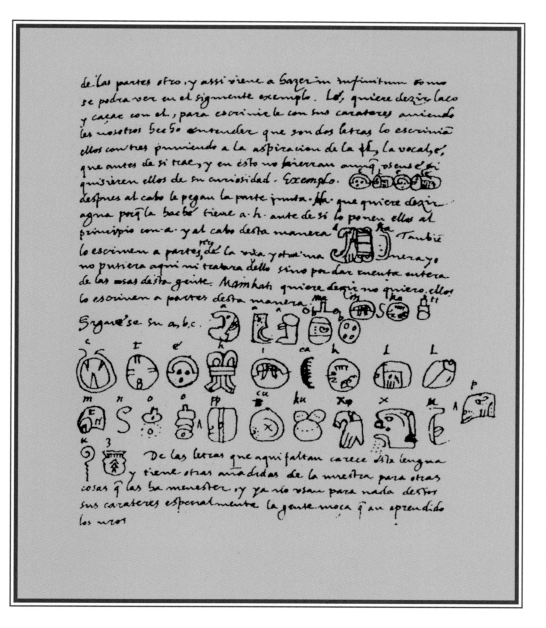

Left *A page from Bishop Diego de Landa's 16th-century* Relacion de las losas de Yucatan, *his ethnographic record of the Mayan peoples and their language. This page shows some of the Mayan symbols and the Roman letters to which Landa supposed they corresponded.*

which in turn gave rise to the Greek letter H. Surely this proved that alphabets on either side of the Atlantic derived from a single source – an original alphabet used by a race from a land situated between the Old and New Worlds?

Unfortunately for Donnelly, one of his primary sources – Landa – was wrong. The Mayan glyphs were not an alphabet (they did not symbolize word sounds such as vowels and consonants), but were mainly logograms (pictures that symbolize or represent whole words/concepts). While it is true that Old World languages and alphabets of the Indo-European family do have common roots, modern scholarship traces these roots back to the lands around the Black Sea *c.*4000 BCE, and not to Atlantis *c.*10,000 BCE, and they have no links, linguistic or otherwise, to New World systems of writing.

ARCHITECTURE AND OTHER TECHNOLOGY

For Donnelly, the most obvious symbol of the shared Atlantean heritage of the Old and New Worlds was the pyramid – 'this singular edifice' as he described it. Pyramids had been built by the ancient Egyptians and Mesopotamians, and by the Maya, Aztecs and Incas. They can also be found in many other places around the world (see, for example, the Canary Islands on pages 72–73). Construction of these mighty edifices required considerable skill and ingenuity, and even today many aspects of pyramid-building remain mysterious. Donnelly pointed to the link between pyramids and the sun-worshipping religions of the Old and New Worlds, and claimed that these civilizations had inherited their pyramid-building skills from Atlantis, and raised them in imitation of the central mount of the capital of Atlantis.

There are several problems with this contention. Plato does not mention pyramids in his account of Atlantis, and there are significant differences between Old and New World pyramids. The latter tend to be step-pyramids with flat tops, used as platforms for religious rituals. In Egypt, however, the famous pyramids are smooth-sided and pointed, and were used as tombs. There is also a clear progression of pyramid evolution on both sides of the Atlantic, so it is not necessary to hypothesize an 'inventor' or source civilization.

Other technologies that Donnelly pointed to included metallurgy – especially the use of copper and tin to make bronze; navigation and maritime technology (which he traced back to Plato's record of the canals, docks and great military and commercial fleets of Atlantis); the compass; plant and animal domestication (that is, the beginnings of agriculture); and pottery.

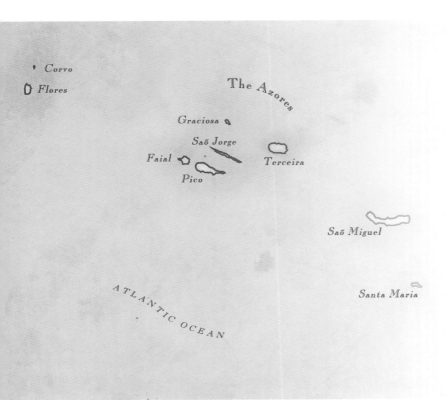

The Azores – Atlantic archipelago

Regarded by Atlanteans as actual remnants of Atlantis, the Azores are volcanic islands in the Atlantic. Mysterious archeological findings raise intriguing questions about the islands, as do modern surveys of the seabed around them.

The Azores are an archipelago of nine volcanic islands in the centre of the Atlantic Ocean, about 1,500 km (930 miles) from Lisbon and nearly 4,000 km (2,485 miles) from the coast of North America. They have high peaks (the summit of Mount Pico on Pico Island is at 2,351 m/7,700 ft), and since they rise up from the sea floor they constitute some of the tallest mountains on Earth if measured from their bases. The name 'Azores' supposedly derives from *Açor*, Portuguese for goshawk, because the early sailors misidentified the islands' buzzards as goshawks.

Officially the uninhabited Azores were discovered in 1427 by Portuguese ships exploring the Atlantic, although there is circumstantial and archeological evidence that they were known to ancient sailors such as the Phoenicians, Etruscans and Romans. The ancient Greek geographer Diodorus Siculus, writing *c.*49 BCE, reported that the Phoenicians and Etruscans competed for control of unnamed Atlantic islands, which were probably the Azores, while Roman sources describe islands nine days' sail from Portugal, matching the location of the

Azores. Ancient writers also mention various, possibly mythical islands in the Atlantic, such as Ogygia, which may reflect ancient knowledge of the islands. More conclusively, a cask of Phoenician coins was discovered on the island of Corvo. To Atlantologists, this ancient familiarity with the archipelago was due to its former role as part

of Atlantis, and an alternative derivation of the name is from Azaes, one of the original kings of Atlantis named by Plato.

DONNELLY AND THE AZORES

Donnelly believed – based on his interpretation of the newly discovered topography of the Atlantic seabed, which showed that the Azores were the highest points of the Mid-Atlantic Ridge – that the Azores were among the last parts of Atlantis to project above the waves. In particular he pointed to the presence of black and red rocks and hot and cold springs, all mentioned by Plato as features of Atlantis, and went so far as to claim that the Azores were the highest peaks

Left *Phoenician coins similar to this were discovered on the remote Azorean island of Corvo.*

of the mountain range at the northern end of Atlantis: 'One has but to contemplate their present elevation, and remember the depth to which they descend in the ocean, to realize their tremendous altitude and the correctness of the description given by Plato.' Donnelly suggested that the coins found at Corvo might have been Atlantean rather than Phoenician, and put the uninhabited state of the islands down to the cataclysm that sunk Atlantis and must have ravaged even those parts that remained above water.

DROWNED RIVER VALLEYS

Retired industrial geologist and 'fringe' archeologist Christian O'Brien, in his 1997 book *The Shining Ones* written with his wife Barbara Joy, claims that detailed explorations of the topography of the seabed around the Azores clearly show huge river valleys sunk far below the waves. This is proof, he argues, that the Azores were once part of a larger land-mass that sank beneath the waves in a volcanic cataclysm. O'Brien even claims to have identified a large sunken plain that matches the one described by Plato. He proposes that drilling into the sunken river beds will reveal geological and biological evidence (in the form of fossils, sediments and ancient pollen) proving his contentions. Mainstream geologists insist, however, that the Azores are simply peaks raised far above the seabed by intense volcanic hotspots (like the Hawaiian islands, for instance), and that they have never been part of a larger land-mass.

Below A vast volcanic crater on the island of Corvo, where Phoenician coins were recovered. Craters like these show the volcanic origins of the Azores, which were not formed in the same way as continental land-masses, despite the claims of Atlantologists.

The Canary Islands

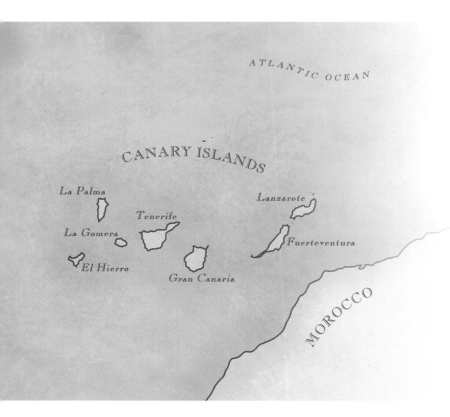

Best known today as a destination for package holidays, the Canary Islands actually conceal a number of mysteries, from the origin of the indigenous peoples to the true story behind the pyramids of Guimar.

The Canary Islands are an archipelago of seven islands of volcanic origin off the coast of North Africa. They were inhabited by a Stone Age people collectively known as the Guanches.

DONNELLY AND THE CANARIES

For Donnelly, the Canary Islands (like the Azores) stood as proof that volcanic land-masses could appear in the Atlantic, while the volcanic convulsions could explain what had happened to Atlantis. He went further, claiming that 'the Canary Islands were probably a part of the original empire of Atlantis'. He argued that the Guanches shared practices such as head-boarding (tying a board to an infant's head to deform the skull) and post-mortem skull-boring with other cultures on both sides of the Atlantic, suggesting that they had a common source.

THE MYSTERIOUS GUANCHES

Genetic and linguistic evidence suggests that the Guanches probably came from North African Berber stock, but one of several mysteries is that neither the Berbers nor the Guanches seem to have had any maritime skills. The Guanches had no boats and did not exploit the ocean, while the currents and winds around the Canaries make the islands hard to reach – so how did the Guanches colonize the islands? To add to the mystery, Pliny the Elder (23–79 CE) records that the islands were visited by the Carthaginians, who found them uninhabited, but saw the ruins of great buildings.

These ruins might have been the pyramids of Guimar on Tenerife – a group of six step-pyramids topped with broad platforms, 'discovered' by Norwegian archeologist and anthropologist Thor Heyerdahl, after having been dismissed for generations as simple agricultural terracing. Excavation revealed that they were in fact skilfully constructed, oriented along astronomical lines, and probably had a religious or ceremonial purpose. According to the foundation that looks after them, 'They were painstakingly built step-pyramids, constructed according to similar principles as those of Mexico, Peru, and ancient Mesopotamia.' It is generally assumed they were created by the Guanches, but perhaps they are Atlantean relics.

① **PYRAMID COMPLEX**

The pyramids of Guimar form part of a complex of multiple levels, platforms and stairs, built on sloping ground in front of a huge volcano. There are six main step-pyramids, with a maximum height of 12 m (40 ft).

② **SOLSTICE ORIENTATION**

Many prehistoric and ancient monuments are aligned with important astronomical or solar co-ordinates, and the Guimar pyramids are no exception. The three main ones are orientated to sunset on the summer solstice, suggesting that they played a role either in helping the Guanches to calculate on which day the solstice occurred or in ceremonies to mark this day. Such an orientation tells us that the Guanches must have had relatively sophisticated astronomical and surveying skills.

③ **FLAT TOP**

The top of each pyramid is a broad, perfectly flat platform covered in gravel, presumably to provide a space for ceremonies and sun-worship.

④ **SUN-WORSHIP**

The Guanches worshipped a solar deity above all others, and the pyramids may well have been used for sacrifices to the sun god, probably involving goats. Sunset on the summer solstice was probably the most important day in the ceremonial calendar.

⑤ **THE BLACK PYRAMIDS**

The pyramids are constructed of black obsidian with jagged edges, arranged so that the flat sides face outwards to give a smooth black facing. This led to the complex being dubbed the Black Pyramids. Behind the facing is a looser filling material.

⑥ **GOAT PENS**

Around the bases of the pyramids the same building materials have been used to create a network of walled enclosures, which may have been holding pens for sacrificial goats. One Guanche practice was to prevent kids feeding for several days so that they would bleat continuously – this was believed to help bring rain.

⑦ **WESTERN STEPS**

The steps up to the top of each pyramid run up their western sides, so that anyone climbing to the highest platform would have ascended into the light of the setting sun on the longest day of the year. Climbing the steps would probably have formed part of a ceremony to mark the occasion.

⑧ **IN THE SHADOW OF THE VOLCANO**

The slopes of mighty Mount Teide, the third-largest volcano on Earth, loom over the pyramids. The Guanches knew it as Echeyde, and thought it was a gateway to hell.

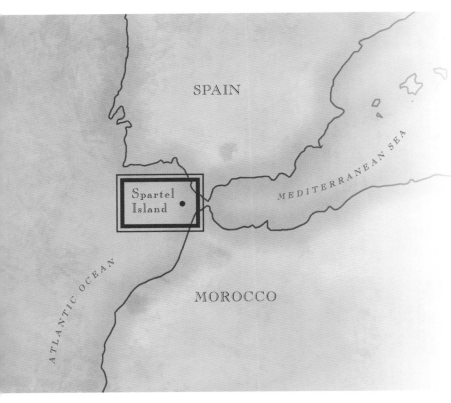

Spartel Island – beyond the Pillars of Hercules

Perhaps the most obvious place to look for Atlantis is exactly where Plato tells us to – beyond the Pillars of Hercules. One radical theory identifies a sunken 'palaeo-island' called Spartel Island located in just such a position.

In terms of geological history (that is, on a timescale of millions or tens of millions of years), current sea levels are relatively low, owing to the large – albeit diminishing – amounts of water locked up as ice at the Poles. Nonetheless, during previous Ice Ages even more water was locked away, and sea levels were sometimes more than 100 m (330 ft) lower than they are today. This meant that huge tracts of near-sea-level continental shelf, which today lie not far beneath the waves, were dry land.

Much of this land simply extended modern coastlines, but some of it would have poked above the waves as islands. The early Stone Age is technically known as the Palaeolithic Era, and islands that existed at this time are sometimes called palaeo-islands. Given that the last Ice Age ended and sea levels rose dramatically around 10,000–12,000 years ago (the time when Plato tells us Atlantis existed), it has been suggested that perhaps Atlantis was such a palaeo-island.

THE SPARTEL HYPOTHESIS

Perhaps with this logic in mind, French geologist Jacques Collina-Girard, from the University of the Mediterranean in Aix-en-Provence, used coral-reef data to estimate sea levels between 19,000 and 11,000 years ago. He discovered that a palaeo-island, named Spartel Island, would have existed just 50 km (31 miles) west of the Straits of Gibraltar during this period, when sea levels were as much as 130 m (422 ft) lower than today, before rising and drowning the island.

Left Satellite view of the Straits of Gibraltar, flanked by the Pillars of Hercules (Gibraltar in Europe and Monte Hacho in Africa).

Now it lies 60 m (196 ft) beneath the Atlantic waves. (Hispanic-American Atlantologist Georgeos Diaz-Montexano claims to have first come up with this theory, and accuses Collina-Girard of plagiarism.)

Collina-Girard's original interest had been in possible migration patterns of Palaeolithic humans, and he theorizes that an island such as Spartel could have been an important stepping stone between Spain and Africa, and maybe even the hub of an early inter-continental trading route. But when he discovered the ancient island on maps of the sea floor, it occurred to him that the right place to look for Atlantis was 'obviously near Gibraltar'. 'Nobody seems to have thought of the clearest indication given by Plato – that of an island at the mouth of the Pillars of Hercules,' Collina-Girard told *New Scientist* magazine.

There were a number of obvious objections to Collina-Girard's identification, of which he was well aware. Firstly, the maximum extent of Spartel Island was just 14 x 5 km (9 x 3 miles), whereas Plato's Atlantis was at least 550 x 370 km (340 x 230 miles) – the size of the central plain, as described in *Critias*. In fact the *Timaeus*

dialogue states that it was 'greater than Asia and Libya combined', although this may be a reference to its political and military clout. Plato's Atlantis also had mountains, and extensive earthworks and buildings, which might be expected to have left some trace. Sonar pictures of Spartel show nothing of this sort, and Collina-Girard simply suggests that Plato's account is an exaggerated version of faint memories of a much less impressive Stone Age waypoint. The problem with this line of reasoning is that Collina-Girard expects us to follow Plato's directions in order to locate Atlantis, but then disregard everything else he says about it – in other words, it is not logically consistent.

TSUNAMI TRACES

However, a 2005 paper by another French geologist, Marc-André Gutscher of the University of Western Brittany in Plouzané, France, has provided unexpected support for Collina-Girard's theory. Gutscher points to the Lisbon tsunami of 1755 – triggered by a massive sub-Atlantic earthquake, which nearly wiped the Portuguese capital off the map – as an example of what might have struck Spartel Island. Donnelly himself

mentioned the Lisbon tsunami as evidence that the Atlantic region could be afflicted with cataclysms and deluges.

Gutscher examined a sea-floor survey that showed a thick layer of turbidite deposits on Spartel, dating from around 12,000 years ago. Turbidite is a layer of heavily disturbed sediment regarded as the telltale trace of a tsunami. The evidence therefore seems to suggest that just as rising sea levels were threatening to submerge Spartel (at roughly the same date that Plato gives for the cataclysmic earthquake and drowning of Atlantis), a massive earthquake hit the region, possibly causing sudden, dramatic subsidence and definitely causing a huge tsunami. Just as Plato describes, Spartel would have been swamped by the ocean in the space of a few hours. Perhaps memories of this event survived from the Palaeolithic to Plato's time and provided the basis for the tale of Atlantis.

Of course even if this hypothesis were true, the Spartel Atlantis would have been a far cry from Plato's grandiose conception, presumably consisting of little more than a Stone Age village or group of villages, albeit perhaps with a far greater concentration of population than was usual for the era.

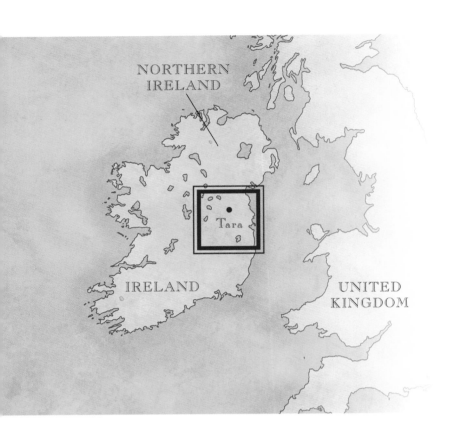

NORTHERN
IRELAND

Tara

IRELAND

UNITED
KINGDOM

Ireland and Tara

A radical theory attempts to link Stone Age events and cultures in western Europe with Plato's tale, to arrive at the startling conclusion that Atlantis was Ireland, the city of Atlantis was the ancient Irish capital at Tara, and the drowned land of the legend is now Dogger Bank beneath the North Sea.

STONE AGE HISTORY

The author of this radical theory is Swedish geologist Ulf Erlingsson, whose book *Atlantis from a Geographer's Perspective: Mapping the Fairy Land* sets out a series of logical steps to arrive at what initially seems like a far-fetched conclusion. His basic contention is that Plato's dating was accurate, but that the rest of his tale was a fantasy based on legends of an impressive prehistoric civilization that really existed. Because Plato's account clearly describes a high Bronze Age civilization, Atlantis revisionists have been tempted to assume the Platonic dating was inaccurate, probably by an order of magnitude. Erlingsson suggests that the dating is fundamentally correct, which puts Atlantis deep in the Stone Age, and this in turn corresponds with events that could have inspired major elements of the Atlantis story.

DOGGER BANK AND THE STOREGGA SLIDE

Erlingsson points out that around the end of the last Ice Age, from about 12,000 to 8,000 years ago, major changes affected the North Sea. While water was still locked up in the ice, the sea levels were low and large areas that today lie beneath the North Sea would have been dry land. In particular, a large plain in the south of the North Sea was protected from northern winds by the Dogger Hills, and would have been a rich hunting ground for Stone Age peoples of the region, where mammoths roamed free (hence the elephants of Plato's account, see page 21).

As the sea levels rose, the Dogger Hills became Dogger Island. Then, 8,100 years ago, global warming triggered an explosive release of frozen methane sediments on the Storegga continental slope off Norway, setting off a huge submarine landslide, which in turn triggered an immense tsunami, the marks of which can still be seen high above modern shorelines in Scotland. This giant tsunami would have swamped Dogger Island in a cataclysm that, Erlingsson theorizes, might have inspired legends of a deluge. Further rises in sea level ensured that Dogger Island became Dogger Bank, a mud shoal that for many centuries might have made the area impassable to navigation – just as Plato says.

Below The entrance to the Newgrange tomb, a massive stone and earth construction that predates the Great Pyramid at Giza by 500 years.

THE MEGALITHIC EMPIRE

Erlingsson suggests that legends of the Dogger deluge could have been adopted and perpetuated by the culture that grew up in western Europe in the centuries that followed. This culture is best known today for the huge stone monuments, or megaliths, that it left behind, including henges, dolmens, barrows and so on. The megalithic culture successfully extended its influence and practices all the way to the eastern Mediterranean, just as Plato describes Atlantis doing. Erlingsson contends that this megalithic 'empire' was Atlantis, and had its headquarters in Ireland.

IRELAND AND TARA

There is no doubt that Ireland played a very significant role in the Stone Age megalithic culture. Erlingsson points out that it is the only large island in the world with dimensions matching those given by Plato in *Critias* (see page 20), with a broadly rectangular central plain, sheltered on most sides by mountains. He points to the ancient capital of Tara as the possible original for Plato's Atlantis city, citing in particular the immense tomb/earthwork of Newgrange. This impressive structure predates the pyramids and was one of the largest buildings in Europe for millennia. Perhaps, the Swede proposes, it was the model for the mighty Temple of Poseidon in Plato's account.

Erlingsson argues that the megalithic culture survived long enough to become known to the ancient Egyptians, who preserved its legends, including tales of Tara, Newgrange and the deluge of Dogger Bank. These legends eventually – via the Egyptian priests and Solon – reached Plato, who used them to weave a legend of his own.

Above An aerial view of the Hill of Tara, showing the two ring forts that sit within the Iron Age hill fort known as the Ráith na Rig *(Fort of the Kings).*

'*Ireland played a very significant role in the Stone Age megalithic culture.*'

SOUTH
AMERICA

PART 5

THE PACIFIC – ATLANTIS, MU AND LEMURIA

Myths and legends of lost lands are not restricted to the Atlantic. The wide open spaces of the Pacific have attracted their share of legends, speculations and wild flights of fantasy. In particular, the Pacific has been suggested as the location of two lost continents that are either similar to or cognate with Atlantis: the lost lands of Lemuria and Mu (names that some writers use interchangeably to indicate the same land).

The path from Atlantis to Lemuria and Mu is a tangled and confusing one, which takes in a cast of larger-than-life characters and frequently bizarre blends of the occult and the pseudo-scientific. This section looks at the main lost-continent theories from the Pacific region, including the Lemurian and Atlantean theories of Madame Blavatsky and her Theosophist successors, and the Mu theories of James Churchward. It also looks at Yonaguni, a Japanese site that may represent the actual equivalent of Mu, and at Sir Francis Bacon's fictional Pacific utopia, Bensalem.

Lemuria

Lemuria is a lost continent of variable size (depending on the proponent), usually situated in the Indian Ocean, but often spreading right across the Pacific. To properly understand Lemuria, it is necessary to understand the fervid atmosphere of scientific and religious debate that dominated Victorian intellectual life.

The 19th century was one of discovery and turmoil in the sciences. It was fast becoming clear that, contrary to the Classical/Christian dogma of the previous millennia, the Earth was not basically immutable and neither were the species that inhabited it. While previously the orthodoxy had been that the Earth had existed for only as long as delineated in the Bible (with a start date of 23 October 4004 BCE, as calculated by Bishop Ussher), new discoveries suggested that in fact it was unimaginably older than had previously been thought, with rocks and landscapes being formed over what are now called 'geological' periods of time – tens to hundreds of millions of years or more. Most controversially, various doctrines of transmutation – or evolution as it is better known today – were being suggested to explain the diversity and distribution of the natural world. Thanks to his brilliant use of the evidence and the careful construction of his argument, Charles Darwin's theory of evolution (initially propounded publicly in 1859) was the most successful of these.

It was against this backdrop that the concept of Lemuria was born and in this medium that it developed, along with the strange and disturbing racial doctrine that accompanied it.

***Right** A portrait of Ernst Haeckel in 1876 at the age of 42. Haeckel was a keen student of Darwin and vigorously promoted radical views on human evolution.*

FROM LAND BRIDGES TO LEMURIA

Naturalists and geologists exploring the world had discovered strange parallels between the strata and natural history of widely separated areas. For instance, almost identical beds of rock had been observed in India and South Africa, while closely related creatures could be found, in either existing or fossil form, in places as far apart as Africa, Madagascar, India and Malaysia. How was this possible when huge tracts of ocean separated the various land-masses?

The religious answer was that God had used different 'centres of creation', but supporters of evolutionary theory wanted to find a 'scientific' explanation. At that time there was no concept of continental drift – instead, it seemed more logical to propose that there had once been land bridges between the existing land-masses, which had

distinctive primates that had inspired it. Today many people are confused about this name. Later occult and New Age authors have suggested it was the name given to the continent by its prehistoric inhabitants, and point out that there is a Roman festival of the same name – supposedly this is proof of the word's antiquity and shared cultural roots. But this is to reverse the order of causality. Lemuria, the place, gets its name from the lemurs. These, in turn, gained their name from their nocturnal habits, reflective eyes and ghost-like presence among the trees, which led to them being named after the baneful spirits of Roman legend, the *lemurs*, for whom the festival is named.

LEMURIA REINVENTED

Ernst Haeckel, an influential German proponent of Darwinism, suggested that Lemuria was not only home to the lemurs, which seemed to be a very primitive order of primates, but might also have been home to the early stages of human evolution. At this point fossils representing these stages had not been found and the 'missing link' was a hot topic in science and cultural debate. Haeckel suggested that the fossils in question might be missing because they were located on the sunken portions of Lemuria. Although this idea did not prove to be scientifically viable, and the development of continental drift theory did away with the need to hypothesize land bridges, Haeckel had sown the seeds that would grow into Lemuria, the pre-Atlantean continent of the Theosophists. When Madame Blavatsky got hold of the idea, Lemuria would blossom into a vast, globe-spanning super-continent intimately connected with the incredible story of human evolution.

since sunk beneath the oceans as the result of earthquakes, rising sea levels or simple erosion. Variations on this theme came from several theorists. One such land bridge was proposed as having existed between Africa, Madagascar, India and Malaysia, linking them together in a giant super-continent.

A smaller version, linking India and Madagascar, was proposed by geologist Philip Sclater in 1864, based on the puzzle posed by the presence of fossil lemurs in India and live ones in Madagascar. Sclater suggested that both had once been part of a larger land-mass, which he called Lemuria after the

Madame Blavatsky and the Theosophists

Among the many colourful characters in the history of Atlantology, Madame Blavatsky may be the most striking. Synthesizing traditions, myths and legends from many world cultures, she created Theosophy, a new discipline that would have a wide-ranging impact.

Much of her life history was obscured by time and self-mythologizing, but it is known that Helena Petrovna Blavatsky – known as HPB to her disciples, and as Madame Blavatsky to the rest of the world – was born in the Ukraine (then part of Russia) in 1831 of aristocratic stock. She had a peripatetic childhood dominated by strong female role-models and was nurtured in the belief that she had supernatural gifts from an early age. Her CV included such diverse occupations as bareback rider in a circus, piano teacher, ostrich-feather importer, interior decorator and medium. She claimed to have travelled extensively in Central Asia, and to have studied with mystic gurus in Tibet.

Right *Madame Blavatsky in a photographic portrait probably taken around 1888, just three years before her death, by which time she was living in London with an inner circle of disciples and friends.*

Travelling to Egypt, she began to move in occult circles and gained a reputation as a powerful medium, capable of feats from clairvoyance to levitation. She was also (and not for the first time) accused of fraudulent activities. In 1873 she arrived in New York and gathered a coterie of devoted disciples. With their help and backing she founded the Theosophical Society to propound an eccentric blend of esoteric wisdom, garbled Oriental philosophy, spiritualism, religion, occult lore and pseudo-scientific thinking. In particular, she claimed to receive letters (later shown to have been self-penned), and

subsequently telepathic communications, from spirits and mystic gurus, such as the 'ascended masters' who controlled human history from lairs in the Himalayas.

The Theosophical Society soon had branches around the world – HPB herself moved to new headquarters in India. Theosophy (from the Greek for 'wisdom of the gods') was based on the belief that all religions shared fragments of a greater truth, and was committed to exploring these truths to found a universal brotherhood of humanity. It is considered to be the foundation of New Age thought, although it also had sinister progeny in

terms of its influence on fascist and Nazi philosophy. HPB died in 1891, reportedly uttering this final exhortation: 'Keep the link unbroken! Do not let my last incarnation be a failure.'

THE SECRET DOCTRINE

Blavatsky tended to make use of any esoteric idea that was current. In her first book, *Isis Unveiled*, subtitled 'A master key to the mysteries of ancient and modern science and theology' (1877), she touched on ideas of mythological and cultural links between the Old and New Worlds, mentioning Lemuria, and possible lost continents in the Pacific. In

1882 Donnelly had great success with his book on Atlantis, and perhaps not coincidentally Blavatsky's next book, *The Secret Doctrine* (1888), adopted the theme of lost continents in great detail. Apparently her mystic sources had vouchsafed her the entire, incredible history of humanity. Humankind had evolved in phases, or Root Races, each of which had corresponded to a land-mass. The map of the world had looked very different with current land-masses absent either in whole or in part. Lemuria had been a giant super-continent stretching across the Pacific and Indian Oceans and into other parts, while Atlantis was a later development.

LEMURIA EXPLORED

Later Theosophist writers explored the story of Lemuria in greater detail, most notably William Scott-Elliot, an English merchant banker and amateur anthropologist, in his books *The Story of Atlantis* (1896) and *The Lost Lemuria* (1904). These two books combined the writings of Blavatsky and her followers alongside poorly understood contemporary science and the products of Scott-Elliot's own 'astral clairvoyance' (a kind of channelling whereby he received information from an otherworld), with no clear demarcation between them. Scott-Elliot explained in great detail what had become of the various races and sub-races of Lemuria and Atlantis, focusing in particular on the 2.4 m (8 ft) tall, coppery-skinned Toltecs (from whom the historical Toltecs, a 10th–12th-century Central American culture, allegedly descended) and their marvellous achievements (see pages 86–87).

Below Blavatsky and her Theosophists issued a series of world maps showing the various stages of evoluthon of the continent of Lemuria and its related land-masses, including Atlantis. This one shows Atlantis 'during the period of its decadence', prior to be being broken up in a series of catastrophes.

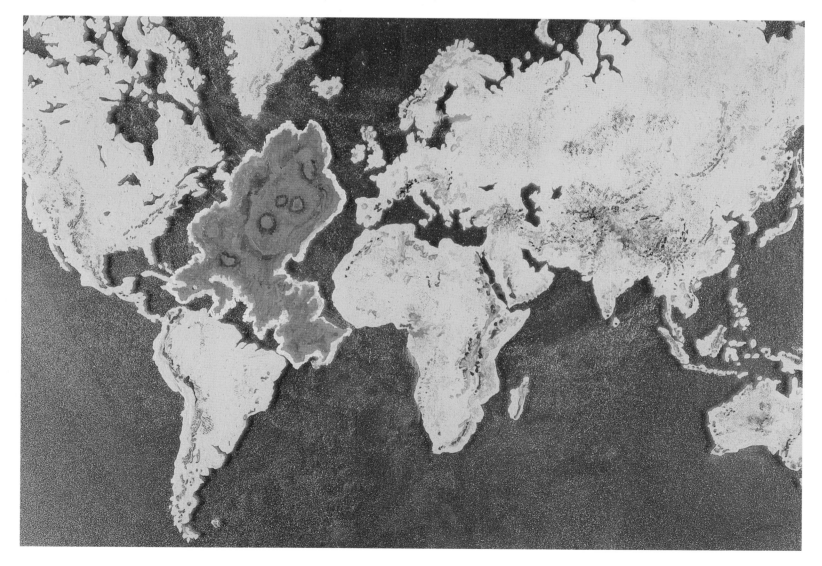

Root Races

For the Theosophists, Lemuria and Atlantis were important as parts of the stage for an immense drama of human evolution (also known as anthropogenesis), which the mystic communications vouchsafed to Madame Blavatsky had elucidated – the drama of the Root Races.

The Victorian era witnessed a growing obsession with issues of race. The evolution debate had raised questions about the true genesis of humankind, while with hindsight we can see that it served the colonial projects of the Western white powers to develop a 'scientific' rationale for their racist agendas. Debates about race were increasingly framed in 'evolutionary' terms that involved progress and ladders of evolution. Spiritual matters also came to be discussed in this fashion, with the assumption that religion as practised by the colonial powers was the end-stage of a progressive developmental process.

It was in this context that Blavatsky concocted her complex and fantastical anthropogeny. She combined new scientific ideas about changing continents and sunken land bridges (such as Lemuria) with spiritual ideas such as the Hindu notion of Yugas – vast epochs of time in which life undergoes cycles of evolution. Instead of Yugas, however, she spoke of Root Races, which were not cyclical but progressive in their development.

RACES AND SUB-RACES

In the Theosophist anthropogeny there are seven Root Races. Four existed previously in history, we are the fifth, and the sixth and seventh are yet to evolve (but will appear in North and South America respectively). Each Race is divided into seven sub-races, although these only really become important in the fourth Root Race.

The first Root Race originated 150 million years ago and was made of pure spirit energy, and was therefore invisible. It lived in a sort of non-physical Imperishable Sacred Land. The second Root Race comprised the Hyperboreans, who lived in Hyperborea – lands around the Arctic Circle. After them came the Lemurians, the third Root Race, who in turn were superseded by the Atlanteans. A sub-race of the Atlanteans evolved into the fifth Root Race, the Aryans, who account for most of the people in the world today, although Theosophists spoke of much complex cross-breeding between sub-races from earlier Root Races that accounted for some ethnic groups.

Right *A Tasmanian Aborigine in 1837. By this time most of the island's indigenous population had already been wiped out by colonists. According to Theosophy, races such as the Aborigines were Lemurian-Atlantean hybrids. Theories such as this were used to help justify the genocide that was visited on them.*

LEMURIANS AND ATLANTEANS

The Lemurians were the first recognizably human-like beings, although Blavatsky describes them as huge egg-laying hermaphrodites, with four arms and eyes in the backs of their heads. As the Lemurians evolved they split into two sexes, which proved to be their downfall because they became sex-crazed. However, they also developed many of the arts and technologies of civilization, thanks to the teachings of visitors from Venus. Descendants of the Lemurians still exist in the form of Lemurian-Atlantean 'hybrid races', described as 'semi-animal' creatures – they include the more primitive peoples of the world, such as Tasmanian Aborigines and Kalahari Bushmen.

When Lemuria broke up in a cataclysm of 'subterranean fire', one of the remnants was Atlantis. Here the fourth Root Race developed, with important differences between the sub-races. The 3.6 m (12 ft) tall, black-skinned Rmoahals lived in the south and invented warfare, going on to colonize Africa. In the north, a lighter-skinned people became Cro-Magnons, and remnants of this race can still be found in places such as the Canary Islands. Other important sub-races include the Toltecs, who created high Atlantean civilization (see pages 86–87); the fierce Turanians, who became the Aztecs and the Mongols; and the Semites, who eventually evolved into the fifth Root Race, the Aryans, sub-races of which include the Persians, Greeks, Hindus and Europeans. Like Lemuria, Atlantis broke up in a series of cataclysms, leaving smaller and smaller remnants until eventually one little island called Poseidonis remained. It was Poseidonis that Plato was actually writing about – situated opposite the Pillars of Hercules it perished beneath the waves in 9565 BCE.

Left The 'Atlantes', a group of statues at the Toltec site of Tula, dating from around the 10th century CE Although the name given to the grouping is suggestive, it is thought they actually represent the god Quetzlcoatl in his human guise.

IS THE ROOT RACES THEORY RACIST?

Theosophists defend the Root Races theory by pointing out that Madame Blavatsky often spoke of her belief in a universal brotherhood of humanity, and insisted that all humans were of essentially the same physical and spiritual origin. But this is clearly contradicted in many of her writings, where she explicitly refers to spiritually degenerate and semi-human peoples. It is also noticeable how white-skinned races, especially the Aryans, are considered to be the natural rulers and most advanced peoples, while surviving Semites are specifically described as 'abnormal and unnatural'. To some extent it is anachronistic to expect anything different from someone writing in late Victorian times, but Theosophical theories were to bear dark fruit when they helped to inspire Nazi philosophies on race and anti-Semitism.

The Toltecs of Atlantis

For the Theosophists, the greatest of the Atlantean sub-races were the Toltecs (not to be confused with their descendants, the Toltecs of pre-Colombian America). Dominating the other sub-races, they rose to prominence and spread their glorious civilization across the entire continent, using their magical powers to attain great wonders.

SCOTT-ELLIOT AND THE TOLTECS

Merchant banker William Scott-Elliot gave the most detailed description of the Toltecs' ways and works. He based his books *The Story of Atlantis* and *The Lost Lemuria* on the work of Madame Blavatsky and on mysterious astral clairvoyance of 'occult records', through which he was able to access amazingly detailed information on events, people and places in the past. It is tempting, on reading his material, to assume that he simply mixed in whatever theories were fashionable at the time.

MASTER RACE OF ATLANTIS

According to Scott-Elliot, the Toltecs were the third sub-race of Atlantis, which 'ruled the whole continent of Atlantis for thousands of years in great material power and glory'. The Toltecs were of a coppery reddish-brown complexion, on average 2.4 m (8 ft) tall with 'straight and well-marked features, not unlike the ancient Greek'. Current thinking at the time, based on fossil discoveries of giant mammals and the like, was that most species evolved from giant to reduced size, so the Theosophists assumed this rule applied to human evolution as well. They originated on the north-west coast of Atlantis, but soon spread their influence over the whole continent. The language they spoke survives today as the Nahuatl of pre-Colombian Mexico, while they survived as a race into the early Middle Ages as the Toltecs of Mexico, precursors of the Aztecs.

ACHIEVEMENTS OF THE TOLTECS

At first the Toltecs formed small, warring tribes who fought constantly with other races on Atlantis. About one million years ago, however, they banded together into a confederation that conquered all the other races, enslaving many of them. An epoch of great peace and prosperity ensued, in which the arts and sciences achieved their greatest extent until modern times.

① CITY ON A HILL

Probably the greatest achievement of the Toltecs was their wondrous capital, the City of the Golden Gates or City of the Waters. The city was built in three concentric rings around a hill, upon which sat the palace of the emperor. However, each ring of the Toltec capital was at a lower level than the one before it.

② HIGHEST LEVEL

The centre of the city was occupied by the emperor's palace and gardens. Water rose from a central spring and flowed out via four channels – one at each point of the compass – to cascade into a moat or canal at the next level down. Four more channels radiated out from here to the edge of this level of the city, before cascading down to the next, and so on.

③ MIDDLE LEVEL

The middle level of the city, just below the palace, featured a circular racecourse and public gardens. The Strangers' Home was a great palace on the middle level that provided magnificent hospitality for visitors and travellers.

④ LOWEST LEVEL

The lowest level was still elevated above the plain. When the channels carried the water down to the plain, they linked up with a fourth, rectangular canal that enclosed an area 19 x 16 km (12 x 10 miles) square.

⑤ AIRSHIPS AND VRIL

The main form of transport for Toltec aristocrats was the airship, a boat-like vessel made of wood or metal that appeared seamless and smooth and was luminous in the dark. Like much of Toltec technology, the airships were powered by vril – magical psychic energy that everyone could generate to greater or lesser degree. Eventually the Toltecs used this for evil ends, practising sorcery, which triggered the destruction of Atlantis.

⑥ STATUES

Temples and gardens were decorated with statues. We can get an idea of what they looked like from the Atlantes – a group of statues that still stand in the pre-Columbian Mexican city of Tula, and which were erected by the people whom conventional history recognizes as the Toltecs (see page 85).

⑦ BUILDINGS

Temples were built in the style of ancient Egypt, but with square pillars and columns rather than round ones. Buildings were ornamented with colourful stones, frescos, murals and carvings, so that the overall effect was kaleidoscopic. The most obvious characteristic of a typical Toltec dwelling was the tower that rose from one corner. A spiral staircase wound round the outside of the tower, which terminated in a pointed dome often used as an observatory, the Toltecs being great astronomers.

Rudolf Steiner, Lemuria and Atlantis

One of the greatest visionaries and most influential gurus of the 20th century, Rudolf Steiner left his mark in fields as diverse as agriculture, education and banking. He also used occult powers to learn about Atlantis.

Steiner was born to an Austrian railway telegraph operator and stationmaster in 1861, and proved to be a prodigious scholar. At a young age he became involved in the literary legacy of the great German polymath Goethe, making a name for himself as a diligent academic. At the same time, however, he was developing a profound interest in spiritual and esoteric matters, stemming from an encounter on a train as a 21-year-old. While travelling to Vienna he met a herb-gatherer called Felix Kogutski, whose simple but profound spirituality made a deep impression on the young Austrian, and who introduced Steiner to a guru figure he referred to only as a 'master'.

Steiner's esoteric interests led him into contact with the burgeoning Theosophical Society founded by Madame Blavatsky and subsequently managed by her successor Annie Besant. Steiner gave lectures to the German branch and eventually became its head, although he always resisted becoming an actual member, insisting that he was evolving an independent spiritual philosophy specifically for the West, rather than espousing Theosophy's supposedly ancient, Oriental spirituality. Eventually, Steiner and his growing band of followers were forced out of Theosophy and he set up Anthroposophy, a movement of his own.

Steiner's influential ideas on education and child-rearing led to the setting up of a network of institutions known as Waldorf Schools, which are still popular today. His notions on what he called biodynamic farming helped foster the modern organic farming movement. He formulated a theory about speech, emotion and movement called eurhythmy, which is still used today in speech therapy. He also set up a form of co-operative community lending that still operates.

THE AKASHIC RECORD

Steiner wrote and lectured about Lemuria and Atlantis. He was heavily influenced by Theosophical views on the evolution of humanity, agreeing with the standard Theosophical account of Root Races, lost lands and so on. He supplemented this information through his highly developed spiritual consciousness, which he claimed allowed him to access the Akashic Record. This is the record of all human experience and knowledge since the beginning of time, imprinted upon (and therefore stored in) the ether – the nebulous, non-physical plane of existence; it is a staple of New Age thought.

According to Steiner, the Akashic Record revealed many fascinating details about the

Left *Rudolf Steiner, one of the most remarkable polymaths, mystics and visionaries of the 20th century. Through his occult investigations into the history of Atlantis, Steiner helped to introduce the now broad assumption in New Age circles that the Atlanteans had psychic powers.*

Atlanteans and Lemurians. For instance, they had no skeletons and were therefore 'soft and pliable'. They also had no power of logical or arithmetical thought, but had immense powers of memory. Instead of calculating the answer to a sum or problem, they would simply remember previous experience of it. They also had control over vital energies or the life force, which enabled them to use natural, growing things, such as plants, as a power source. One use of this power was to drive flying vehicles that sound very similar to those of William Scott-Elliot (see pages 86–87). Their predecessors, the Lemurians, did not even have the faculty of memory and therefore had no language. But their ideas were so powerful that they could be transmitted to – and have an effect on – other people and things, effectively through telepathy and psychokinesis (the ability to move things or exert force using only the power of the mind).

Above *Among his many achievements, Steiner was a ground-breaking architect. Here he is seen with a model of his design for the Goetheanum, a centre for his movement where lectures and theatrical events could be held.*

'Steiner was heavily influenced by Theosophical views on the evolution of humanity, agreeing with the standard Theosophical account of Root Races, lost lands and so on.'

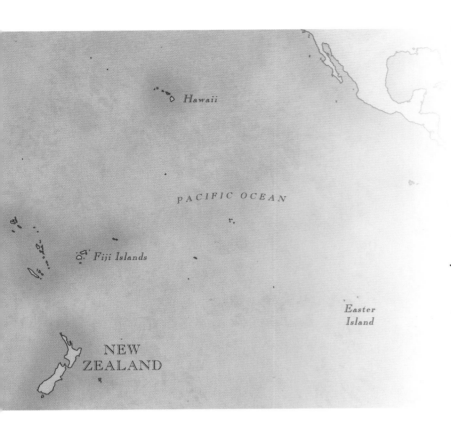

Mu – the lost Pacific continent

Mainly through the work of British-American writer James Churchward, the story of the lost Pacific continent of Mu has become a popular alternative to Donnelly's conception of Atlantis, with which it had much in common.

According to James Churchward (1851–1936), Mu was a vast continent 'extending from north of Hawaii, down towards the south. A line between Easter Island and the Fijis formed its southern boundary '… It was over 5,000 miles [8,000 km] from east to west, and over 3,000 miles [4,800 km] from north to south.' It was composed entirely of gently rolling hills, unbroken by mountain ranges of any sort, and was a lush tropical paradise where mastodons (extinct elephant-like mammals) and mammoths roamed the forests and where winding rivers watered the fertile plains.

EMPIRE OF THE SUN

In this land lived 64 million Muvians, which Churchward explained were split into ten tribes or peoples, as were the Atlanteans, but unlike the Atlanteans they were united in one government, called the Empire of the Sun. Elsewhere, however, Churchward said that the Muvians were also divided up into races with different skin colours and – in an uncomfortable example of the prevalent racism of his era – claimed that the white-skinned race ruled the others.

Echoing Donnelly's claims for Atlantis, Churchward's Mu was the cradle of human civilization on Earth, and the Empire of the Sun attained the highest level of cultural and social sophistication, as well as inventing

Below *A mural of the Egyptian sun god Ra in the solar boat.*

most of the technologies and attributes of civilization. The continent was criss-crossed with a network of paved roads, built with such ingenuity that even when the roads were left untended, grass could not grow in the cracks between the stones (a claim that probably refers to the discovery of the sophisticated masonry of the Incas, a technology that so impressed the Victorians that they found it hard to believe a Bronze Age culture could have achieved it without some quasi-mystical/magical inspiration).

The Muvians also built magnificent constructions, including their seven main cities, which were centres of science, education and religion. Although not militaristic, the Muvians were also great navigators and colonizers.

THE RELIGION OF MU

The priest-king of the Empire of the Sun was known as Ra-Mu, while their principal god – a sun god – was simple called Ra, from whom the ancient Egyptians derived their own sun god. Despite this apparently pagan basis, the religion of Mu as Churchward described it was essentially a monotheistic Christian one, albeit dressed up slightly differently. Churchward's translations of the creation myth of Mu reveal it to be very similar to that of the Bible. Supposedly the Muvians had spread their religion around the world through colonization and disseminating their civilization, much as Donnelly describes for the Atlanteans.

THE DESTRUCTION OF MU

Mu flourished for an amazing 200,000 years, but around 12,000 years ago it perished in a terrible cataclysm: 'the greatest tragedy of mankind'. Churchward explained that underlying the Earth's crust was a series of gas-belts or chambers – great hollow spaces filled with high-pressure gas. When the pressure in these gas-belts fell, they collapsed under the weight of the crust above them, causing most of Mu to plummet suddenly, amid an apocalypse of volcanoes and earthquakes, whereupon the waters of the Pacific rushed in to cover the subsided land. Only a few chunks of the continent, rent into jagged, mountainous shapes, were left above the waves as the island chains of the Pacific we know today. About one million Muvians survived the cataclysm, but found themselves crammed onto tiny islands and soon fell into savagery and cannibalism, which explained the 'savage state' of the Pacific islanders when they were encountered by Europeans.

The discovery of Mu

If Churchward's account of the lost continent of Mu seems far-fetched, the exciting story of how he came to learn the secrets of this phenomenally ancient super-civilization is scarcely less incredible.

Churchward claimed that while in India and supposedly helping with relief work following a massive famine, he befriended an Indian priest or rishi, at the monastery of Hemis in Ladakh, in north-western India. Hemis is an ancient Buddhist monastery full of copies of documents and scriptures, among which were ancient texts that set Churchward on the trail of 10,000 clay tablets in the ancient language of the Naga. The Naga are an Indian tribe, but also a mythical race of powerful snake-beings, best known in South-East Asia. The even more ancient people, the Naacal, who supposedly created the language had come, Churchward would eventually learn, from Mu, the motherland.

The tablets of the Naacal had been written between 12,000 and 14,000 years ago, around the time of the destruction of Mu, by scholars who were in Asia as part of the Muvian colonization and diaspora. Eventually they were split up between libraries and temples of several ancient Asian civilizations, while the Naacal people themselves went on to found the civilizations of ancient Mesopotamia and Egypt.

DECIPHERING THE ANCIENT TABLETS

Churchward says that with the help of his friendly rishi he was able to teach himself Naacal over the course of seven years of diligent study, and thus set about deciphering the ancient tablets, piecing together broken ones and travelling all over Asia tracking down others. Eventually he was able to read the amazing tale of Mu, its creation myth, the story of its religion, its founding of daughter civilizations around the world and its destruction.

THE EVIDENCE FOR MU

Galvanized by his incredible discoveries, Churchward set out to gather evidence from a detailed comparative study of all the world's myths, religions and ancient civilizations, until he was able to point to a range of Donnelly-style evidence for the existence of his ancient super-civilization. In particular he

Above The complete Troano Codex *from which Churchward deciphered the amazing tale of the lost continent of Mu.*

> 'The tablets of the Naacal had been written around the time of the destruction of Mu.'

claimed to have travelled all over the Pacific, seeing evidence of monumental masonry (such as pyramidal platforms and massive sculptures), which, he assumed, could not possibly have been built by the 'primitive' peoples who now lived there. He also gathered myths and folklore that seemed to point to Mu, and looked for evidence of the distinctive Muvian symbolism he had deciphered. However, since the central element of this symbolism was the rectangle, such proof was not hard to come by.

THE *TROANO CODEX*

Churchward also met Augustus le Plongeon and his wife, the team who had done pioneering work on the recently uncovered Mayan sites of Central America (see pages 52–53). He was impressed with le Plongeon's

analysis of Mayan carvings and writing, especially his translation of the *Troano Codex*. Cynics might even claim that he 'stole' the idea of Mu from le Plongeon before reworking it into a grander version in an attempt to become the new Donnelly. What is not in question is that Churchward arrived at a quite different interpretation of the Mayan material, arguing that it actually recorded the story of Mu in the Pacific, and the subsequent colonization of the Americas from the west, not from the east. Churchward further claimed that the *Troano Codex* confirmed his translation of the Naacal tablets, in particular the tale of Mu's destruction. Unfortunately, like le Plongeon's translation, Churchward's was ultimately based on the faulty 'alphabet' of Bishop Landa and was therefore completely mistaken.

James Churchward

As colourful as Donnelly (see pages 64-65) and as suspect as Blavatsky (see pages 82-83), James Churchward's life story is a tangle of doubtful claims and genuine drama, constituting a fascinating tale that should assure his place in the pantheon of Atlantologists.

Born in England in 1851, James Churchward claimed to have been educated at Sandhurst and Oxford and to have spent his early adulthood in India. According to his own account, he went there as a very young man serving with the British Army, helping with famine relief in the wake of the 1868–70 Rajputana famine, and achieved the rank of colonel with (according to some sources) both the Engineers and in a regiment of Lancers. In later life he was known as (or called himself) Colonel James Churchward. However, there is some suspicion about this part of his life. The census of 1871 lists him as living with his parents in Croydon, south London, while employed as a banker's clerk, although in later censuses his occupation *is* listed as East India tea planter. There are no records of his military career, although this does not mean that it never happened.

As well as travelling around India and Tibet, he also claimed to have visited South-East Asia from Burma to Malaysia and beyond; including Siberia and the Arctic; the Maldives; New Zealand; and all over the Pacific, from Fiji and Tonga to Hawaii and Easter Island. Later he travelled extensively in Mexico and Central America to investigate pre-Colombian sites.

Right *The well-travelled Colonel James Churchward. He claimed to have visited almost every corner of the world in his quest for the hidden origins of human civilization.*

TRAVELLING TO AMERICA

During the 1880s he established himself in Brooklyn, New York, taking up a new career as an engineer and inventor, with side excursions into writing (on angling and Freemasonry, both of which were hobbies of his). He was particularly involved in the burgeoning railway industry, patenting railway spikes, locknuts and other railway technology, and acting as a sales representative. Around the end of the century he turned his hand to metallurgy, inventing a new alloy of extra-hard steel that would be suitable for armour-plating for battleships. He claimed to have derived his metallurgical expertise from his studies of ancient wisdom in India, especially the mysteriously rust-resistant 1,600-year-old iron Pillar of Delhi (the secret of which

Left *The rust-resistant Pillar of Delhi. Almost 7 m (24 ft) high and weighing more than 6 tonnes, it was erected by Chandragupta II Vikramaditya (375–414 CE) and is composed of 98 per cent pure wrought iron, which makes it one of the world's great metallurgical mysteries.*

was recently revealed to be the formation of a microscopically thin patina of oxidization on the pillar's surface).

PUBLISH AND BE DAMNED

The Colonel's invention, named NCV Steel, apparently did not go down well with major industrialists and he was dragged through a series of damaging patent battles and contract disputes, eventually selling up for a sum that enabled him to concentrate on his more esoteric researches. During the 1920s he turned his attention to his theories about

Mu and Atlantis, drawing on (some might say stealing) the theories and work of many others. Donnelly is the most obvious influence, but for more specific ideas about a Pacific super-continent Churchward must have drawn on Blavatsky, Steiner (see pages 88–89) and Scott-Elliot (see pages 86–87), and in particular on Augustus le Plongeon and Paul Schliemann (grandson of Heinrich Schliemann, discoverer of Troy), who like Churchward claimed to have discovered important documents and artefacts in Himalayan monasteries.

In 1926 he finally published his first book on Mu, *The Lost Continent of Mu*, followed by several more: *The Children of Mu* (1931), *The Sacred Symbols of Mu* (1933) and *Cosmic Forces of Mu* in two parts (1934–35). They were not well received by conventional scientists and historians, who regarded them as pure fiction. Yet more books were on the drawing board when he died in the midst of giving a lecture in California in 1936. Today his books are more popular with a New Age/occult audience than with serious scholars of the roots of civilization.

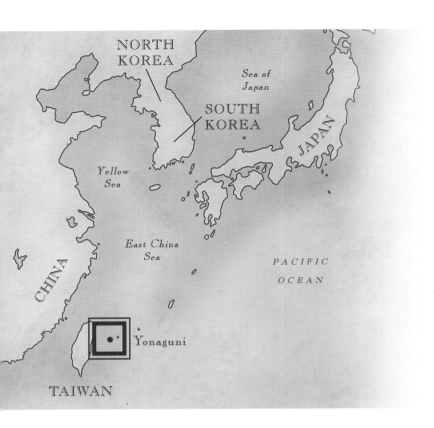

The ruins of Yonaguni

Beneath the waters surrounding Japan's westernmost islands lie amazing, apparently man-made structures that may represent the best evidence yet found for the existence of a sunken proto-civilization – perhaps the actual remains of Mu itself.

The extreme western islands of the Japanese archipelago are Okinawa and its smaller neighbours, including the most westerly of all, Yonaguni. The waters of the Pacific in this area can be rich in coral and wildlife and wonderfully clear, attracting many divers. Beginning in 1995, divers stumbled upon a series of what looked like massive man-made structures hewn out of the sandstone of the sea bottom, some 7–30 m (20–100 ft) below the surface. The first structure to be found was what appears to be a titanic castle off the coast of Okinawa, sparking comparisons with the castles, or *gusuku*, on the mainland, the origins of which are not entirely clear.

Even more impressive finds were to follow in the waters off Yonaguni. Fierce currents in the area mean that, unlike the structures off Okinawa, which are encrusted with a layer of coral and other marine life, the structures off Yonaguni have not been colonized by coral, and their stark outlines remain uncluttered and unsoftened. Straight lines and right-angles clearly suggest that the sandstone of the area has been hewn into massive blocks, steps, ramps and platforms, to create what

Right A view of the underwater ramps, steps and platforms in the waters off Yonaguni. In this picture it is easy to see why some people argue that they are artificial, and links have been drawn between them and megalithic complexes on Polynesian islands such as Hawaii.

has been called an underwater pyramid, although a platform complex might be a more accurate description.

These amazing finds triggered more searching, and at least eight similar undersea sites have now been found. It is even claimed that almost the entire seabed between Yonaguni and nearby Taiwan may have been a vast megalithic complex of which the detected sites are only remnants.

MAN-MADE OR NATURAL?

The key question about the Yonaguni ruins is whether they really are what they appear to be. At first glance it is hard to imagine how anyone could doubt the artificial provenance of the structures, but geologists know that erosion can produce some remarkable structures, especially when molten rock has cooled under special conditions, or where tectonic stress has caused very regular fault lines. Erosion then exploits these faults to carve off slabs of rock and leave remarkably regular surfaces, edges and corners. The mainstream academic view is that this is what has happened with the Yonaguni structures, and sceptics point to the lack of

archeological evidence to corroborate the man-made hypothesis. For instance, it is claimed that no tools have been recovered from the site, although this is disputed; a Japanese academic who has studied the site for a decade claims that stone adzes have been found. An exciting discovery is the presence of what look like post-holes, circular depressions into which wooden posts could be fitted, so that wooden structures could be erected on the stone platforms.

If the structures *are* man-made, it could have immense repercussions for the conventional view of the history of civilization. The depth of the remains below sea level, the coral accretions on some of them, and the discovery of features such as stalactites (which could only be formed above water) suggest that the latest date at which the structures could have been carved would be around 12,000 years ago, when this was last dry land. Given their size and complexity, this would suggest that a civilization to rival the ancient Egyptians or Mesopotamians existed on the east coast of Asia at least 7,000 years before civilization is 'supposed' to have started.

Above Sceptics suggest that all of the apparently man-made structures can be explained by natural geological and erosion processes.

MU AND JOMON

The prospect that actual remains of an Ur-civilization have been uncovered in the Pacific has prompted many to make the obvious link to Mu/Lemuria. It is claimed that the undersea platform-complex/pyramid closely resembles structures on Polynesian islands such as the *heiau* of Hawaii: temples made from ramparts, staircases, platforms and plazas carved into the rock. The ancient peoples of the area from the equivalent time are known as the Jomon; they apparently had a simple Stone Age culture until around 5,000 years ago, and there is certainly no record of them having left ruins that are anything like the Yonaguni structures. Perhaps the Jomon peoples were more advanced than is currently believed, or perhaps there was an entirely different, highly advanced civilization in the Pacific, just as James Churchward claimed.

Sir Francis Bacon and the *New Atlantis*

A notable instance of a marvellous continent in the Pacific occurs in Sir Francis Bacon's New Atlantis, *a philosophical adventure tale concerning a voyage to an unknown land of scientific wonders.*

Born to an important court family in 1561, Francis Bacon proved to have a precocious intellect. He studied science and philosophy from an early age and began to develop ideas about the correct way to think and do science. His father died before making a proper settlement for him, leading him to run into debt, and coping with this would prove to be one of the main themes of Bacon's life. He spent 20 years trying unsuccessfully to get Queen Elizabeth I to give him a lucrative official post of some kind, studying law and becoming a Member of Parliament in the meantime.

When James I acceded to the throne, Bacon's fortunes improved. He was knighted (and later made a viscount) and appointed to a series of important roles, culminating in Lord Chancellor in 1618. However, he was soon accused of corruption and taking bribes and apparently pleaded no contest, his glittering career thus ending in disgrace.

Afterwards he retired to a life of writing and scientific research, which led him to become interested in the possibility of preserving meat through refrigeration. In 1626 he purchased a chicken for an experiment, stuffing it with snow to see if it would keep, but caught a fatal dose of pneumonia in the process. The ghost of the chicken is still said to haunt Pond Square in Highgate, London, where he died.

Left *An engraving of the pioneering philosopher of science, Sir Francis Bacon.*

THE NEW ATLANTIS

Bacon's works included several books on philosophy, some of which were published after his death, among them *New Atlantis*, a kind of early science-fiction adventure in which a boatload of shipwrecked Europeans find themselves adrift in the Pacific and about to run out of food and water. Fortunately, they come across the previously unknown land of Bensalem, which proves to be the very model of an enlightened society – a kind of new Atlantis. Indeed, one of the natives specifically discusses Plato's original Atlantis, which he explains is what Europeans call America. The Bensalemite scoffs at Plato's elaborate description of the capital city, but confirms that the Atlantean nation equating to modern-day Mexico did launch an expedition to the Old World, reports of which came down to Plato 'from the Egyptian priest whom he citeth'. For Bacon, Bensalem was the new Atlantis, as it represented his version of Plato's idealized state.

BACON'S *NEW ATLANTIS*

At the heart of Bacon's philosophy was the idea that the scientific method he had invented – a kind of inductive reasoning process based on progressing from observation of facts, through testing of hypotheses, to formulation of natural laws – could be applied for the benefit of all humankind. He believed that a society run on scientific principles would also be a happy and prosperous one. In Bensalem and in particular in its central institution, Salomon's House (also known as the College of Six Days Works), a kind of research and technology facility, these principles were applied to great effect, and Bacon spent much of the book describing Salomon's House in detail.

As a utopian-philosophical novel, *New Atlantis* is considered to be a direct descendant of Plato's *Republic* (and by extension his prelapsarian Atlantis). Salomon's House is often said to have inspired a real-life equivalent – Britain's Royal Society, the institution that helped to trigger the Enlightenment, which was always conscious of its debt to Bacon.

THE OAK ISLAND MYSTERY

There is a very bizarre mystery that ties together Francis Bacon, Atlantis, the Knights Templar and pre-Columbian trans-Atlantic exploration. In the late 19th century stories began to circulate of a mysterious treasure pit on Oak Island off the coast of Nova Scotia. Numerous attempts to excavate this 'Money Pit' yielded nothing more than suggestive clues, but the apparently ingenious construction of the shaft, with false bottoms and traps, has led to wild speculation about who built it and what they buried there, from pirates secreting gold to 14th-century Knights Templar hiding the Holy Grail.

One suggestion is that Bacon, who had been given some land in the Americas, concealed within the Pit the evidence that he was the true author of Shakespeare's plays; another is that it was constructed using technological know-how passed down from Atlantis, in order to hide some sort of Alantean treasure.

'Bacon's New Atlantis *is a kind of early science-fiction adventure in which a boatload of shipwrecked Europeans find themselves adrift in the Pacific and come across a previously unknown land.'*

Below *Gresham College in London in 1616. It was here that the Royal Society – the learned institution said to have been, at least in part, inspired by Bacon's fictional Salomon's House – convened from 1660 until 1710.*

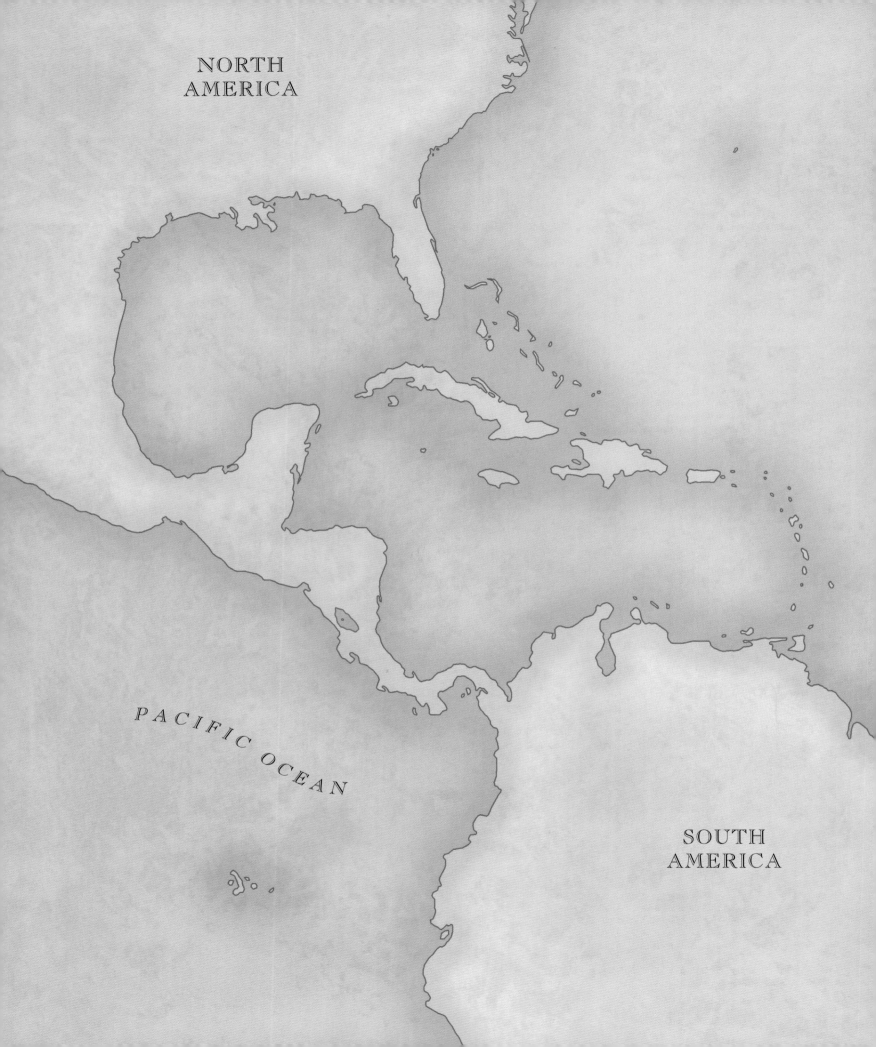

ATLANTIC OCEAN

PART 6

THE WEST INDIES

The West Indies received their collective name when
Columbus, the first European to reach them, thought he
had reached the shores of East Asia (also known as the
Indies). His discovery opened up the New World and
triggered a number of theories linking the new continent
to Atlantis.

However, the islands that sit in the Caribbean and
western Atlantic also have connections with Atlantis. They
are often associated with the mythical western islands
referred to by many ancient writers, and have also been
explicitly linked to Atlantis. In particular, the prophet and
seer Edgar Cayce, who had numerous visions of Atlantis
and explained its history in unprecedented detail, focused
on the Bahamas as a site of major Atlantean importance.
More recently the writer Andrew Collins has made a
serious and convincing case that Cuba could be the true
inspiration for Plato's lost land.

Edgar Cayce

Known as the 'Sleeping Seer', American psychic Edgar Cayce profoundly influenced 20th-century conceptions of Atlantis, its people and history and its spiritual significance, not to mention giving us a precise location for Atlantean remains of potentially Earth-shattering significance.

Cayce (pronounced 'Casey') was born into a poor Kentucky farming family in 1877, and was forced to give up school and go to work from an early age, despite an incident in which he allegedly absorbed the information from a school book through his pillow while he slept. A devout Christian throughout his life, Cayce also had strange dreams and psychic intimations as a child. For instance, when he was baptized in 1890 at the age of 13 he had a vision of an angel, and it has been suggested that his healing readings began in 1892, when he was knocked unconscious during a baseball game and suggested his own treatment (the application of a poultice).

Among the various jobs that Cayce did were several stints in bookshops. One of the things that has been most impressive for Cayce believers and enthusiasts – that is, those who believe he was a genuine psychic and seer – is that his trance readings seemed to access a universe of ideas, philosophies and information that a poorly educated farm boy with limited experience of the world would not have come across on his own. Sceptics have suggested that his bookshop work could explain this, as it would have given him the chance to read widely and pick up information about everything from Atlantis to homeopathy. It is not hard to imagine the young Edgar devouring Donnelly's *Antediluvian World* and Madame

Blavatsky's *Secret Doctrine*, and in later life unconsciously integrating them into his trance readings.

HEALTH AND HYPNOSIS

It was not until Cayce sought hypnotic treatment for a psychosomatic ailment (paralysis of the vocal cords that left him unable to talk) at the age of 24 that his apparent psychic gifts fully surfaced. While under hypnosis he proved able to diagnose himself and prescribe a treatment. Soon he was able to put himself into a trance and perform the same service for others. By 1910 word of Cayce's gifts had spread and he was giving readings for a stream of visitors. His wife or children would put questions to him and a secretary would keep notes. He did not even need to see clients, who could request readings by letter.

PAST LIVES AND METAPHYSICS

At first the readings dealt mainly with health matters, but in 1923 a client asked him some metaphysical questions and Cayce began to speak about reincarnation and past lives. Although this was deeply troubling for the religious Cayce, these themes developed into accounts of ancient civilizations, philosophies of life and predictions for the future.

As his fame spread, Cayce began to make a good living from his readings, while the

support of generous benefactors enabled him to set up hospitals and foundations to advance his work (some of which, such as the Association for Research and Enlightenment, are still very active today). As his fame spread in the 1940s, the demands for readings became ever more insistent and in 1945, burnt out from attempting to do eight readings a day, Cayce suffered a stroke and died. His family and foundation continue his legacy today.

CAYCE AND ATLANTIS

Cayce described the more than 40,000-year history of this great civilization, detailing its location in the Atlantic, its phases of evolution, the periodic disasters that broke up the original continent into smaller islands, the development of advanced technology by the Atlanteans and their final destruction in the calamity that is familiar from Plato's account.

Piecing together the fragments provided by Cayce's 700-odd readings that deal with Atlantis, it is possible to get a coherent picture of the lost continent's development and history. In terms of his overall view, Cayce seems to owe a heavy debt to previous concepts of Atlantis, especially those of the Theosophists (see pages 82–83). He is said to have had dealings with Theosophists, or may have picked up material from published works (see pages 104–105). Like the Theosophists,

'Cayce described Atlantis as a huge continent between the Mediterranean and Central America.'

AFTERMATH AND REAPPEARANCE

Cayce followed writers such as Ignatius Donnelly in attributing to Atlantean colonists and refugees the founding of ancient civilizations, from the Maya to the Egyptians. He also made a number of predictions for the future, in particular that one of several Atlantean Halls of Records – enormous hidden chambers containing the ancient wisdom of the lost civilization – would be discovered and opened, ushering in a new phase in human history. One such Hall, he predicted, would be discovered between 1996 and 1998 on or near the Caribbean island of Bimini, which he claimed was the last remnant of the lost land's western approaches (see pages 110–111).

the Sleeping Seer described the lost Atlantis as part of a vast span of human evolution.

Cayce described Atlantis as a huge continent between the Mediterranean and Central America. Originally, he said, the eastern United States and areas of western Europe had been part of it. It was broken up in successive cataclysms in 50,700 BCE and

28,000 BCE and was eventually destroyed altogether in 10,000 BCE (as described by Plato). The original Atlanteans were unisex pure-energy beings who began to assume material forms varying in stature 'from … midgets to giants … 10 to 12 feet [3–3.6 m] in stature'. They wore 'coats of the skins of the animals' and had an extra eye in their heads.

The Law of One and the Sons of Belial

Edgar Cayce's trance readings gave him access to one of the most detailed explanations of Atlantean history ever produced. According to his visions and past-life readings, Atlantis was the stage for an epic struggle between the forces of good and evil.

CHILDREN OF THE LAW OF ONE

The original Atlantean energy beings were simply vibrations of pure thought and light, and they existed in a state close to harmonious oneness with the Creator. As the Atlanteans began to assume material forms and become physical beings, they were exposed to greater risk of corruption and split into two groups. One group, the Children of the Law of One, followed the Law of One (the supreme creator deity) and upheld the strongest moral and ethical standards, at the same time maintaining a purity of consciousness that meant they were able to vibrate at a high level of light and energy.

THE SONS OF BELIAL

The other group, which fell into evil ways, was the Sons of Belial (Belial was an Old Testament demon who, in later Christian tradition, was the fallen angel of confusion and lust). In the words of one of Cayce's readings, they 'had no standard, save of self, self-aggrandizement'. They used all their gifts to base, corrupt ends, becoming entangled in carnal and materialistic pursuits. Alas, this was as seductive as it sounds, and many of the followers of the Law of One were seduced to the dark side. In particular, the Sons of Belial used their spiritual gifts and intelligence to devise powerful technologies, but only in order to increase their own power and pleasure. This was to have disastrous consequences as they became victims of their own scientific creations, like ancient Frankensteins.

A particular point of contention between the Children of the Law of One and the Sons of Belial was the treatment of a class of Atlanteans that Cayce described as 'things' or 'mere machines'. Atlantean society was organized not by family, but by role – a bit

Right *The Copper Scroll, part of the Dead Sea Scrolls. The Copper Scroll is a treasure list, inscribed on a sheet of copper, which was then rolled up. To access it, researchers had to cut it into the thin strips, as shown here.*

Left A medieval woodcut showing a rather jaunty Belial cutting a caper before the jaws of Hell itself. Belial was an Old Testament demon who was later ascribed dominion over the sins of confusion and lust.

like a colony of insects. There were farmers, craftspeople, priests, and so on, and one group of slave-like automatons who existed at a very low level of consciousness. The Children saw it as their responsibility to help these unfortunates attain a higher level, while the Sons simply wanted to take advantage of them.

AGENTS OF DESTRUCTION

Eventually the scientific and materialistic hubris of the Sons of Belial was to prove their downfall. Their attempts to harness spiritual energies to material ends eventually resulted in a release of energies, which destroyed the Atlantean lands (for the third time), finally wiping them off the face of the planet.

In fact the Atlanteans had had plenty of warning of their impending doom, but the Sons of Belial were too proud and greedy to heed them and many perished in the cataclysm, whereas the Children of the Law of One had supervised major population movements to lands we know today, such as Egypt and Mexico. It was they who built the Sphinx and the pyramids, for instance. Below the Sphinx, and in the Yucatán peninsula and in the vicinity of Bimini, they excavated great storehouses for vast libraries of their wisdom and technology, to keep it safe until the time of the Second Coming when its discovery would transform humanity. Cayce also claimed that many people today are reincarnated Atlanteans, who might be able to regain their power and purity if they could access their true spiritual nature.

> '*The Atlanteans had plenty of warning of their impending doom.*'

THE DEAD SEA SCROLLS

In an extraordinary parallel with Cayce's trance pronouncements, the ancient religious texts of the Dead Sea Scrolls, discovered in the late 1950s and early 1960s (more than a decade after Cayce's death), told a similar story. One of the scrolls is called *The War of the Sons of Light Against the Sons of Darkness* and tells of an epic struggle between the forces of good and evil in which the latter are led by Belial, whose purpose is to bring about 'wickedness and guilt'.

Atlantean technology

One of the most remarkable elements of Cayce's account of ancient Atlantis was the range of strange and wonderful technologies he spoke about, many of which would prove to have disturbing parallels in the modern day within a few years of his death.

During the long history of Atlantis that Cayce described, the civilization reached heights of scientific and technological mastery unparalleled in the rest of history, even today. The Atlanteans were able to channel their spiritual powers into material, physical and technological forms, creating devices that Cayce describes as electrical and mechanical. He also talks of their mastery of gaseous and ferrous elements, their metallurgical skills and, crucially, their crystal technology.

CRYSTAL POWER

The Atlanteans used crystals (sometimes referred to as 'firestones') to capture and transform different types of energy, including sunlight, starlight, etheric and psychic energy. The firestone transformed these energies into electrical and motor forces, and could even be used to generate what Cayce described as 'death rays'. The destructive use of these tremendous energies by the Sons of Belial caused a titanic disaster, blasting a hole in their continent that became the Sargasso Sea, and helping to trigger one of the episodes of destruction that split Atlantis into smaller parts.

When lasers were invented during the 1950s it was assumed by many of his devotees that lasers and death rays were one and the same thing. Since Cayce had predicted that Atlantean technology would start to make a comeback, this invention was widely seen as confirming his predictions.

AIRSHIPS AND SUBMARINES

As well as describing technologies akin to modern-day computers, radio, television and telephones, Cayce also talked about the various modes of transport the Atlanteans had invented. They were masters of the seas, having both ships and submarines, and also invented at least two types of aircraft. One was like a modern-day balloon or zeppelin, made from elephant hide and filled with lighter-than-air gas. The other was more like a hovercar or aeroplane, but was powered by the energies gathered by the crystal firestones.

The firestones were fitted in ground stations, like observatories with retractable domes that slid back to reveal the crystal in the centre, which collected sunlight or starlight and beamed it to the airship to provide power. Amazingly, this technology is similar to modern plans to build solar collectors on Earth that would convert solar radiation to microwaves, and then beam these to power stations, satellites or wherever they were needed.

In practice Cayce's 'foresight' in talking about wireless transmission of energy and beam weapons may not be quite so amazing after all. At much the same time Cayce was producing his pronouncements, the electricity pioneer Nikola Tesla was vigorously promoting inventions along exactly these lines. Sceptics might suggest that Cayce simply 'saw' technology that was cutting-edge and popular at the time.

① **POWER STATION**

The station was constructed of non-conductive, heatproof insulating material. When the retractable roof slid back, the firestone collected sunlight or starlight and beamed the energy wherever it was required. Aircraft, factories and even submarines were powered with this energy source.

② **SUBMARINES**

These plied the waters around Atlantis and were also used in warfare.

③ **AIRCRAFT AND AIRSHIPS**

Airships were similar to today's zeppelins, with gasbags stitched from 'pachyderm' hide (the hide of a large, thick-skinned mammal) and fittings of brass and other metals, these craft were similar to today's zeppelins. Aircraft were mosty one- or two-seaters for personal use by the Atlantean aristocracy, but military versions were also produced by the Sons of Belial.

④ **HEALTH CLINIC**

The Atlanteans could use crystal power to heal and rejuvenate their bodies.

⑤ **PSYCHIC TRAINING FACILITY**

Although the Atlanteans had natural psychic powers, they were also able to use their technology to train and enhance those powers, enabling them to practise telepathy, astral travel (where the astral body, akin to a soul or spirit, leaves the physical body and travels in the etheric realms), and psychokinesis.

⑥ **WEAPONS OF MASS DESTRUCTION**

The firestone technology could be used for destructive purposes. The Sons of Belial invented laser-like death rays, powerful explosives and what sound like atomic devices. These were used in civil wars, for suppressing other races and even in attempting to fight off an invasion of giant animals.

'The Atlanteans used crystals to capture and transform different types of energy, including sunlight, starlight, etheric and psychic energy.'

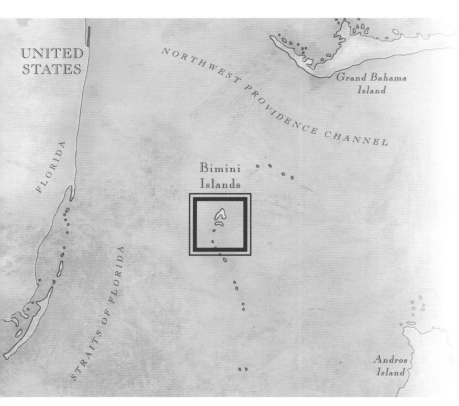

The Bimini Islands

Edgar Cayce gave a specific time and date for what would be one of the greatest events in human history: the time when Atlantis would rise again. The Sleeping Seer pointed to the Bimini Islands in the Caribbean, and sure enough suggestive structures have been discovered on the sea floor in this area.

CAYCE AND BIMINI

According to Cayce, most of America did not exist when Atlantis was around. Some areas of what is now its eastern seaboard formed part of the western reaches of Atlantis. In particular, the area that is now the Caribbean was an important part of Atlantis, and the present-day West Indies were Atlantean mountains and hills that survived the break-up and final deluge of the continent to remain projecting above the waters.

Cayce focused particularly on the tiny Bahaman island of Bimini, explaining that this unlikely spot was the location of one of the Atlantean Halls of Records, and predicting that the remains of Atlantis would be discovered here:

In the sunken portions of Atlantis, or Poseidia [one of the islands that remained after the penultimate Atlantean cataclysm], where a portion of the temples may yet be discovered, under the slime of ages of sea water –near what is known as Bimini, off the coast of Florida.

He even gave a date for this momentous event: 'And Poseidia will be among the first portions of Atlantis to rise again. Expect it in 68 and 69.'

THE BIMINI ROAD

Incredibly, 1968 saw the discovery of two exciting formations in the area, apparently confirming Cayce's amazing predictions. First, following up aerial surveys performed in 1967 by the Association for Research and Enlightenment (the foundation that carries on Cayce's work), Dr Manson Valentine led an expedition to waters off the Bahaman island of Andros, where they discovered an apparently ancient rectangular building, 30 x 22 m (100 x 75 ft), covered in seaweed, which was thought to be an Atlantean temple. Then, in the waters just off Bimini, divers discovered what looked like cut blocks or flagstones, arranged in two straight parallel lines, one of which had a distinctive and artificial-looking curve at one end to give it a J-shape. The road-like appearance led to the formation being christened the 'Bimini Road'.

The discoveries generated massive excitement and the area is still being investigated and surveyed to this day. More recent finds include the Andros Platform, a sea floor formation off the coast of Andros Island, similar to the Bimini Road, but with

blocks arranged into a platform. There are apparent tool marks on the stones of the Platform, and sea floor mounds in the shape of animals, including one that looks like a shark, apparently aligned with the positions of important stars *c*.1000 CE.

ROAD, DOCK OR HARBOUR?

These findings have triggered great controversy, with believers and sceptics vying to prove their interpretations and pouring scorn on each other's efforts. The Andros 'temple' has been convincingly explained as a relatively recent structure – a storage area for sponge harvesters, probably built in the 1930s. The Bimini Road has proved more resistant to sceptics. The conventional explanation is similar to that applied to the Yonaguni structures (see pages 96–97); it is the result of natural erosive processes. Such 'beach rock' formations are known all around the world. They are formed by wind and wave action operating on sand and rocks on the coastline, but can subsequently end up on the sea floor as a result of rising sea levels. Sceptical geologists who have studied the Bimini Road insist that all the evidence points this way: for

Right View of divers inspecting the famous Bimini Road. Although it is easy to see how this rock formation could be interpreted as the surface of a road or other structure of monumental masonry, geologists claim that it is simply a beach-rock formation, eroded into this suggestive shape by natural processes.

instance, if the rocks had been quarried and placed, the grain of each slab should point in a different direction – apparently this is not the case. It is also claimed that seashells from the rock have been dated and are 3,000 years old, considerably younger than the claims made by Atlantologists.

Atlantologists say these sceptical studies are flawed. They claim that this area of the Caribbean seabed was last above water 12,000 years ago, and that there is clear evidence that the Bimini Road is a man-made structure (the Platform too). It is variously suggested that the Bimini Road might be the remains of a road, a harbour or port structure, a dry dock or even, according to clairvoyant Carol Huffstickler, part of a labyrinth built by space brothers from the Pleiades (a constellation of stars that feature heavily in UFO lore as a point of origin for various alien races visiting the Earth). Whatever their original function, the Road and the related structures are seen as clear evidence that a prehistoric civilization was active in the area around 12,000 years ago, and that Cayce may be right about its potential rediscovery after thousands of years.

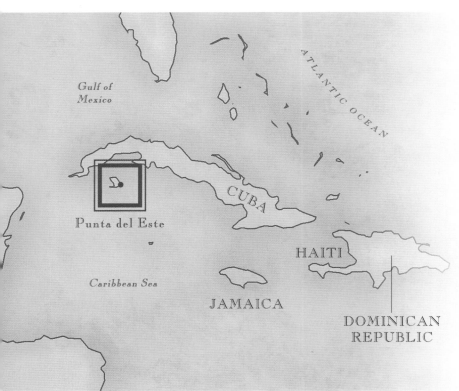

Cuba – cradle of New World civilization

Writer Andrew Collins has made a persuasive case that the island of Cuba closely matches many aspects of Plato's description of Atlantis. This identification was strengthened when extremely ancient ruins were apparently discovered on the sea floor off the coast of Cuba.

In his book *Gateway to Atlantis*, Andrew Collins argues that Cuba was the true site of Atlantis. He suggests that the Cuban Atlantis was the birthplace of New World civilization, and that it was destroyed by tsunamis and sea level rises triggered by asteroid impacts and the extremely rapid thawing of the American ice sheet at the end of the Ice Age (itself the result of these impacts). Refugees fleeing Cuba made it to the mainland (modern-day Mexico and Central America), where they founded the long chain of pre-Colombian civilizations that culminated in the Maya and Aztecs.

Collins argues that this epic tale is reflected in the myths and legends of the Meso-American peoples. Many groups (including the Maya and Aztecs) had origin myths explaining how they came to be, and these often speak of culture heroes/ founding fathers coming from islands to the east. In particular, the story of the Seven Caves is widespread – it is a myth that tells of how the ancestral tribes of the Meso-Americans emerged from seven caves and founded seven cities or tribes. Collins says that the only place in the Caribbean that matches this description is the 'seven caves complex' at Punta del Este on Cuba's Isle of Youth.

PASSING ON THE STORY

How did this tale reach Plato? Collins marshals evidence to suggest that ancient Old World seafarers such as the Phoenicians and Carthaginians had extensive traffic with the New World, and learned from the ancient Native Americans about their myths, including Atlantis. This information was disseminated throughout the ancient Old World, reaching Plato, and was also preserved by the North African Berber peoples, who eventually passed it on to Iberia during the Moorish conquest, inspiring the Iberian legends of Antillia and the Seven Golden Cities (see pages 48 and 156). These in turn, claims Collins, inspired explorers and mariners such as Columbus to cross the Atlantic in search of the lost lands.

MATCHING CRITERIA

Collins points out that Cuba is the only Caribbean island large enough to fulfil Plato's description, and in particular is the only one with a large, south-facing plain ringed by high mountains to the north, which protect it from cold winds in winter, just as Plato detailed. Before its southern end was submerged 9,000 years ago, during the cataclysms mentioned above, this plain would have been much larger, closely matching the dimensions carefully described by Plato in *Critias*.

A DROWNED CITY OFF THE COAST OF CUBA?

Collins' theory received an unexpected boost in 2000 when sea floor survey work off the coast of Cuba revealed what has been described as a lost city at a depth of about 700–800 m (2,300–2,600 ft). Paulina Zelitsky, part of the husband-and-wife team running the survey, described what she saw on the sonar monitor:

It is stunning. What we see in our high-resolution sonar images are limitless, rolling, white sand plains and, in the middle of this beautiful white sand, there are clear man-made large-size architectural designs. It looks like when you fly over an urban development in a plane and you see highways, tunnels and buildings ...

It was subsequently reported that a submersible had returned video footage of large, apparently crafted blocks of stone.

Little additional information has been forthcoming, but if the shapes really are artificial, the depth suggests that the 'lost city' must be about 12,000 years old (although Zelitsky argues that subsidence caused by sudden tectonic shifts could mean they are only half that age). Conventional opinion is that the shapes are either natural formations or that there is simply too little data to make any attribution. The Association for Research and Enlightenment suggests that the shapes may be concrete sections of missile silos, broken up and dumped at sea in the wake of the Cuban Missile Crisis.

'Cuba is the only Caribbean island large enough to fulfil Plato's description.'

Below *Cave art in Cuba's Punta del Este cave complex. The caves are believed to have been a pre-Columbian solar temple, for some of the cave art is aligned with shafts of sunlight coming through skylights at particular equinoxes.*

ANTARCTICA

PACIFIC OCEAN

PART 7

ANTARCTICA

In many respects Antarctica is the single least-likely place on the face of the planet to make a convincing candidate site for the lost land of Atlantis, but incredibly there is an apparently plausible theory locating it there. Based on a 500-year-old cartographic mystery and a radical and controversial theory about planetary geology, the 'Atlantis in Antarctica' theory references historical enigmas such as the pyramids at Giza and the true face of the Sphinx to build a case for a prehistoric super-civilization.

Currently the prime motivator behind this theory is Graham Hancock, perhaps the best-known Atlantologist in the world today, which is ironic, given that he does not actually call his putative prehistoric civilization Atlantis. This section examines his controversial theory and the fascinating trail of historical clues that led him to develop it.

The Piri Reis map

Does a medieval map by an Ottoman admiral hold the key to the greatest mystery in human history? Could it represent proof of both an ancient tradition of secret geographical knowledge and a revolutionary theory of plate tectonics that could literally turn the accepted model on its head?

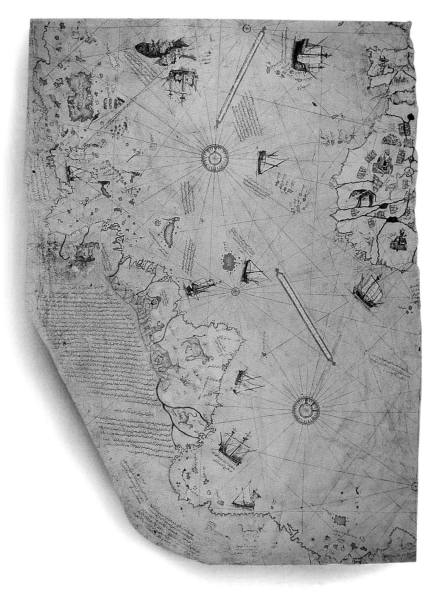

Left *The Piri Reis map of 1513. The coasts of the Iberian peninsula and West Africa can clearly be seen at top right, while at the bottom of the map is the mysterious coastline said to resemble the Antarctic as it would appear without a covering of ice.*

ADMIRAL PIRI

Hadji Muhiddin Piri Ibn Hadji Mehmed was a brilliant and battle-hardened Turkish sailor in the 15th and 16th centuries, whose diligent service for the Ottoman empire earned him the title 'Reis' (admiral), but could not spare him the indignity of a gruesome end – beheaded for treason at the age of 90. Today Piri Reis is best remembered for the world map he drew up *c.*1513, a fragment of which was discovered in 1929 during works to transform the Topkapi Palace in Istanbul into a museum. According to Piri's own notes, he drew on a number of pre-existing maps and accounts of voyages and discoveries, including a number of Ptolemaic maps (that is, ones dating back to the Classical era), an Arabic map and some Portuguese ones describing recent discoveries in the New World.

THE MAP

Drawn on gazelle skin, the extant portion of the map is the western third, showing the Iberian peninsula, West Africa, several islands (real and imagined) in the Atlantic, and what looks like the eastern coast of the New World, including the West Indies, the coastline of South America and a mysterious southern land with which it is contiguous. The conventional reading of the map is as follows:

- The north-western portions actually show what was thought to be the eastern coast of Asia, including Japan. Columbus and the rest of the Old World assumed that he had discovered a new, direct route to the East Indies (which is how the Caribbean islands came to be known as the West Indies in the first place), and that islands such as Cuba were actually just to the east of Japan. This idea lasted for nearly two decades until further voyages of discovery showed it to be false.
- The coast of Brazil is portrayed reasonably accurately.
- The southernmost portions of the map show either an imaginary southern continent (known as Terra Australis Incognito) or the coast of Patagonia and Tierra del Fuego, but reoriented to run west-east rather than north-south, possibly in order to fit on the vellum.

> *'Hapgood theorized that the thin crust of the Earth could suddenly shift on the molten mantle layer beneath, especially if it was unbalanced by the build-up of ice caps at the Poles.'*

Right *A portion of Antarctic coastline where the true coastline is actually visible. The actual land coastline of much of the rest of the continent is hidden beneath kilometres of ice sheet.*

ANTARCTICA REVEALED?

The alternative reading of the map – most influentially disseminated by the American academic Charles Hapgood (1904–82) and later by the popular writer on alternative history, Graham Hancock – is that the southern land-mass is actually a depiction of the coastline of part of the Antarctic, as it looks beneath the massive ice sheet that smothers it. Since Antarctica itself was not even discovered until the 19th century, while the sub-glacial coast was not mapped until the 20th century, it has been suggested that Piri Reis' information derived from an ancient cartographer who had mapped the polar continent when it was ice-free. However, since Antarctica was last ice-free at least several thousand years ago (in fact, modern research suggests at least several million years ago), this assertion challenges the conventional view of history. Hapgood and his successors see this as direct evidence that a highly advanced civilization must have existed thousands of years before Egypt or Sumeria, the earliest known civilizations. Somehow their detailed cartographic information was passed on to one of the sources that Piri Reis used to draw up his map.

CRUSTAL DISPLACEMENT

Hapgood went still further, suggesting that the reason why the Antarctic had been ice-free was because it was, at that time, in temperate latitudes, but through an abrupt and cataclysmic process of crustal displacement had suddenly shifted to the South Pole. Hapgood theorized that the thin crust of the Earth could suddenly shift/slip on the molten mantle layer beneath, especially if it was unbalanced by the build-up of ice caps at the Poles (although conventional geology says this is impossible). Everything on the Earth's surface would then find itself displaced: shifted by several degrees of latitude or longitude. Perhaps such a shift caused the destruction of the prehistoric super-civilization, for it would necessarily be a cataclysmic event with earthquakes and tsunamis on an unprecedented scale.

Antarctic super-civilization

If a prehistoric super-civilization did exist, did it leave behind any evidence? According to Graham Hancock and others, this evidence exists in the form of some of the most famous and mysterious monuments in history, including the Sphinx and the Great Pyramid at Giza.

Much of Hancock's work has been devoted to tracking down what he says is evidence of a super-civilization that existed around 12,000 years ago, and which perished in some sort of disaster, probably linked to rising sea levels at the end of the last Ice Age. Although he does not actually call it Atlantis, he obviously means as much. For Hancock, the Piri Reis map and other suggestive medieval maps are documentary evidence that highly advanced cartographic knowledge of the world was somehow available to the Old World medieval cartographers and explorers, presumably because it had been preserved for millennia and transmitted through generations of initiates.

As additional evidence, Hancock points to submerged, apparent megalithic structures around the world, including the Bimini Road (see pages 108–109), the ruins of Yonaguni (see pages 96–97), structures off the coast of India (see pages 128–129) and elsewhere. He claims that these prove that an advanced global civilization, mainly sited on low-lying coastal lands, existed until *c*.10,500 years ago, but that most of the evidence has been drowned by the rising waters. Perhaps the centre or homeland of this civilization was Antarctica, at that time a fertile land in the temperate or tropical latitudes, but now (thanks to crustal displacement) covered in thick ice that has obscured or obliterated all remnants of the once-mighty culture.

Right *The Sphinx is conventionally held to be a representation of the Old Kingdom Pharaoh Khafra or Khephren, who was said to have ordered its construction c.2500 BCE, or at least to date to around this time. Alternative historians like Graham Hancock, however, have argued that it is much older.*

Conventional archeologists, Egyptologists, archeo-astronomers, geologists, scientists and historians of all stripes dismiss Hancock's theories as half-baked and spurious, and point to numerous flaws in his reasoning. For instance, it is said that the actual angle of deviation from a straight line made by the three pyramids does *not* match that of Orion's Belt, and in fact bends the wrong way, so that star maps must be reversed in order to match up. A much simpler explanation for the deviation of the third (and youngest) pyramid is that a large outcrop of rock makes the directly aligned site unsuitable.

Above View of the Great Pyramid at Giza, emphasizing the extraordinarily precise alignments the ancient Egyptians were able to achieve in its design and construction.

THE ANCIENT SPHINX

Important evidence dating the prehistoric super-civilization does survive, says Hancock, in the form of ancient monuments including the Sphinx and the pyramids that were constructed to reflect astronomical events *c.*10,500 BCE. He and others propose that erosion and weathering patterns on the Sphinx suggest that they were made by heavy rainfall, indicating that it must have been carved when the Sahara was relatively wet and fertile, thousands of years before the conventional date of construction. He also says that the Sphinx's current face, which seems to be too small for the rest of its body, is the result of recarving ordered by the

pharaohs, in the process obliterating the pre-existing lion's head. In other words, the Sphinx was originally a great lion, carved in honour of the constellation of Leo, which would have been visible on the horizon at the spring equinox (a sacred time) in 10,500 BCE.

THE PYRAMIDS AND ORION'S BELT

Hancock further claims that the orientation of the three pyramids at Giza also reflects an important constellation, namely the stars in Orion's Belt. The first two pyramids are precisely aligned so that a single line can be drawn from the corner of the first to the far corner of the second, but the third pyramid is offset from this line. The stars in Orion's

Belt follow a similar pattern. Orion was a sacred constellation to the ancient Egyptians, and 12,000 years ago it would have been visible on the horizon at the spring equinox. In other words, the arrangement of the pyramids reflects the night sky as it was *c.*10,500 BCE, Hancock's magic date.

AUSTRALIA

PART 8

THE INDIAN OCEAN

Like most of the rest of the world's cultures and civilizations, contemporary and historical, those bordering the Indian Ocean have a rich mythology of floods, cataclysms, culture heroes and lost lands. For instance, the ancient Hindu myth of Matsya tells how King Manu was visited by a god in the shape of a fish, called Matsya, who warned him of an incipient universal flood and instructed him to build a great boat, thus saving him from the deluge so that he could repopulate the Earth. Myths such as these tie the region into the network of associations surrounding Atlantis and related theories about lost prehistoric progenitor civilizations.

Above all, however, this region possesses broad, shallow continental shelves that would have been above sea level during the last Ice Age, and would have made hospitable habitats for Stone Age civilizations. This section examines two fascinating theories based on these facts, which may offer the best explanation yet for the mystery of what inspired Plato.

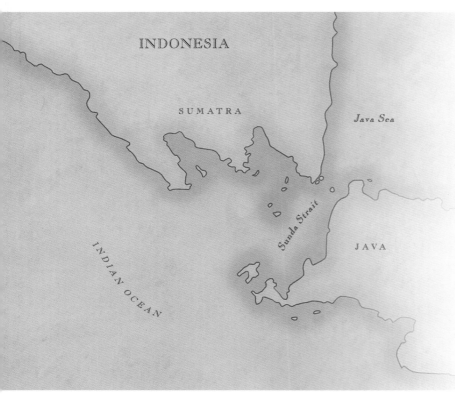

INDONESIA

SUMATRA

Java Sea

Sunda Strait

JAVA

INDIAN OCEAN

Sundaland – the Cradle of Civilization

Where the scattered islands and peninsulas of South-East Asia now lie, there once existed a vast, contiguous land-mass known as Sundaland. Strong archeological, genetic and linguistic evidence suggests that it may have been home to an influential prehistoric civilization that perished beneath a deluge.

Many cultures in the Indo-Pacific region share flood myths about lost civilizations and lands submerged by rising waters. These myths can be found from India to Thailand, and from China to the Pacific islands. To mystical writers like James Churchward (see pages 94–95), these were proof of the former existence of Mu or Lemuria. It is now known that neither Mu nor Lemuria could have existed in the sense that Churchward, Blavatsky and others described, but the ubiquity of these myths and legends suggests they might have some common root.

THE WALLACE LINE

Sundaland was originally a biogeographical concept, based on the Wallace Line. Alfred Wallace was a pioneering naturalist and co-originator of the theory of evolution. One of his key findings was the strange discontinuity between flora and fauna in the Indo-Pacific region. He identified a line through the Malay Archipelago – now known as the Wallace Line – on the west and north of which the flora and fauna were Asian (including many species found on the Asian mainland, such as rhinos and elephants), while on the other side they were Australasian (such as marsupials). Wallace proposed that the western region was once contiguous land, with today's islands and peninsulas connected by land bridges

Below *The Wallace Line – a boundary between biogeographical regions first noticed by Alfred Wallace during his voyages in the area in the 19th century.*

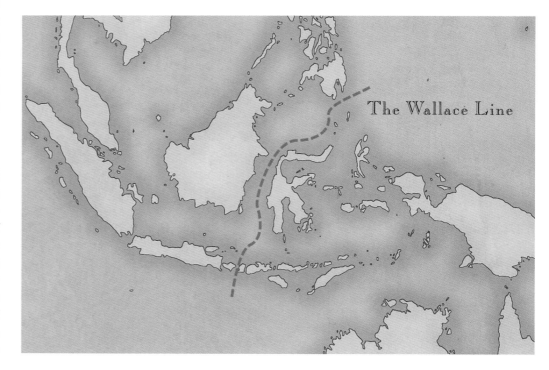

The Wallace Line

(enabling the same animals and plants to colonize areas now separated by water). It is now known that this was indeed the case, thanks to the relatively shallow continental shelf in this area, which was largely uncovered during the last Ice Age. The shelf is called the Sunda Shelf, and so the biogeographical region is known as Sundaland.

AN ORIGINAL EDEN

Several writers and theorists, most prominently and convincingly scientist Dr Stephen Oppenheimer, have suggested that Sundaland could have been the home of a Stone Age civilization that later inspired tales of Atlantis. Oppenheimer's theory, articulated in books including *Eden in the East*, is that early humans migrated from Africa to the Arabian peninsula and followed the coast east around India and into South-East Asia, settling in the broad plains of Sundaland. Thanks to the same Ice Ages that uncovered the Sunda Shelf, much of the rest of the planet at this time was inhospitable and was lightly colonized (or not at all) by early Stone Age people.

Prehistoric peoples generally lived at very low population densities as nomadic hunter-gatherers, with a sophisticated but essentially static set of basic technologies – the opposite of what we call civilization. However, there is strong archeological and genetic evidence that on the hospitable plains of Sundaland things began to change. Population density increased and agriculture may have been invented here. The full extent of the Stone Age civilization that may have developed is unclear because the lands involved are now at the bottom of the sea, but it is possible to speculate (see page 122).

THE DESTRUCTION OF EDEN

Sundaland was eventually drowned by the sea level rises that accompanied the end of the last Ice Age from 20,000 to 8,000 years ago. Oppenheimer and others suggest that some of these rises may have been catastrophically rapid; in particular when Lake Agassiz – an enormous meltwater lake beneath the ice sheet that covered North America – suddenly drained into the Atlantic around 8,000 years ago. Oppenheimer

further argues that the inhabitants of Sundaland fled west to lands that had now become more hospitable, and marshals considerable genetic and linguistic evidence to show that regions as far afield as the Levant, Egypt and the Caucasus had an influx of people who brought with them advanced Stone Age technologies. Perhaps memories and tales of these incomers survived to the time of Plato and inspired his Atlantis.

Eden in the East

If Sundaland genuinely was the cradle of prehistoric civilization and the progenitor of Atlantis, what would this Stone Age Eden have been like? How closely might it have matched the classical description of Atlantis written by Plato?

There is very little chance that the prehistoric Sundaland identified by Oppenheimer and others as a possible model or inspiration for the biblical Garden of Eden would have resembled the Atlantis of Plato, still less the advanced super-civilization beloved of Theosophists, seers and New Age dreamers.

Plato clearly describes a High Bronze Age civilization with massive public works, monumental construction, advanced engineering and highly developed metallurgy and associated technologies. The people of Sundaland may have been taking the first tentative steps on the road to civilization, but it is likely that their culture fell well short of Plato's Atlantis, as it was very much a Stone Age rather than Bronze Age culture.

THE SIMPLE LIFE

The Sundalanders were probably a culture in transition from a nomadic hunter-gatherer way of life to a settled pastoral-agrarian society. It is likely that they lived in small groups of a few families, settling in semi-permanent villages for part of the year and moving at other times or in response to poor weather or other environmental conditions. While they may have employed basic agriculture, such as the domestication of wild plants or wild pigs, to supplement their diet, the bulk of their food probably still came from hunting and gathering. Archeological evidence also suggests that they invented milling of grain to make flour and were among the earliest people to make pottery (a hallmark of settled rather than nomadic peoples, because of its fragility), but they may have used these skills only when convenient, relying on hunter-gatherer strategies much of the time.

Left A Melanesian family in their canoe off Vanuatu in the Pacific. The Melanesians are an ethnic grouping possibly descended from the original inhabitants of Sundaland, who may have shared similar technology and even culture with their modern-day descendants.

Possibly they would occasionally gather together for social, ceremonial or religious purposes, and it is conceivable that they might have pooled labour to undertake collective works, such as building sacred mounds or digging basic irrigation ditches. To what extent this kind of activity can be extrapolated to match Atlantean fantasies is purely speculative.

THE LANGUAGE TRAIL

Speculation about prehistoric civilization starting in Sundaland and spreading from there is all very well, but what evidence is there to back up these incredible claims?

Scientists trace population movements and the spread of cultural influences through normal archeology, but also through linguistic archeology – that is, by examining languages around the world to see if it is possible to identify common elements, and then trace these back to common origins.

Oppenheimer points to work showing that language families that originated in South-East Asia, and therefore probably in Sundaland, have extended tentacles of influence all over the Old World. For instance, words from the Austronesian language family, which probably started in Sundaland, can be found in Indian languages (the root word for mother is *ayi* in Austronesian, *bayi* in Indic languages; other examples include the words for honey, bamboo and fruit) and even in Indo-European languages. For example, the Malay word for 'two' is *dva*, which looks and sounds similar to the English word. Perhaps the most striking example is the Malagasy language of Madagascar, which is an Austronesian language (as are such far-flung languages as Malay, Tagalog, Hawaiian and Maori), proving that the early Austronesians possessed the naval technology to cross the ocean and settle long distances away.

'It is likely that the Sundalanders lived in small groups of a few families, settling in semi-permanent villages for part of the year and moving at other times or in response to poor weather or other environmental conditions.'

Could Sundaland be Atlantis?

What today constitutes the submarine Sunda Shelf once roughly matched Plato's description of a broad plain surrounded on three sides by high mountains that came down to the coast. Unlike Plato's description, however, it mainly faced the sea to the east, but cardinal directions may easily have become scrambled during the 5,500 years that it took for the story to reach Plato.

Dr Sunil Prasann has suggested that Natuna Besar, an Indonesian island halfway between the Malay peninsula and northern Borneo, would have formed an isolated and relatively low mountain in the centre of the Sunda Plain during the last Ice Age, roughly matching Plato's description of Atlantis' Acropolis hill. Could Natuna Besar have been the centre of the true Atlantis?

RICE PADDIES AND IRRIGATION DITCHES

It may be ambitious to suggest that the people of Sundaland domesticated rice and grew it in paddies like today's South-East Asians, but there is certainly evidence that they were the first people in the world to practise agriculture and made extensive use of nuts, fruits, medicinal plants and stimulant or narcotic plants. If the Stone Age Sundalanders did domesticate rice, beans or other staple crops, they might also have dug simple irrigation works. Perhaps these were the inspiration for the mighty canals of Plato's Atlantis.

ELEPHANTS AS A FEATURE OF THE TROPICS

One of the most notable features of Plato's Atlantis is his specific mention of elephants. The forests and plains of Sundaland would have been teeming with elephants. Might the Sundalanders even have domesticated them, like today's South-East Asians? Elephants are among several features of Plato's Atlantis that suggest a tropical location. For instance, he mentions that the climate was so clement that the Atlanteans could grow two crops a year – a hallmark of the tropics.

STONE AGE TECHNOLOGY AND NAVIGATION SKILLS

Archeological evidence suggests that the Sundalanders were among the first to invent technology such as pottery and quern-stones (for milling grain), along with their other agricultural advances. Migrating

> *'The ancient Sunda peoples are thought to have been expert seafarers because of their ability to colonize even far-flung islands in the Pacific and Indian Oceans'*

Left *The island of Krakatoa before it was obliterated by a colossal volcanic explosion in 1883, which devastated the local area.*

Right *An Asian elephant at work in India. Elephants would have been numerous in antediluvian Sundaland.*

Sundalanders, fleeing the devastation of their homeland and arriving in western Asia, might have brought this technology and introduced it to the natives, inspiring enduring legends of culture-heroes from across the seas.

The ancient Sunda peoples are also thought to have been expert seafarers because of their ability to colonize even far-flung islands in the Pacific and Indian Oceans; indeed, they probably arrived from Africa to Sundaland via the coast. This expertise in navigation and colonization ties in with Plato's description of empire-building Atlantis.

In Stone Age times, today's river systems would have extended into huge, wide rivers on the flat lands. Underwater mapping of the Sunda Shelf (what was then the Sunda plain) shows that the mighty rivers of today that drain Indonesia, Malaysia and Indo-China once extended across the lowlands and may have combined to create vast 'super rivers'. The Sunda Plain would have been watered by several of these rivers, providing extensive possibilities for navigation and trade within Sundaland and with communities in the lands surrounding it. Perhaps giant waterways such as these inspired Plato's description of the canals and waterways linking Atlantis to the ocean and its trade.

NATURAL RESOURCES

Plato specifically mentions the abundant forestry resources of Atlantis, and Sundaland would have been rich in tropical hardwoods.

Like Plato's Atlantis, this part of South-East Asia is also rich in tin and other ores; indeed, a large portion of the resources are found on the now-submerged land of the Sunda Shelf. Perhaps the Sundalanders were truly ahead of their time and invented basic metallurgy, inspiring Plato's description of their metallic wealth.

THE END OF SUNDALAND

One theory suggests that the devastating event that destroyed Sundaland and its Stone Age civilization was the titanic eruption of a prehistoric Mount Krakatoa or similar volcano. This super-volcano would have blasted its immediate surrounds with lava and flames, smothered most of Sundaland under thick ash, set off enormous tsunamis and shattering earthquakes, and possibly triggered the melting of the ice plug holding back Lake Agassiz, by depositing sunlight-absorbing ash on to the normally reflective North American ice cap. This in turn could have unleashed the flood that raised global sea levels and finally drowned the devastated Sundaland.

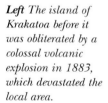

Kumari Kandam

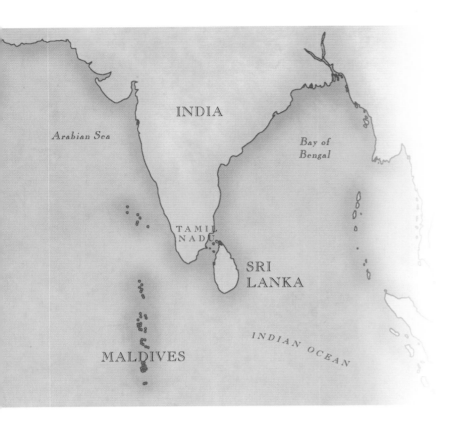

A major inspiration for the Lemuria of the Theosophists was the plethora of Indian legends concerning lost lands to the south that had been submerged by great floods. Prime among these was the legendary Tamil homeland of Kumari Kandam.

Like Sundaland and many other parts of the world (see, for instance, the theories about Dogger Bank on page 76 and Yonaguni on page 96–97), a considerable amount of India's continental shelf was dry land during the last Ice Age. Most palaeontologists agree that early humans probably first explored and colonized this coastal strip that now lies underwater, and that this is where the bulk of prehistoric human settlement, and therefore early civilization and culture, took place.

TAMIL HOMELAND
The prehistory of India is complex and confusing. The aboriginal peoples were conquered and/or displaced by waves of invaders, but there is still great uncertainty over who invaded whom, and where the interlopers came from. The traditional view is that the aboriginal Dravidian peoples of India were overrun from the north-west by Indo-Aryans, who pushed them south and took control of most of the subcontinent, even where they did not replace the original inhabitants. But the Dravidians themselves, especially the Tamil peoples of the southern tip of India, have their own legends, which

tell of them migrating north out of a southern homeland that is now submerged – Kumari Kandam. It was either a separate land-mass or one joined to India; either way it encompassed both Sri Lanka and the Maldives, possibly stretching as far as South-East Asia or even Australia.

THE SANGAMS
Central to the myth of Kumari Kandam is the Sangam, the ancient body of Tamil literature, and also the conclave or academy that drew it up. According to Tamil tradition, there were three Sangams, each one convened to draw up works of literature, law, commentary, and so on. The first Sangam sat for thousands of years at the mythical Mount Mahedra, until a terrible deluge forced it to relocate. This happened twice more, until eventually Kumari Kandam was completely submerged and the Sangam had to relocate to Madurai, a city now on the coast of India.

The chronology of the Sangam potentially matches up quite well with Plato's Atlantis, for at least one stage of the destruction of Kumari Kandam dates to around 12,000 years ago. It also matches well the

accepted chronology of sea level rises after the last Ice Age. In other words, the Sangam may actually be an incredibly ancient record of events usually thought to lie far back before the dawn of recorded history.

UNCOVERED REMAINS
The Tamil legends speak of *kadaktol* – the devouring of the land by the sea. Modern scholars now believe this is probably a reference to tsunamis and earthquake-related subsidence, which could result in large areas of land being catastrophically submerged.

Graphic illustration of the power of tsunamis, and of the archeological treasures that may lie off the Indian coast, was provided by the Boxing Day tsunami of 2004. After the wave had struck India's south-eastern coast and the waters had retreated, ancient structures off the coast of Mahabalipuram were left high and dry, scoured clean of the sand and silt that had obscured them.

Archeologists had already been exploring the waters off Mahabalipuram, site of the last remaining temple of the legendary City of

'Like Sundaland, a considerable amount of India's continental shelf was dry land during the last Ice Age.'

the Seven Pagodas. After the tsunami they were presented with stone remains, including a granite lion. Although these are thought to be relics from just 1,200 years ago, they illustrate the archeological wealth that may yet be discovered.

Potentially even more significant was the uncovering of the remains of a beachfront temple dating back more than 2000 years. Deposits at the site clearly show the tell-tale traces of tsunami damage, and the evidence now suggests that tsunamis on the scale of the one that supposedly doomed Atlantis may have struck the area around 200 BCE and again in the 14th century CE. Could even older cataclysms have fed into the Kumari Kandam legend?

Finds from much further north and west, in the Gulf of Cambay, also offer us a glimpse of India's drowned past. Divers exploring the sea bottom in 2001 and 2002 spotted what look like megalithic remains that may date back to 7000 BCE – far older than any known civilization. Like the finds at Yonaguni and Bimini, however, these are contentious and may simply be natural features.

The marvels of Madurai

Madurai in Tamil Nadu is one of the oldest cities in southern India. Officially it is at least 2,500 years old and, according to the Tamil Sangam legends, it was founded by refugees from lost Kumari Kandam. Today it is best known for its breathtaking temple complex of Meenakshi.

MANY MADURAIS

According to the legend of Kumari Kandam and the story of the Sangams, present-day Madurai, despite being one of the oldest cities in India, is only the most recent incarnation in a line of cities bearing this name. Each was the site of one of the epic Sangams – the meeting place for scholars, priests and poets for thousands of years during the Muthal Sangam (the first) and the Idaii Sangam (the second). Both of these previous Madurais were consumed by monstrous deluges, a fate that seems more plausible given recent findings about the frequency of tsunami devastation in the region (see page 126). The illustration on page 129 imagines how the original Madurai would have looked before it was consumed by the flood.

According to legend, the temple was founded millennia ago when the legendary King Kulasekhara Pandya found a sacred stone (lingam) in a clearing in the forest, and built the first temple around it. He then founded a lotus-shaped city around the temple, which was visited by the god Shiva who shook his locks over it, showering it with divine nectar, whence it got its original name of Madhurapuri (from the word *madhu* meaning honey).

The present-day temple was constructed mainly in the 16th and 17th centuries CE, but myth and legend connect it to the days of Kumari Kandam, and the layout of the temple and the streets around it reflect ancient Tamil traditions. Could they, in fact, have been inspired by prehistoric settlements in the lost Tamil homelands of Kumari Kandam?

① THE TEMPLE

This is known as Meenakshi Sundareswar, after the fish-eyed goddess Meenakshi (an incarnation of Shiva's wife Parvati), and Sundareswar, an incarnation of Shiva himself in the form of the god of beauty. It is one of the largest and most magnificent temples in all India, and among the greatest examples of Dravidian architecture.

② GOPURAMS

The most eye-catching features are the lofty towers or gopurams. There are 12 gopurams covered with a riot of sculpture and colour. There are four main Rajagopurams at the corners of the temple complex. The largest rears up 49 m (160 ft) from the southern gatehouse, and features 1,511 sculptures. For many years it was one of the tallest structures in India.

③ GOLDEN LOTUS POND

In one of the temple courtyards is a giant pond or tank, 73 x 50 m (240 x 165 ft), said to be older than the temple itself and to have been created when Shiva thrust his *soolam* (trident) into the ground. It is believed to grant prosperity to all who bathe in it. According to Sangam tradition, the Golden Lotus Pond was used to rate the products of the Sangam – manuscripts would be dropped into the water and, if they floated back up to the surface, they were accepted as worthy.

④ MULTI-PILLARED HALL

One hall of the temple, the Ayirangaal Mandapam, is filled with an extraordinary profusion of geometrically arrayed pillars. There are 985 ornately carved and sculpted pillars, each cut from a single block of granite. Some are engineered to be musical, so that when they are struck, they emit a note.

⑤ AS ABOVE, SO BELOW

Around the temple the streets of the city are laid out in a rectangular fashion that is said to mirror the structure of the cosmos.

⑥ LANDSCAPE

The landscape of Kumari Kandam, a lush green paradise of rolling hills and verdant forest, was of such beauty that the Sangam poets were moved to write verses in praise of it.

'Present-day Madurai, despite being one of the oldest cities in India, is only the most recent incarnation in a line of cities bearing this name.'

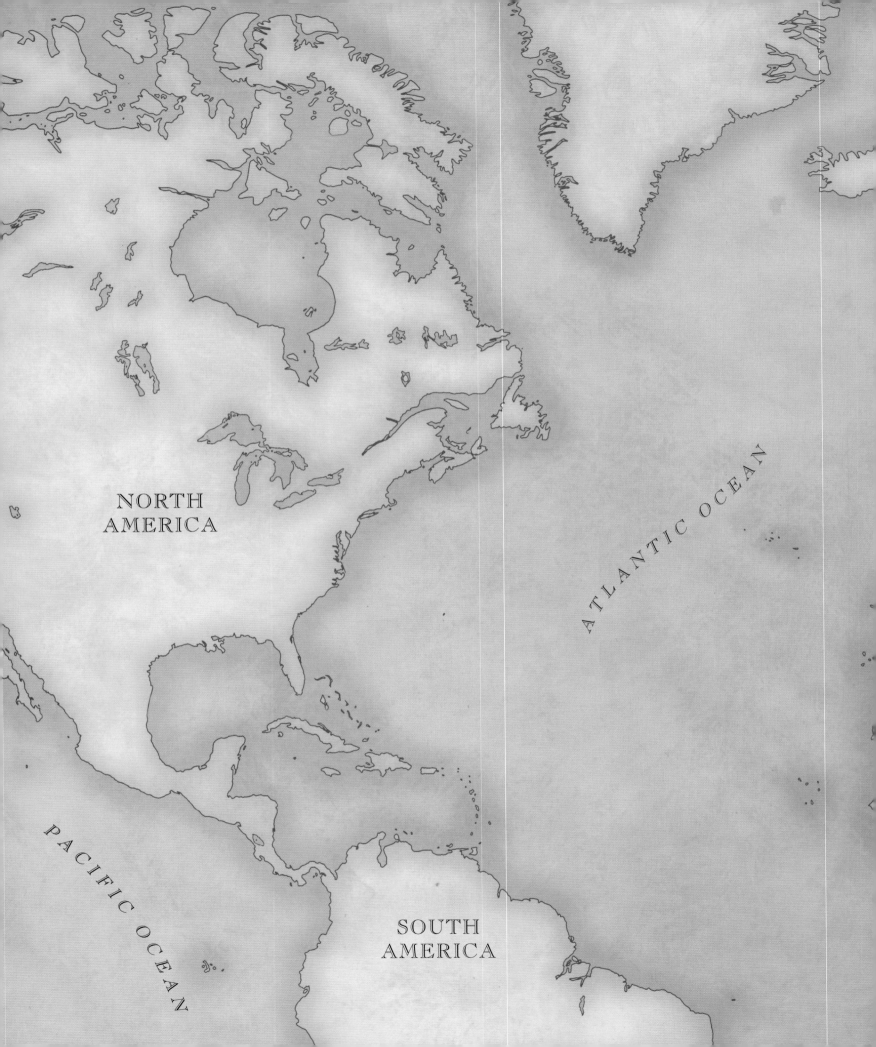

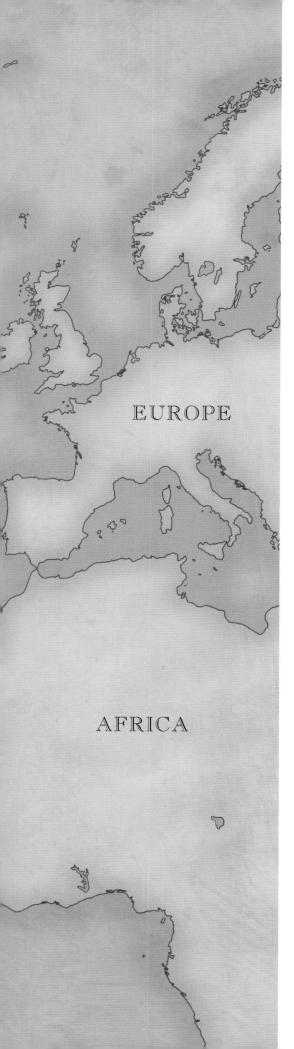

EUROPE

AFRICA

PART 9

LEGENDARY LANDS OF THE CELTS

The Celtic peoples have some of the richest lore of any culture concerning lost and/or legendary lands. These fantastic otherworlds are variously described as islands, submerged cities, drowned lands or even alternative dimensions, and they are almost always located to the west. Many of them were actually believed to exist, to the extent that expeditions were commissioned to go in search of them, helping to kick-start the Age of Discovery and the opening of the New World.

This section reviews four of the most important Celtic legendary lands: the submerged kingdoms of Lyonesse and Ys, the semi-legendary island of Hy-Brasil and the eldritch (unearthly) fairyland of Tir Nan Og.

Lyonesse – the lost land of Tristan

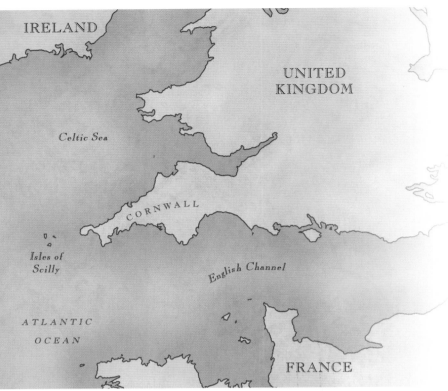

IRELAND

UNITED KINGDOM

Celtic Sea

CORNWALL

Isles of Scilly

English Channel

ATLANTIC OCEAN

FRANCE

Best known today for its Arthurian associations, the lost land of Lyonesse has roots in Celtic folklore and Pictish history, as well as reflecting uniquely Cornish traditions concerning Lost Lethowstow, a drowned land near St Michael's Mount. These lost lands may even have a basis in reality.

Lyonesse was a mythical kingdom said to stretch from the Cornish mainland to the Isles of Scilly and beyond, before it was submerged beneath the waves. In Arthurian legend it was the homeland of Tristan, of the tale of Tristan and Isolde; and in the 19th century, Tennyson, in his *Idylls of the King*, made it the scene of the last battle between Arthur and Mordred. Late medieval literature also records the specific legend that Lyonesse was lost beneath the waves on the night of 11 November 1099, and that the only escapee from the deluge was a man called Trevelyan, who outran the waves mounted on a white horse, which subsequently became the emblem of his family on their coat-of-arms (this legend probably derives from the Breton story of Ys, see pages 134–135).

The capital of Lyonesse was said to be a place of marvels called the City of Lions, while the land itself was home to an amazing 140 churches, the bells of which can still be heard tolling beneath the waves. Looking from Land's End (the westernmost tip of Cornwall and by extension mainland Britain) towards the Scilly Isles to the south-west, it is possible to see rocks jutting from the sea. These are called the Seven Stones, and are said to mark the site of the City of Lions. Fishermen claim to have pulled doors and windows from the water, and to have seen buildings and ruins beneath the waves.

FROM LOTHIAN TO LETHOWSTOW

In the Arthurian cycle, Sir Tristan was the son of the king of Lyonesse. His uncle, King Mark of Cornwall, charged him with the task of travelling to Ireland to bring back his own bride-to-be, Princess Isolde, but Tristan and Isolde accidentally drank a love potion and fell for one another. Tristan eventually ended up married to another Isolde, had numerous adventures and died tragically.

IDYLLS OF THE KING

*Then rose the King and moved his host by night,
And ever push'd Sir Mordred, league by league,
Back to the sunset bound of Lyonesse –
A land of old upheaven from the abyss
By fire, to sink into the abyss again;
Where fragments of forgotten peoples dwelt,
And the long mountains ended in a coast
Of ever-shifting sand, and far away
The phantom circle of a moaning sea.*

Alfred, Lord Tennyson, *Idylls of the King*

This Arthurian figure is based on a historical Tristan, one of the four recorded kings of Lyonesse. Since Lyonesse probably never existed (although see below), where did these historical figures come from? The real Tristan was probably King Drust of Lothian, a Pictish kingdom in what is now Scotland. The family of Drust was associated with Celtic kingdoms in Wales and the north of England, where the name becomes Drystan. Meanwhile an alternative form of Lothian was Leonais. Since this was also the name of part of Brittany, which had close Celtic connections with Cornwall, it is likely that legends of Drust of Leonais in Scotland became attached to Cornwall, where he became Tristan of Lyonesse. This was possible because Cornwall had legends of a sunken land known as lost Lethowstow. Lethowstow was conflated with Leonais, which became Lyonesse.

DROWNED FORESTS AND SUNKEN LANDS

Lost Lethowstow itself may have a basis in reality. Around Mount's Bay, location of St Michael's Mount, there is a local tradition that the bay is home to a drowned forest, which once covered lands stretching to the Scilly Isles and beyond. Could the sea bottom between Cornwall and the Scillies once have been dry land? In prehistoric times it almost certainly was, as sea levels were much lower during the last Ice Age.

There is also intriguing evidence that some lands in the area have been drowned in historical times, perhaps as late as the Classical Era (Late Bronze Age/Iron Age in Britain). When sea levels rose, low-lying land bridges between some of the islands may have flooded, breaking up large islands into smaller islets. Some Roman sources describe the Scilly Isles as a single island, while the ancient geographer Strabo records that there were ten Scilly Isles – and today the archipelago is made up of 140 rocky islets. Meanwhile, in 1997 a Russian Atlantis-hunting expedition focused its attentions on Little Sole Bank, a submarine hill off the coast of Cornwall that may have been above sea level relatively recently (in geological terms). Perhaps ancient memories and traditions of Little Sole Bank, of a single large Scilly Isle or of now-submerged tracts of Cornish coastline were responsible for the legend of lost Lethowstow and, by extension, the story of Lyonesse.

Left A view from Land's End looking towards the Isles of Scilly. The rock that is visible is called the Armed Knight, but beyond it are other rocks, which are also said to mark the site of the City of Lions, the lost capital of Lyonesse.

The lost city of Ys and Douarnenez Bay

Perhaps the most famous folktale of old Brittany is the story of Ys, a fabulous city built for love that perished beneath a deluge of divine wrath, leaving only two survivors. Where did the tale come from, and what does it mean?

According to the traditional Breton folktale, which became popular and widely known when it was recorded in a book of Breton folksongs in 1839, Ys – also known as Is or Ker-Is (probably from the Celtic *Caer Ys*) – was a fabulous city in Douarnenez Bay in south-west Brittany. It was built by Gradlon, king of Armorica (the pre-Roman name for Brittany). He had married a beautiful pagan woman who had died in childbirth, leaving him a daughter named Dahut, upon whom he doted.

Besotted with his beautiful daughter, Gradlon built the marvellous city of Ys for her. It was the most beautiful city in the world, with white palaces and grand temples to the old pagan gods, for Dahut followed the religion of her mother even though Gradlon had converted to Christianity and relied upon the wise counsel of St Winwaloe (or Guenuole) as his main advisor. Ys grew fantastically rich, thanks to its extensive trade links.

THE GATES OF DESTRUCTION

Ys was built on land that lay below sea level, and therefore relied upon an extensive system of dykes and dams to keep back the waves. In the centre of the main dam was a mighty gate, which enabled out-flowing tidal water to exit, but held back the sea. Gradlon wore the key to the gate on a chain around his neck.

Unfortunately, his daughter Dahut was wicked and depraved, and encouraged the citizens of Ys to indulge their vices with feasts, orgies and worship of the old gods. Eventually, besotted with a new lover (or in some versions tricked by the Devil himself), Dahut stole the key from around her father's neck and opened the gate to let the Devil in. Immediately the sea rushed in and began to drown the iniquitous city. Perceiving that the vengeful wrath of God was upon them, St Winwaloe advised the king to mount his steed Morvac'h (which in some versions was noted for its ability to run on water) and flee. The king tried to carry his daughter to safety with him, but the horse could not carry them both, and either Winwaloe or God himself ordered Gradlon to cast 'the fiend' into the waves. The king and his saintly advisor were the only two to escape – Gradlon going on to found the city of Quimper. Dahut was transformed into a crow or a mermaid (depending on the version) and still haunts the rocks of Douarnenez Bay to this day. When the tide is very low, the tops of the towers of Ys can be glimpsed below the waves, and the bells of its temples can still be heard.

THE LEGEND IN CONTEXT

Many elements of this tale are familiar: the drowned church bells and escapees fleeing the rising waters on horseback link it to Lyonesse. There are also parallels with Atlantis: a kingdom of fabulous wealth, ringed with massive earthworks, that was drowned in divine vengeance for its hubris and degeneracy. This last theme is also related to the biblical tale of Sodom and Gomorrah, and features in similar tales of drowned cities from all over the Celtic world. For instance, there is a Welsh legend of the city of King Gwyddno, drowned beneath the waters of Cardigan Bay, which is almost identical to the story of Ys. The tale has also been seen as an allegory of the victory of Christianity over paganism in the Celtic lands. Ys is the city of Dahut, the wicked pagan witch, whose dealings with Satan bring destruction, while the good Christians, King Gradlon and St Winwaloe, survive and prosper.

THE LOWLAND HUNDREDS

Welsh legend tells the story of King Gwyddno Garanhir ('Longshanks'), who ruled a country known as *Cantre'r Gwaelod* – the Lowland Hundreds. Located in what is now Cardigan Bay in West Wales, this was a fertile area protected from the sea by a great dyke known as *Sarn Badrig* (St Patrick's Causeway). As with Ys, the dyke was breached by a gate, which was left open by Prince Seithenyn, a feckless drunk. Gwyddno was able to escape to the mainland, where his basket would later become one of the legendary Thirteen Treasures of Britain. It has been suggested that submarine petrified forests and sunken but natural offshore ridges gave rise to the legend of the lost land and the dyke that protected it.

Above *An 1885 engraving showing King Gradlon fleeing the encroaching sea upon his steed Morvac'h.*

'When the tide is very low, the tops of the towers of Ys can be glimpsed below the waves, and the bells of its temples can still be heard.'

Hy-Brasil

① **THE DIVIDED CIRCLE**

Hy-Brasil was believed to be a circular island divided in two by a central river or canal. According to some sources, this belief also accounts for the circle with a line through it that features on the modern Brazilian flag.

② **THE FOG**

In some versions of the legend, the island is usually concealed by a shroud of fog, which lifts once every seven years to allow lucky mariners a glimpse of the fabulous land.

A legendary island in the Atlantic that inspired transatlantic voyages of exploration, Hy-Brasil featured on maps until well into the modern era. Could the legend have been a record of pre-Columbian discovery of the Americas?

The period from the Middle Ages to the dawn of the modern era in the 18th century was a golden age for cartographic Atlantic fictions, in the form of phantom islands depicted on maps of the Atlantic Ocean. Even serious geographers and cartographers, whose charts were depended upon by pioneering mariners to direct them across vast expanses of unknown ocean, included mythical, legendary and folkloric islands alongside real lands. Among the most persistent of these so-called 'phantom islands' was the wonderful land of Hy-Brasil – also known as Brasil, Brazil, O'Brasail, *Beg Ara* (in Irish) and many other variations. Hy-Brasil first appeared on a map in 1325, and still featured on charts as late as the 1870s.

GO WEST

Primarily the product of Irish folklore traditions, Hy-Brasil was said to be a fabulous land of plenty somewhere in the Atlantic Ocean. As voyages of exploration filled in more and more of the blank spaces on maps, so the mooted location of Hy-Brasil shifted westward. Originally it was said to lie just off the coast of Ireland and to be visible occasionally from the westernmost mainland. Later Hy-Brasil was identified with the Azores, Newfoundland and other real places. Mariners from Bristol were among those said

to have chanced upon Hy-Brasil, and when in 1497 John Cabot 'officially' became the first European since the Vikings to reach the North American mainland, it was assumed that his discovery confirmed these tales. Writing to Christopher Columbus, Bristol merchant John Day explained:

It is considered certain that the cape of the said land was found and discovered in the past by the men from Bristol who found 'Brasil' as your Lordship well knows. It was called the Island of Brasil, and it is assumed and believed to be the mainland that the men from Bristol found.

③ HARDWOODS AND DYES

Among the bountiful natural resources, it was thought that the island was thick with valuable hardwood trees that could be used as sources of precious dyes.

④ TOWERS AND DOMES

In some of the Irish folktales of Hy-Brasil, travellers who returned from it spoke of the inhabitants living in golden-roofed towers and domes, marking them as a rich and sophisticated culture. There are definite echoes of Atlantis here.

⑤ ISLAND OF PLENTY

As a paradisial land of Edenic bounty, Hy-Brasil was depicted as being covered in fruit trees groaning with produce, along with every other bounty of the Earth. In fact, in accounts such as the story of Brendan the Navigator, Hy-Brasil is explicitly linked to Paradise. It was said that it was always autumn in Hy-Brasil, so that trees and crops were eternally in season. It was also claimed that the sun never set, so that it was always warm and sunny. This suggests that the legends of Hy-Brasil were inspired by genuine trips to the Polar region during summer.

⑥ CORACLES ACROSS THE OCEAN

Brendan the Navigator was a real historical figure noted for his piety and for founding monasteries in Ireland and Britain in the 6th century. He also features in legendary tales about how he and a party of monk companions sailed across the Atlantic in a traditional Irish coracle (a small boat made of hides). They made landfall on the shores of Hy-Brasil, explored and were greeted by an angelic figure.

WHAT'S IN A NAME?

The name Hy-Brasil was thought to be derived either from the Irish *Ui Breasil* – 'descendants of Breasal' – an ancient Irish tribe, or to be a reference to a type of tree or plant that provided the rare red dye also called brasil (this was how the real country of Brazil got its name). Hy-Brasil was also cognate with several other phantom islands such as the Fortunate Isle, the Blessed Isle, St Brendan's Isle (after the legendary Brendan the Navigator, who was said to have visited it on his transatlantic voyage), Island of the Saints and the Isle of Delight.

'It was said that it was always autumn in Hy-Brasil.'

Tir Nan Og

The rich fairy lore of the Celts speaks of an exotic and alluring otherworld where the fairy folk live. It goes by many names, including the Irish Tir Nan Og, Land of the Young.

Fairies, elves, Little People, Fair Folk, goblins, pixies, piskies, sprites, gnomes, knockers, kobolds, brownies and boggarts – there are dozens, if not hundreds, of names for the eldritch (unearthly) race of supernatural beings that feature so heavily in Celtic folklore. Traditionally, the fairy folk were said to have been earlier inhabitants of the lands where humans now live, who had been driven out of their lands and eventually into another plane of existence entirely. Although they could still visit the human world, they lived primarily in some sort of alternative reality or dimension, which itself went by many different names, including Fairyland, Elfhame, Mag Mell and Annwn. Among the most popular versions of this fairy otherworld was Tir Nan Og (spellings vary), which translates as Land of the Young.

Tir Nan Og is cognate with the other Celtic otherworlds, including Hy-Brasil, Lyonesse, Avalon, the Fortunate Isles, and so on. It is also related to Greek concepts such as the Elysian Fields and to the Valhalla of the Norse. In Tir Nan Og there was no unhappiness or illness; everyone was young, healthy and happy; and all feasted, hunted and played amid abundance and wondrous delights. It was, variously, the home of the fairies, the land of the dead, and the realm of heroes and gods. In later Christian traditions, which frowned upon heathen paradises, Tir Nan Og was a much more dangerous and scary place.

GETTING TO FAIRYLAND

Like most Celtic otherworlds, Tir Nan Og was assumed to lie to the west, possibly as an archipelago of some sort. However, since it did not actually exist in this reality, geography (including its exact location and dimensions) was not strictly applicable. While some figures of folklore and legend managed to reach it by travelling across the sea, others were carried there by fairies or elves aboard their steeds, or were transported there instantaneously via magic portals (for example, in fairy mounds or fairy rings) or simply by walking anti-clockwise around a church. Obstacles along the way included fog, rivers, torrents of blood (one tradition was that all the blood

Left *An illustration of the tale of* Thomas the Rhymer. *Thomas is swept off to Faeryland by the Queen of Elphame. On his return home he finds that seven years have passed, and that he is gifted with the power of prophecy.*

shed in the mortal world flowed past Tir Nan Og), and wrong turnings could lead to hell. Fairyland itself was, in Christian tradition, neither Paradise nor hell, just as the fairies were entities somewhere between angels and demons (according to some traditions, they were the angels who did not take sides in the war between heaven and hell).

VISITORS TO FAIRYLAND

There are many folktales, legends, ballads and poems about humans who visited Tir Nan Og, or one of its incarnations. Oisín (pronounced 'uh-sheen') was a folkloric hero who was taken to Tir Nan Og by a beautiful fairy maid named Niamh (pronounced 'neeve'). She was a queen of the Tuatha de Danaan (the People of the Goddess Dana, as the pre-human inhabitants of Ireland were called before they were driven out and became the fairies). They fell in love and had a child, but Oisín grew homesick and so Niamh lent him her steed, Embarr, to carry him back to Ireland. She

warned him not to touch the ground, for although only a few years had passed in Fairyland, 300 years had passed in the mortal world; but Oisín failed to heed her and the years instantly caught up with him, although he lived long enough to relate his tale to St Patrick.

RULES AND REGULATIONS

Oisín's fate illustrates the dangers of visiting Tir Nan Og, where the rules are different. Time passes at a different rate there (it can be either fast or slow). Most mortals who visit risk losing their immortal souls, or at least becoming trapped there forever if they eat or drink anything, and it is frequently unwise to speak to anyone, take anything or believe anything you see. The worst danger is that a mortal may be used in place of a fairy as part of the *teind*, a regular tithe of souls owed to the Devil. A particular practice of the fairy folk was to steal human babies and replace them with weak and sickly fairy infants, known as changelings.

Above *Richard Doyle's* Triumphal March of the Elf-King *is an example of the degeneration of the fairy archetype in Victorian times, where what had once been supernatural entities of power and danger became cute flower fairies.*

'Traditionally the fairy folk were said to have been earlier inhabitants of the lands where humans now live.'

ASIA

OCEAN

AUSTRALIA

ANTARCTICA

PART 10

OTHER LOST WORLDS

History, myth, legend, folklore and fiction have thrown up a multitude of lost or hidden places. To give a completely exhaustive list is beyond the scope of this book, but this section explores as many as possible of the lands, cities and continents that do not fit any of the other categories already covered.

Inevitably this is a disparate group, ranging from esoteric and occult locations, such as Shambhala and the Hollow Earth worlds, to legendary kingdoms such as El Dorado and the Kingdom of Prester John. What unites them is that you will not find them on any modern map, but they are nonetheless rooted firmly in the geography of the imagination.

Shambhala and Shangri-La

The remote mountain fastnesses of the Himalayas were not fully explored by Europeans until well into the 20th century, leaving plenty of imaginational space for dreamers, visionaries, mystics and madmen to fill in the blanks for themselves.

Shangri-La has become a familiar term or concept, in popular usage akin to the phrase 'Holy Grail', meaning an ultimate goal or prize sought for, but practically impossible to reach. It derives from a fictional place invented by author James Hilton in his 1933 book *Lost Horizon*, which was subsequently made into a popular film of the same name. In the book and film the survivors of an air crash discover a utopia in the Himalayas, where a mighty monastery-citadel sits at the head of a fertile valley, the inhabitants of which are happy, enlightened and long-lived.

THE REAL SHANGRI-LA

Today many places in and around the Himalayas compete for tourist dollars by claiming to be the 'real' Shangri-La, obscuring the actual basis of Hilton's fiction, which was the Tibetan-Buddhist concept of Shambhala. Shambhala is a mystical kingdom, where everyone is enlightened, ruled by the Kulika king in the capital city of Kalapa.

Shambhala is mentioned in ancient texts, particularly a body of teachings known as the *Kalachakra tantra*, said to have been drawn up at the request of King Suchandra of Shambhala in around 900 BCE. In its original form, Shambhala was a mystical concept and allegory, as well as an actual place. According to the *Kalachakra*, a huge army will issue forth from Shambhala and defeat the forces of evil just as they are on the verge of conquering the world.

THE HIJACKING OF SHAMBHALA

Shambhala (and by extension Shangri-La) has become well known in the West because the concept was appropriated by Western esoteric groups, starting with Madame Blavatsky (see pages 82–83). Her philosophy included elements of Tibetan Buddhism, often recast using terminology and concepts from Hinduism and elsewhere to make it more palatable to a Western market. Blavatsky claimed that she had received her secret wisdom from mystic gurus in the Himalayas, who guided world affairs from hidden lairs, the mightiest of which was Shambhala. Those who are pure enough can reach Shambhala and access the ancient wisdom and power that resides there. Blavatsky's successors developed the story of Shambhala into a central part of

New Age philosophy. It was said to be the home of creative and spiritual energies that could regenerate or destroy the world. One development was Agartha, a hidden land within the Earth, related to Hollow Earth ideas (see pages 148–149).

② PASSAGE TO PARADISE

Buddhist teachings claim that physical journeying can only take the seeker of Shambhala so far, and that the voyage can only be completed by spiritual progress. Nonetheless, if mighty armies are to issue forth from Shambhala at some point in the future, they will need physical access to the outside world – perhaps over hidden passes known only to adepts.

③ TUNNELS AND CAVERNS

Shambhala is said by some to be connected to other hidden kingdoms, sacred spots and places of power by a network of underground passages and caverns. Supposedly much of the Himalayan massif is honeycombed with them.

④ THE SECRET GARDEN

At the heart of Kalapa lies a grove of sandalwood trees, in the midst of which is a sacred mandala (a circular design symbolizing the cosmos) representing the wisdom and knowledge of the Kalachakra tantra.

⑤ SELF-SUFFICIENCY

Despite the extreme height of the surrounding country, Shambhala itself is said to lie in a deep, fertile valley with a hospitable climate all year round. The kingdom is supposed to be entirely cut off from the outside world, so that all the food and water its inhabitants require comes from within the valley. Presumably sophisticated and efficient terracing and irrigation works for agriculture and animal husbandry, together with village industries and cottage crafts, help to ensure that all the material wants of the people of Shambhala can be met within the secret valley.

⑥ CAPITAL OF SHAMBHALA

The capital of Shambhala is the citadel of Kalapa. Presumably it might resemble other Himalayan mountain citadels, with their combination of temple, palace and fortress characteristics. According to the ancient Buddhist scriptures, Shambhala is ruled by the Kulika king, who sits atop a lion throne in the main palace or temple of Kalapa.

⑦ ARMS AND THE MEN

Buddhist scriptures prophesy that when the world is on the verge of being overwhelmed by the forces of darkness, the Kulika king will lead a great army of warriors out of Shambhala to defeat them. Presumably, therefore, Shambhala has an extensive garrison and training facilities for a mighty army.

① HIMALAYAN HIDEAWAY

Shambhala is hidden somewhere in the deepest and most inaccessible part of the Himalayas or the Tibetan Plateau. It is shielded from the cares and travails of the outside world by lofty mountain peaks.

The search for Shambhala

As befits an esoteric Buddhist concept, Shambhala has developed many layers of meaning. The concept has been appropriated and extrapolated by different groups and movements, becoming (among other things) a symbol of the highest spiritual attainment.

To understand the historical basis of Shambhala, it is necessary to comprehend the troubled times in which the Kalachakra, the main source for the legend, was written. Although it is claimed that it dates back to the 10th century BCE, the relevant parts of it probably date back only as far as the late 10th century CE. This was a period when the primarily Buddhist-Hindu region of Afghanistan, where the *Kalachakra* was thought to have developed, was threatened with invasion by aggressive Islamic forces under the Ismaili Shiites of Multan (in present-day Pakistan). The internal anxieties and tensions occasioned by this threat are thought to underlie the *Kalachakra's* apocalyptic prophecies regarding the defeat of Abrahamic forces (those who follow the Judaeo-Christian-Islamic faiths) by messianic Buddhists. So the original significance of Shambhala may have been as a kind of spiritual and historical retreat for threatened Buddhists – a symbol that their beliefs would survive and ultimately triumph.

This political aspect of Shambhala continued into the 20th century, as the forces that warred over Central Asia sought to turn the myth to their own ends. During the civil war that followed the Russian Revolution, both the Bolsheviks and their White Russian foes claimed to represent Shambhala, in an attempt to win over the Mongols and other Central Asian Buddhists – in doing so they were following in the footsteps of Tsarist Russia. Later the Japanese would attempt the same trick after they invaded Mongolia in 1937, spreading propaganda that Japan was Shambhala and therefore the natural ruler of Central Asia.

MODERN MEANINGS

Since the Theosophists got hold of it, however, Shambhala has come to mean something different and more spiritual for Westerners. Russian painter and mystic Nicholas Roerich argued that Shambhala represented an essential truth that was portrayed differently by different traditions – he claimed that the Grail legend, for

Left A Tibetan banner showing the paradise of Shambhala. In the centre is the citadel of Kalapa, where the Kulika king sits atop his lion throne.

instance, was a Christian version of the Shambhala story. Rudolf Steiner (see pages 88–89) saw Shambhala as the home of the Messiah, which would be revealed by Christ at the Second Coming. The Theosophist and white magician Alice Bailey, who is considered the direct founder of the modern New Age movement, described Shambhala as 'the seat of Cosmic Fire', a purifying force that would sweep away the corrupt materialist world and establish a new age of purity.

HOW TO GET TO SHAMBHALA

Many Buddhist concepts are considered to have multiple layers of meaning, including outer, explicit ones and inner, allegorical ones. Shambhala is the same – as well as being a physical place, it is also an inner goal, representative of attaining a high level of enlightenment. According to the *Sham-bha-la'i lam-yig* (*Guidebook to Shambhala*), written in the mid-18th century by the Third Panchen Lama, one can only travel part of the way to Shambhala by physical means. To complete the journey one must perfect arduous spiritual disciplines.

WHERE IS SHAMBHALA?

The *Kalachakra* is indeterminate about the location of the mystic kingdom, but there have been many theories, ancient and modern. In popular legend, Shambhala is assumed to exist within some remote valley in the Himalayas, probably in deepest Tibet. Ancient Zhang Zhung texts that predate Tibetan Buddhism place it in the Sutlej Valley in Himachal Pradesh.

Explorers and mystics seeking Shambhala in the 19th and 20th centuries claimed that it was much further north, in or near Mongolia. Blavatsky placed it in the Gobi Desert, claiming that the desert was once a sea and that Shambhala was an island in the midst of it, to which the Lemurians had fled on the destruction of their continent. Prior to her, the early 19th-century writer Csoma de Körös, who compared Shambhala to a Buddhist Jerusalem, claimed that its location lay in the Kizilkum Desert in Kazakhstan.

Mystic Nicholas Roerich, who actually led an expedition in search of Shambhala, said it was in the Altai mountains of Mongolia. He was probably echoing Mongolian beliefs that their land was indeed the home of the fabled kingdom.

Agartha

Related to Shambhala, but with much darker connections, is the mystic kingdom of Agartha, deep within the shell of the Earth. Here evil energies build, as dark forces gather and plot.

Agartha (also spelled Agarrta, Agharta, Agharti and many variations thereof) is said to be an underground kingdom that either lies beneath the Himalayas or occupies the whole centre of the Earth. Shambhala is variously said to be its capital, a minor colony or even its cosmic enemy. Where did Agartha come from? Its history is peculiar and complex.

During the 19th and early 20th centuries a number of mystic and esoteric writers introduced and expanded theories about ancient races, hidden kingdoms and secret wisdom. There was often a thin line between what was intended to be taken seriously as fact, and what was presented as fiction.

Hollow Earth theories had become popular (see pages 148–149), and novels such as *The Coming Race* by Edward Bulwer Lytton (the book that introduces the concept of Vril, see page 87) and *The Smoky God* by Olaf Jansen spread ideas about powerful beings and spiritually advanced races beneath the ground. Influenced by these, and apparently instructed by an Indian guru, French Orientalist and mystic Saint-Yves d'Alveydre self-published a bizarre collection of essays entitled *Mission de l'Inde* (*The Mission of India*), which reworked the story of Shambhala into a new legend.

Claiming to have used astral travel to spy on an amazing underground civilization,

Right *Ferdynand Ossendowski, the Polish writer, explorer and man of mystery.*

Saint-Yves described the kingdom of Agartha and its mystic ruler, the Brahmatina or 'Sovereign Pontiff'. The Brahmatina had led his millions of followers underground in 3200 BCE, and there built an advanced civilization with sophisticated technology, psychic powers and ideal government. Soon it would reveal itself to the world above and usher in a new age.

PSYCHIC WARS

Despite not having been invented until the late 19th century, the legend of Agartha took on a life of its own, quickly establishing itself as part of the Shambhala legend. The tale that developed spoke of a psychic war between Agartha and Shambhala, with one representing negative energies and the other positive. Which side was 'good' and which 'evil' depended on the person expounding the view, but it is noticeable that the 'Earth' forces who sought to align themselves with Agartha tended to be much less savoury.

THE GREAT GAME

Central Asia had long been a kind of chessboard for geopolitical machinations and intrigue, as powers such as the British empire, Tsarist Russians, the Chinese and later the Bolsheviks and their White Russian enemies contested for supremacy at the roof of the world. During the civil war that followed the Russian Revolution, one of the main players in this Great Game was the barbaric White Russian warlord Baron von Ungern-Sternberg, also known as the Mad Baron for his cruelty and love of mass executions. Into his orbit fell the Polish scientist and Central Asian explorer Ferdynand Ossendowski. Agartha featured in his account of his researches, *Beasts, Men and Gods* (1922), and according to some accounts the Mad Baron was so interested in the prospect of recruiting Agarthan aid for his battle with the Bolsheviks that he dispatched two expeditions in search of it, the second of which allegedly disappeared without trace.

NAZIS IN TIBET

The best-known seekers for Agartha were the Nazis. According to an involved and influential body of legend, they were engaged in a psychic-occult war at the same time as they were fighting the conventional one. In practice these legends have been wildly exaggerated or entirely fabricated (although the Nazi Party did have occult roots, see pages 152–153), but the Nazis did have an obsession with issues of race and the Aryan homeland, and entertained all sorts of wild notions on the subject. One result was the *Ahnenerbe*, the German Ancestry – Research and Teaching Society, set up by Himmler, which dispatched a famous expedition to Tibet in 1937–39. Legend has it that the expedition was actually searching for Agartha, so that Hitler could forge an alliance with the hidden masters of the underground world. The truth is that the expedition was there to measure skulls, research the notion that Tibet was an Aryan homeland and forge political links with a strategically important area.

Above The 1937–1939 Ahnenerbe expedition to Tibet at dinner, entertaining some Tibetan guests. Ernst Schäfer, the expedition leader is seated in the centre.

Despite having been repeatedly debunked, the Nazi-Agartha myth still has many adherents. Later additions include theories about Hitler's survival and escape to the Antarctic, and Vril-powered Nazi UFOs flying out of Hollow Earth bases (Vril was a fictional concept from a novel, but enthusiasts of Nazis and the occult believe the novel was thinly disguised fact and that Vril really existed). Many of the proponents of these theories are neo-Nazis raising funds for Holocaust denial. For more on the links between the Nazis and lost worlds, see pages 152–153.

see pages 152–153

SAINT-YVES D'ALVEYDRE

It is there [in the main cupola of Agartha] that the central hierarchy of Cardinals and Archis, arranged in a semicircle before the Sovereign Pontiff, appears iridized like a view from beyond the Earth, confounding the forms and bodily appearances of the two worlds, and drowning in celestial radiances all visible distinctions of race in a single chromatic of light and sound, singularly removed from the usual notions of perspective and acoustics.
Saint-Yves d'Alveydre, *Mission de l'Inde*

The Hollow Earth

Today it may sound as ridiculous as theories about the Flat Earth, but for a heady time in the 19th century the world was fired with enthusiasm for the idea that the Earth was hollow, and that new and wonderful worlds might be discovered by those bold enough to explore.

Many religions and cultures featured 'underworlds', often lands of the dead or places of punishment, such as hell or Hades, that were below or within the Earth. One of the first 'scientific' theories that the Earth might be hollow was that of Edmund Halley, the Astronomer Royal, who in 1692 attempted to explain anomalous compass readings and the mysteries of the Aurora Borealis by suggesting that the Earth was composed of a series of concentric shells, the outermost of which was about 800 km (500 miles) thick. Luminous gases separated the inner spheres and occasionally issued forth in the Polar regions.

SYMMES AND THE GREAT US EXPLORING EXPEDITION

Hollow Earth fever really caught on in the 19th century, however, with the efforts of John Cleves Symmes, Jr. He formulated a theory similar to that of Edmund Halley, arguing that the natural balance between gravity and centrifugal forces should result in a rotating sphere separating into several concentric spheres. According to Symmes, there should be wide entrances to the Earth's interior at the Poles, the interior sphere should be habitable, and it would be possible for an intrepid polar expedition to prove the truth of these suppositions. In a widely circulated and printed letter of 1818, Symmes announced:

TO ALL THE WORLD! I declare the earth is hollow and habitable within; containing a number of solid concentrick spheres, one within the other, and that it is open at the poles 12 or 16 degrees; I pledge my life in support of this truth, and am ready to explore the hollow, if the world will support and aid me in the undertaking.

Symmes spent much of the last 11 years of his life lecturing and touring to raise support for his planned expedition, and although he never wrote a book on the topic (at least under his own name), many of his supporters did. Eventually their efforts were to bear fruit, in that they were partly responsible for the launching of the Great US Exploring Expedition of 1838–42, an American equivalent to the voyage of the *Beagle* or the earlier journeys of Captain Cook. Although the Exploring Expedition did not search for an entrance to the Hollow Earth, it did visit the South Pole.

LATER DEVELOPMENT OF THE HOLLOW EARTH

Fictional and non-fictional treatments of Hollow Earth theories continued to be popular, even after explorers had reached the Poles and proved that there were no entrances to the underworld. An eccentric American physician Cyrus Teed formulated a theory that the outer surface of the Earth was actually on the inside of a sphere, and that matter is held onto its surface by centrifugal force. The stars and the rest of the Universe are an illusion created by the effects of the giant, battery-operated Sun that sits in the centre. Teed's unusual beliefs formed the basis of Koreshanity, an alternative religion and way of life, which did not long survive his death (neither, despite the expectations of his followers, did he, even though they propped his body in a bath tub and waited for it to reincarnate). According to one story, a later proponent of this idea was the German scientist Dr Heinz

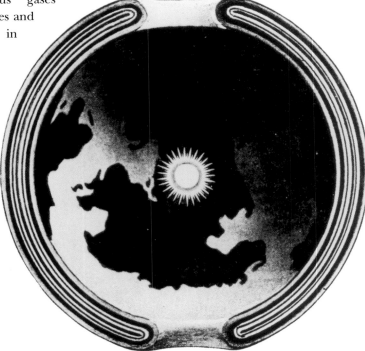

Right *A model of how the Hollow Earth might work, as proposed by 19th-century theorist Marshall Gardner, after the 18th century Swiss mathematician Leonard Euler.*

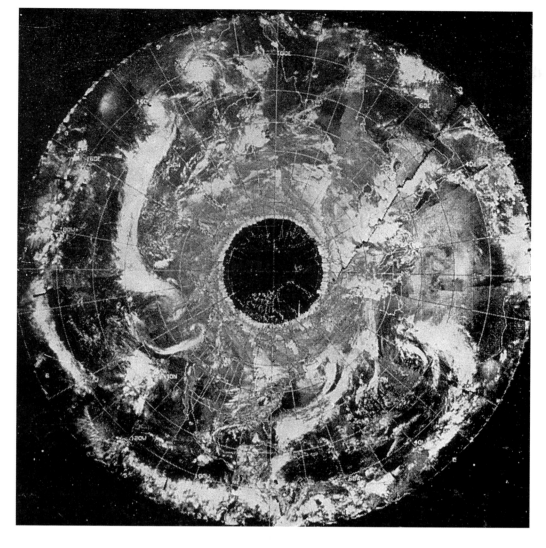

WHAT WOULD LIFE IN THE HOLLOW EARTH BE LIKE?

Most Hollow Earth theories posit some sort of light source to allow life, but with no rising or setting of the 'Sun', concepts of time would suffer, while visiting humans would suffer sleep deprivation and mental problems similar to (but worse than) those who live above the Arctic Circle during the long summers. Meanwhile physicists explain that a Hollow Earth would have practically no gravity, while the centrifugal force beloved of Hollow Earth theorists would, at its strongest (at the Equator), only be 1/300th of ordinary Earth gravity.

Fischer, who convinced the Nazis to send him on an expedition to the Baltic coast so that he could aim his telescope straight up and spy on the British fleet across the North Sea. The expedition was a failure and Fischer paid with his life.

An even more alarming development was the Shaver mythos. Presented as fiction in the pulp science-fiction magazine *Amazing Stories*, the stories of Richard Shaver told a lurid tale of extraterrestrial visitors settling the Hollow Earth in millennia past, with their dangerous progeny, the Deros, still lurking below, sending out evil telepathic assaults on the surface dwellers and occasionally kidnapping one for unspeakable purposes. Many readers took these stories as fact.

'An eccentric American physician Cyrus Teed formulated a theory that the outer surface of the Earth was actually on the inside of a sphere, and that matter is held onto its surface by centrifugal force.'

Hyperborea – the land beyond the North Wind

Atlantis was not the only legendary land of the ancient Greeks. They believed that a blessed land of sunlight and plenty existed in the far north, the abode of the north wind beyond the lands of known nations.

The Greeks had a clearly delineated world view when it came to geography (see pages 48–49) and were happy to let myth, legend and folklore fill in the blank spaces around the edges of the known world. To the north of Greece was the barbarian land of Thrace, where the north wind Boreas lived. But there was another country beyond this, known as '[the land] beyond the North Wind', or Hyperborea. Pliny the Elder tells us: 'Many marvels are told of this people. Some say that the hinges of the world and the limit of the course of the stars lie in their region ...'

LAND OF SUNSHINE AND HAPPINESS

Greek myths and legends about Hyperborea seem to reflect a basic knowledge of lands within the Arctic Circle, and in particular the year-long 'days' produced by the behaviour of the Sun at extreme latitudes. Accordingly, Hyperborea became famous as a land of eternal sunshine, and therefore of warmth, happiness and plenty. According to Pliny, it was 'a blessed nation ... [where] all discord and sorrow is unknown'. Its inhabitants were

said to live to the age of a thousand – in fact, according to Pindar, 'Illnesses cannot touch them, nor is death foreordained for this exalted race.' Pliny goes on to explain:

People there do not die but from the satiety of living. After a festive banquet, full of the joys of old age, the one who wants to die jumps into the seas from a lofty rock. Such is for them the happiest way to die. One cannot doubt the reality of this country, described by many authorities.

In maps from the time of Alexander the Great, Hyperborea is sometimes shown as a long island or peninsula, suggesting that it was based on a vague Greek knowledge of Britain and/or parts of Scandinavia. Another suggestion is that Hyperborea developed from folk memories of an important centre of prehistoric culture in Siberia.

HOME OF APOLLO

Most of the Olympian gods steered clear of Hyperborea, but Apollo made his home there for six months of the year (probably a reference to the fact that the Sun, with which Apollo was closely associated, shone there for six months at a time), and so the

Below Hyperborea, *an etching from 1923 depicting the lost northern paradise.*

Right *The frontispiece from one of Olaf Rudbeck's books, showing him pointing out what he believed was the true location of Atlantis, which he identified as being one and the same as the Hyperborean paradise of the ancients.*

Hyperboreans were said to be special favourites of his. Each year they would send the first fruits of their crops as an offering to the Temple of Apollo at Delos. Originally Hyperborean maidens had delivered the offerings, but they had a tendency to die suddenly on delivery when, beyond the immortalizing influence of their country, their years caught up with them. Instead the Hyperboreans introduced a system whereby the offerings were wrapped in straw to keep them fresh and then passed from one nation or tribe to another, until they reached the Greeks and the Temple at Delos.

HYPERBOREA AND THE ARYANS

Hyperborea developed much darker associations. In the late 17th century Swedish scientist and nationalist Olof Rudbeck identified Hyperborea (ancient Scandinavia) with Atlantis, and portrayed it as the original home of civilization. This association was picked up by Madame Blavatsky, who involved Hyperborea in her Root Races theory (see pages 84–85). When German nationalists began to develop pseudo-historical underpinnings for their philosophy of racial superiority, Hyperborea was identified as the original homeland of the Aryan peoples – an Aryan utopia where proud Nordic warriors had lived in proto-fascist bliss before their world was corrupted by dark, southern races. In this evolving fascist mythology, Hyperborea was said to have suffered Atlantis-like cataclysms, breaking it up into islands that included Thule.

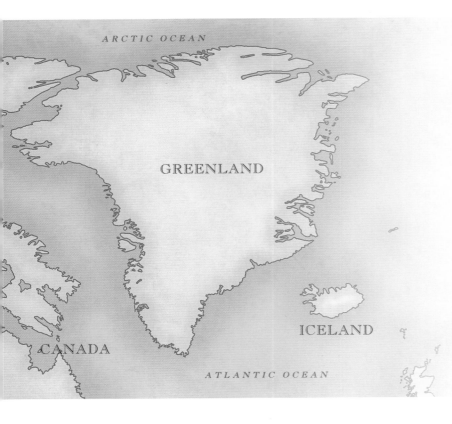

ARCTIC OCEAN

GREENLAND

ICELAND

CANADA

ATLANTIC OCEAN

Thule and the Nazis

As the successor to Hyperborea, Thule started life simply as a legendary place of classical lore – a magical northern land that represented hazy knowledge of north-western Europe – but later became a central element of Nazi mysticism. In Classical times Thule, like Hyperborea, was a far northern land, one of many occupants of the vast terra incognita *beyond the known Classical world.*

Below Rudolf Hess in 1938. He joined the Thule Society shortly after the First World War, possibly even before he met Hitler in May 1920.

Thule was sometimes called Ultima Thule, the 'ultima' signifying its extreme northerly location, although sometimes Thule and Ultima Thule are considered to be two different islands. In Classical times Thule was said to be an island – perhaps Saaremaa in the Baltic – but has also been identified as a name for Scandinavia. In the Middle Ages Thule and/or Ultima Thule were also used as names for Iceland, Greenland and other extreme northern islands. One suggestion is that Thule was Iceland and Ultima Thule was Greenland. More generally, Ultima Thule was a term referring to anywhere at the extreme ends of the Earth.

PYTHEAS AND THULE

The earliest recorded journey to the Arctic regions is that of Pytheas of Massalia (modern-day Marseilles), who lived from *c.*380-310 BCE. At that time Massalia was a Greek colony of merchants and traders. In his account *On the Ocean*, Pytheas relates his travels in north-western Europe, exploring territory unknown to the ancient Greeks, recording the names, customs and lore of

the tribes he met and relating the natural history and geography of the region. He travelled to Cornwall and others parts of Britain, the Isle of Man, probably the various isles of Scotland, possibly the coast of Scandinavia up to the Arctic Circle and even to Iceland, eventually returning via Kent and the Low Countries.

Voyaging north of Britain, Pytheas relates that by sailing for six days he reached the island of Thule (possibly Iceland or Spitsbergen, or perhaps one of the Faroes or Shetlands). Here he found rich and productive land that produced honey, fruit, milk and grain, which the islanders stored in barns. He noted the short nights and reported that on a further day's travel to the north, strange things happened to the sea. According to a report of his travels by the geographer Strabo:

Pytheas also speaks of the waters around Thule and of those places where land properly speaking no longer exists, nor sea nor air, but a mixture of these things, like a jelly, in which it is said that earth and water and all things are in suspension as if this something was a link between all these elements, on which one can neither walk nor sail.

This is probably a reference to 'pancake ice', which forms on the edges of pack ice.

THE THULE SOCIETY

Like Hyperborea, Thule was incorporated into the evolving mythology of German nationalism and Aryan racial supremacy. A number of quasi-Masonic societies sprang up in late 19th- and early 20th-century Germany, promoting a potent brew of mysticism, nationalism, pseudo-scientific racism and virulent anti-Semitism. One of the most influential of these was the *Thule-Gesellschaft* or Thule Society, which promoted pseudo-historical and occult ideas about the origins of the Nordic-Aryan peoples in mythical Hyperborea and its capital, Thule, along with Atlantis, the Hollow Earth and much else besides.

The Thule Society brought together many of the major ideologues and founders of the Nazi movement, and in 1919 leading members of the Society founded the *Deutsche Arbeiterpartei* or German Workers' Party. Later that year Adolf Hitler joined the DAP, and in 1920 it was renamed the *National Sozialistische Deutsche Arbeiterpartei*, also known as the Nazi Party. Although Hitler was only ever an 'associate' of the Thule Society, many leading Nazis were fully paid-up members, including Rudolf Hess, Alfred Rosenberg and Hitler's mentor Dietrich Eckart.

Since the end of the Second World War the Thule Society has occupied a prominent place in persistent myths of occult Nazi activities. A typical suggestion is that Thule exists within the Hollow Earth, where it is home to legions of magical, Vril-powered Nazi UFOs.

***Below** Iceland's dramatic landscape of fire and ice, similar to those that must have confronted Pytheas as he ventured into the far north, to the land he called Thule.*

Caribbean Sea

VENEZUELA

PANAMA

Lake
Guatavitá

GUYANA

PACIFIC
OCEAN

COLOMBIA

ECUADOR

BRAZIL

PERU

El Dorado – lost city of gold

Both a legendary person and a legendary place, El Dorado has become synonymous with an unattainable goal of immense riches. For the conquistadors of the New World it was a siren call to death and madness.

El Dorado means 'the Gilded One', and was originally a reference to a man. In 1538 the Spanish conquistador Captain Sebastian de Benalcásar heard a story about a tribe in the highlands of modern-day Colombia who practised an annual ritual in which their king was coated in gum and then dusted with gold powder, before being rowed out to the middle of a sacred lake on a ceremonial barge. Precious ornaments and gems were tossed into the waters as an offering, before the king himself dived in and washed himself clean. Benalcásar named this legendary figure 'the Gilded One' or 'El Dorado'.

IN SEARCH OF GOLD

Inflamed by the prospect of treasure, conquistadors and adventurers from the Old World spent the next 300 years exploring South America in their hunt for El Dorado, which soon became a place as much as a person. It was sought in the highlands and jungles of Colombia, the mountains and rivers of Guyana and all points in between. Since this was virgin territory filled with hostile Native Americans, impenetrable jungle,

impermeable mountains and impassable swamps, the quest led to starvation, illness, murder, madness and suicide.

Numerous conquistadors led expeditions known as *entradas* into the South American interior in search of El Dorado. The Spanish authorities were happy to encourage these, as they employed vicious and unruly soldiers in exploring and opening up new territories instead of fomenting rebellion at home. Famous examples included the notorious Aguirre (known today from the Herzog film, *Aguirre, Wrath of God*), who led a band of renegade soldiers on a spree of murder, rape, looting and arson before murdering his own daughter and eventually being killed by his men.

Another was Francisco de Orellana, who became detached from the rest of his expedition and accidentally made one of the greatest voyages of discovery in history. Building some river boats to look downriver for El Dorado, which he believed to be just around the next bend, he ended up following a series of increasingly large rivers all the way to the Atlantic Ocean, becoming the first European to travel the Amazon. The river's

Below Sebastian de Benalcazar, the Spanish conquistador who coined the term 'El Dorado'.

name derives from de Orellana's account of meeting a tribe of warrior-women ruled by a fierce queen. Not all the seekers of El Dorado were Spanish. Sir Walter Raleigh lost his son hunting for the fabled city, and eventually his own failed South American adventures cost him his life, as they gave his enemies at court an excuse to have him executed.

OMAGUA AND MANOA

As the El Dorado legend developed, conquistadors and Indian informants brought back tales of a legendary city in the jungle where El Dorado lived. At first this city was known as Omagua, but later its name was given as Manoa. It was said to be paved with gold, while the walls of its buildings were studded with gems. One theory about Omagua/Manoa was that it was the refuge of the last Incas. When the Spanish conquered

the Incas, the remnants of the empire fled into the jungle to continue a guerrilla struggle against the invaders. The Spanish believed they had carried with them the state treasures and had founded a new city deep within uncharted territory.

THE REAL EL DORADO

The original story that inspired the El Dorado legend was probably based on the gilding and ritual bathing practices of the Muisca, a tribe who lived near modern-day Bogotá and on Lake Guatavitá, a crater lake in the Colombian highlands. Unfortunately for the conquistadors, the practice had died out before the Spanish invasion and they were merely chasing shadows.

Lake Guatavitá is a crater lake that may either be an extinct volcano or the result of a meteorite strike. Over the last 450 years

Above Lake Guatavitá, the probable starting point for the El Dorado legend. Numerous attempts have been made to drain the lake and claim its drowned treasures. All have failed.

repeated attempts have been made to drain the lake and access the riches believed to lie at the bottom. For instance, in 1580 conquistadors cut a notch in the crater rim to drain the water away. Only a few pieces of gold were found, but the notch remains visible today. All subsequent attempts failed, and today the Colombian government forbids any further attempts.

The Seven Cities of Gold

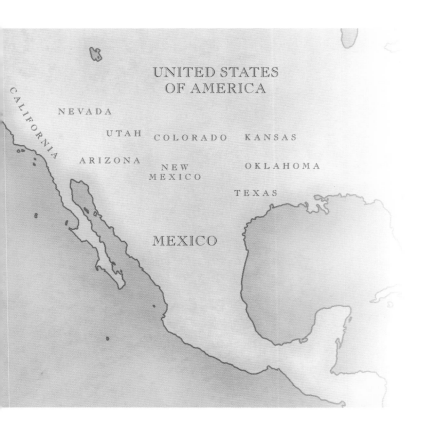

An extraordinary blend of Atlantis and El Dorado, the tale of the fabulous Seven Cities of Gold – a sort of utopian commonwealth of bishoprics – grew from quaint Iberian folklore to deadly mirage, inspiring the European exploration and subjugation of North America and dooming the indigenous inhabitants of today's New Mexico to a miserable end.

THE SEVEN BISHOPS

The Portuguese and the Spanish have matching legends from the time of the Moorish conquest of Iberia, which relate that in order to escape the Muslim invasion, the Archbishop of Porto (or the Bishop of Mérida, in the Spanish version) led six bishops and their parishioners across the western ocean to a new land, where each leader founded a city. In the Portuguese tradition these seven new cities were named Aira, Anhuib, Ansalli, Ansesseli, Ansodi, Ansolli and Con.

According to the legend, these seven cities grew into prosperous and peaceful states, which existed as a kind of utopian commonwealth, free from poverty, injustice and dissent. Accounts of the fabulous wealth of the cities led to them becoming known as the Seven Cities of Gold. The exact location of the *Septe Cidades*, as they were known in Spanish (*Sete Cidades* in Portuguese) was unknown, but a link was drawn with the Classical tradition of Antillia, the Atlantis-like island to the west, which was said to be an Elysium or possibly the true Isles of the Blessed (see pages 48–49).

Antillia, now also known as the Isle of the Seven Cities, was widely assumed to be a real place. Stories circulated of Spanish and Portuguese ships have sighted it, and even of having landed there and come away with reports of a land of plenty, dripping with so much wealth that even sand picked up from the beach was two-thirds gold dust. The island was routinely included on medieval maps, and Columbus planned to stop off there on his way to Japan.

INTO AMERICA

As voyages of exploration started to fill in the blanks on the map of the Atlantic, the proposed location of the Isle of the Seven Cities shifted westward. For a while it was associated with San Miguel, one of the

Azores. Later, the name Antillia was applied to some of the West Indies. But it was in North America that the legend of the Seven Cities of Gold would gain new life.

As with the city of El Dorado in South America, greedy conquistadors always had their ears pressed to the ground for news of treasure. When the four survivors of an ill-fated 1528 expedition to Florida returned to Spanish lands, they brought with them tales picked up from Native Americans of cities of great wealth and splendour, in particular a city named Cíbola. It was immediately assumed that these must be the legendary cities of the Christian refugees, established and flourishing in the heart of the New World. A series of *entradas* were launched through northern Mexico into

'According to the legend, these seven cities grew into prosperous and peaceful states, which existed as a kind of utopian commonwealth.'

what is now New Mexico, Arizona, and so on, to look for what had become the Seven Cities of Cíbola. One was guided by Estevanico, otherwise known as Esteban the Moor, one of the first Africans to feature in the recorded history of North America. Estevanico was the first person from the Old World to explore New Mexico.

CORONADO AND THE PUEBLOS

The largest of these *entradas* was that of Francisco Vásquez de Coronado, whose men discovered the Grand Canyon and ventured as far as Kansas. While Coronado did succeed in discovering the probable inspiration for the tales of Cíbola, he was bitterly disappointed. The magnificent cities he had been promised were in reality the dusty pueblos of the Zuni, canyon dwellings ingeniously constructed of adobe, which could be several storeys high. One suggestion is that, when seen from a distance, the straw in the adobe mix would glisten and sparkle, suggesting to a distant observer that the buildings were made of gold. In reality the Zuni had no gold to offer, and predictably paid for the lack with their lives as the Spanish conquered and abused them.

Below Cliff Palace in Mesa Verde National Park, Colorado, USA. The largest cliff-dwelling in North America, it was built by Pueblo Indians related to the Zuni.

The kingdom of Prester John

Prester John was a legendary Christian monarch who ruled a fabulous kingdom said to lie deep within Asia or Africa. Medieval monarchs attempted to form alliances with him, and explorers travelled to the ends of the Earth to find him. His kingdom was said to be home to such marvels as the Fountain of Youth and the Gates of Alexander.

CRUSADES AND KHANS

Even in the earliest days of Christianity evangelists had not restricted their activities to Europe and the Near East. St Thomas was said to have travelled to India, and important communities and even kingdoms of Christians were established as far afield as Central Asia and the Horn of Africa. To medieval Europeans, whose boundaries stretched only as far as the Holy Land where the Crusades were in full swing, these far-flung Christian outposts, known only by rumour and distant memory, were both exotic and promising, offering the possibility that much-needed allies in the fight against the Saracens might be found to the east.

The legend of Prester John arose from this context, first appearing in the early 12th century with reports of visits from Indian archbishops or patriarchs (such as St Thomas Christians) to the pope and the Byzantine capital. It became firmly established in 1145 when a German chronicler, Otto of Freising, reported in his *Chronicon* the tale of an emissary to the Pope from one of the Crusader princes,

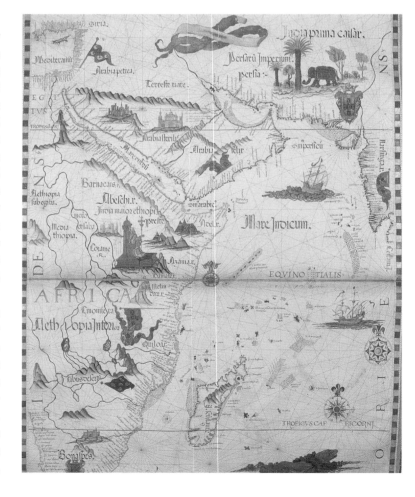

Left A chart of the Indian Ocean from 1558, with the Horn of Africa region labelled as the kingdom of Prester John.

seeking help against the Saracens. The emissary told of a Christian king called Prester John, who was said to have attacked the Saracens from the east, winning a great victory and only being prevented from marching on Jerusalem by the waters of the Tigris.

Prester is short for 'Presbyter', meaning priest or elder, and was said to be the humble honorific with which the legendary ruler preferred to be addressed. (There was actually a potentially real historical figure called John the Presbyter, an early Christian from Syria who was said to have written one of the Epistles of John, but he probably shares little but his name with the later legendary character – John, after all, was a common name, and presbyter was simply a profession.)

This report was probably a garbled version of a real event – the invasion of Persia by Yelü Dashi of the Kara-Khitan Khanate, and his victory over the Seljuk Turks at Samarkand. While Yelü Dashi himself was not a Christian, some of his men were Nestorian Christians (as Asian Christians were generally known). In the European telling, the khan was descended from the Three Magi (who had attended the birth of Christ) and carried an emerald sceptre. It is suggested that Hebrew or Syrian transliteration of the khan's name produced something that read 'Yohanan' or 'Yuhanan', similar to 'Johannes', Latin for John.

RELOCATING TO ETHIOPIA

Accounts such as Marco Polo's began to make it clear that Prester John's land was not to be found in Asia. However, to the medieval Europeans the 'Indies' encompassed Ethiopia, known to be a Christian kingdom, and when diplomatic contact between Ethiopia and Europe was established in 1520, the Ethiopian *negus*, or emperor, was referred to as Prester John by courtiers and chroniclers alike (to the bemusement of the visiting Ethiopians). This African identity was firmly established until the 17th century, with maps labelling Ethiopia as the kingdom of Prester John.

THE LETTER OF PRESTER JOHN

The legend of Prester John really took off in 1165, with the widespread circulation of a letter purported to be from the Eastern potentate to the Byzantine emperor. It began with the proud boast:

I Johannes the Presbyter, Lord of Lords, am superior in virtue, riches and power to all who walk under heaven. Seventy-two kings pay tribute to us. Our might prevails in the three Indies, and our lands extend all the way to the farthest Indies where the body of Saint Thomas the Apostle lies.

The *Letter of Prester John* described him as the king of India and gave many details of his fabulous and semi-magical kingdom, which was said to contain the Fountain of Youth and the fabled Gates of Alexander (set up by Alexander the Great to keep northern barbarians away from the lands to the south of the Caucasus), and to border the Garden of Eden. Prester John commanded many marvels, including a magic mirror through which he could view all his lands. Although it was a fiction, this letter was generally accepted to be true, to the point where the pope dispatched his personal physician to entreat with the marvellous monarch (the doctor was never heard from again).

Further confused reports of events in Central Asia led to stories that Prester John's son or grandson, King David of India, was now taking on the Muslims. The true identity of this King David was none other than Genghis Khan, who had indeed once been fostered by a Nestorian Christian warlord, and who was in the process of conquering Persia. Nonetheless several Europeans, including Marco Polo, set out across Asia to find Prester John.

'The legend of Prester John first appeared in the early 12th century and became firmly established in 1145 when a German chronicler reported that a Christian king called Prester John was said to have attacked the Saracens from the east.'

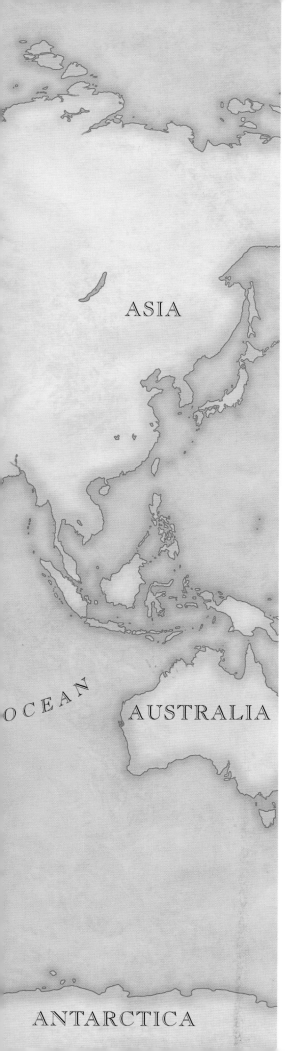

ASIA

OCEAN

AUSTRALIA

ANTARCTICA

PART 11

ATLANTIS AND THE NEW AGE

Atlantis has a come a long way since Plato's original version. From a 'useful fiction' cooked up to illustrate a philosophical programme, which would only have been known to the literate and educated minority, Atlantis has grown to become one of the most prevalent, persistent and influential cultural myths of all time. Today it means so much more than Plato intended. Above all, it has become one of the most central concepts of the New Age movement, the nebulous but pervasive spiritual-cultural phenomenon.

Indeed, Atlantis and the people associated with it have been instrumental in creating the New Age movement – people such as Madame Blavatsky, Rudolf Steiner, Alice Bailey (who coined the term New Age) and Edgar Cayce are the defining figures of the phenomenon, and it is their ideas, beliefs, practices and writings that form its core. In particular, Atlantis and its modern interpretations have been important in defining New Age spiritual values, beliefs and aims, and have informed the burgeoning ecological-environmental movement in myriad ways.

Atlantis and spiritual values

The primary themes of the New Age spiritual movement are linked to, and often derived from, Atlantis and Atlantology. Topics such as reincarnation, vibrations, crystal energy, channelling and spiritual evolution all have their roots in writings about Atlantis.

The modern story of Atlantis is a blend of the versions of Ignatius Donnelly (a highly advanced prehistoric root civilization), Madame Blavatsky (an epic history of human spiritual evolution) and Edgar Cayce (a technologically advanced super-civilization made possible by psychic, spiritual and moral super-powers), together with Plato's original (an Eden blessed by the gods, but later destroyed by hubris). In particular, the central theme is that the Atlanteans were originally close to divine, with such highly developed consciousnesses/spirits/morals that they were almost at one with the Creator or divine principle, except that they had taken physical, material bodies. At first this did not prevent them using their elevated spiritual states to give them psychic and technological super-powers, but later they became spiritually and morally corrupt, and their gifts turned on them and destroyed them.

Discover Atlantis by Diana Cooper and Shaaron Hutton is a typical guide to the psychic and spiritual benefits that study of Atlantis can bring. Its brief synopsis of Atlantean history is a classic example of the New Age interpretation of the lost continent: 'For 240,000 years [Atlantis] was the subject of a divine experiment to see if people could live in a physical body and still keep their connection with All That Is (known as the Creator, God, Godhead or Source).' This modern reading of the story of Atlantis underlies all the spiritual interpretations that derive from it.

ATLANTIS AND GNOSTICISM

One of the primary themes of New Age spirituality is that there is a divine principle to which all can aspire, and that if a person reaches a high enough level of spiritual awareness, he or she can achieve union with this divine principle and in doing so acquire enlightenment, peace, wisdom and entry to Paradise or bliss. This is the core belief of Gnosticism, which can trace some of its principles back to Plato.

Gnostics have not been restricted to any one religion. There have been ancient Persian and Jewish Gnostics, but the movement reached its fullest flowering in the early Christian era. Today Gnosticism has received fresh impetus with the New Age movement and its emphasis on personal paths to spirituality and self-knowledge.

One of the main sources of inspiration for the modern version of Gnosticism has been Atlantean. As explained above, the modern version of the story of Atlantis is a fall from grace – a kind of reverse Gnosis, where the Atlanteans start off in almost perfect union with the Creator or divine Oneness, but become separated from It/Him/Her, with disastrous results. Atlantologists such as Cooper and Hutton believe that by regaining the best of Atlantean values, we can reverse this process and recapture the original blessed state; the subtitle of their book is

Left *Atlantis, the city of temples. Spirituality has played an important part in conceptions of Atlantis ever since Plato emphasized the central role of the Temple of Poseidon and the Atlantean veneration for him.*

that Atlantean state. Sceptics regard past lives, regression, and so on as bogus, and point out that people in a trance state are highly suggestible and will unconsciously fabricate entire life stories, which they will then believe when out of their trance. This can have dangerous consequences, as with people scarred by the belief that they have been ritually abused or experimented upon by aliens.

CHANNELLING WISDOM

Cayce, Blavatsky and other mystic/occult Atlantologists were also responsible for introducing concepts such as channelling (where another consciousness or entity takes control of and communicates through the channeller), astral travel (where a person's astral body – or spirit or soul – leaves the physical body and travels to other places and even in other dimensions) and remote viewing (where, by means of psychic power, the mind's eye is able to view distant places and times). These have all been used to access information about Atlantis and pass it on. Sceptics say that none of these phenomena really happen – in reality the practitioners are only accessing their unconscious and creating fictional accounts without realizing it.

'A Guide to Reclaiming the Wisdom of the Ancients', and their stated aim is 'to bring the energy of pure Atlantis back'.

ATLANTIS AND REINCARNATION

A staple of New Age thought is that some or all of us have walked the Earth before as different people, thanks to reincarnation. Since Edgar Cayce, it has also been widely accepted that the most spiritually, morally and psychically advanced incarnation occurred during the time of Atlantis. If people could get in touch with their Atlantean incarnations, through past-life regression or channelling, they could access some of this ancient wisdom and power. Even better, if they could attain high enough spiritual development, they could return to

ATLANTIS REBORN

So Atlantis has come a long way since Plato used it to illustrate the virtues of his ideal state and the perils of hubris. Today it has been recast in a much more positive light, as an exemplar of the enduring yearning for utopian ideals; as the *locus classicus* of a Golden Age to hark back to; and as an inspiration to light the way to a brighter future amid the darkness of uncertain times.

Atlantis and the environment

As well as its positive spiritual messages, Atlantis has also been interpreted as giving negative or warning messages. In particular, the story of Atlantis' doom and destruction can be seen as a parable for today's environmental crisis.

Today we are faced with an apparently unprecedented range and combination of threats to our civilization. On the environmental front alone, we currently have to contend with global warming, water shortages, pollution, overfishing, deforestation, desertification, soil-fertility degradation, disappearing biodiversity, the spread of invasive and pest species, and many others. On top of this there are threats from extremism, terrorism, weapons of mass destruction, energy shortages and a lack of raw materials. This is without even mentioning natural disasters such as epidemics, super-volcanoes or asteroid impacts. Many people feel that the threats are too extreme and numerous for our civilization to respond effectively, and the ultimate doomsday scenario is that the ecosphere will collapse completely, leaving the oceans, atmosphere and land barren and polluted, and the majority of humankind dying of disease, malnutrition, poisoning, starvation and thirst. Are these threats really unprecedented, or does history offer an example from which we can learn?

THE END OF ATLANTIS

Atlantologists claim that Atlantis *is* that historical example, but different accounts present different versions of what destroyed Atlantis. In Plato's original version the gods themselves visited a natural disaster on the continent, while Ignatius Donnelly and others posited a purely natural catastrophe of geological activity, earthquakes, volcanoes and tsunamis.

From Blavatsky onwards, Atlantis is doomed by the hubris of its inhabitants in a very direct fashion, in that they destroy the continent themselves, either through psychic power gone awry or through rogue technology. Whatever the precise means of destruction, however, the moral of the Atlantis story is clear: even the greatest civilization can end in calamity, quite possibly *because* of its achievements. More specifically, some versions of the story warn

Right *A still from* Terminator 3: Rise of the Machines, *which tells the tale of how machine intelligence runs amok almost as soon as it becomes sentient and destroys humanity who created it. Similar Frankensteinian themes are apparent in many modern versions of the Atlantis story.*

of the dangers of unchecked technology, while others concern the perils of unchecked greed.

FRANKENSTEIN SCIENCE

In Edgar Cayce's conception of Atlantis, it is the sophisticated and powerful technology invented by the Atlanteans that ultimately spells their doom, as their death rays and other weapons cause catastrophic damage on a continental scale. In the years immediately following Cayce's death this was seen as an obvious warning about the perils of nuclear weapons – among the greatest achievements of human endeavour, but with the power to wipe out the species.

This warning is still relevant, and has been joined by other concerns. There is the fear that genetically modified technology may somehow contaminate the natural world. Nanotechnology could get out of control, reducing the planet to a 'grey goo' as self-replicating nano-robots break down all organic matter to make more copies of

themselves. Or artificial intelligence might prove to be malevolent and inimical to humans, as in the *Terminator* or *Matrix* films. More generally, the pollution that we pump into our planet's ecosphere (especially carbon dioxide) is the result of our industrial and transport technology – in a sense, technologies that are already running out of control.

GREED AND OVERCONSUMPTION

Ultimately, whether in Plato's version or the New Age retelling, the Atlantis story is about a society that enjoyed all the blessings of God and nature, but, rather than being content with its lot and remaining true to its founding principles, overreached itself and paid the price. It is all too easy to see this as a parable on modern consumer-capitalist society. In the post-industrial West we have all the benefits of a highly advanced civilization; however, our desire to have more, but pay less, is matched only by the desire of the rest of the planet to match our exalted living standards. Already the globe is

Above The Boxing Day tsunami – proof that disasters of Atlantean proportions are a real threat.

struggling to meet the burden of exploitation of resources and pollution that results, but both of these problems are set to worsen exponentially as the Third World raises its living standards and the West refuses to lower its. The story of Atlantis illustrates the consequences.

A MESSAGE OF HOPE

Despite this gloomy reading, the Atlantis legend also offers hope. Firstly, it illustrates the heights to which humanity can aspire. Secondly, although Atlantis perished, *we* are here now. Many Atlantis enthusiasts believe that time is cyclical in nature, and that although great civilizations may founder and fall, humankind will bounce back, perhaps next time better than ever before.

Bibliography

Literally thousands of books have been written on Atlantis and related topics. The list below includes books used as reference, those mentioned in the text and those that are important in the development of Atlantology.

Allen, James M., *Atlantis: The Andes Solution: The Discovery of South America as the Legendary Continent of Atlantis*, Palgrave Macmillan, 1999

Ashe, Geoffrey, *Atlantis: Lost Lands, Ancient Wisdom*, Thames & Hudson, 1992

Babcock, William H., *Legendary Islands of the Atlantic: A Study in Medieval Geography*, American Geographical Society, 1922

Blashford-Snell, John, *Atlantis: The Andes Solution*, Weidenfeld & Nicolson, 1999

Blavatsky, Helena, *The Secret Doctrine: An abridgement*, Quest Books, 1967

Brennan, Herbie, *The Atlantis Enigma*, Piatkus, 1999

Cayce, Edgar, *Edgar Cayce on Atlantis*, Little, Brown, 1996

Churchward, James, *The Lost Continent of Mu*, C.W. Daniel Co. Ltd, 1987

Collins, Andrew and Rohl, David, *Gateway to Atlantis*, Carroll & Graf, 2002

Cooper, Diana and Hutton, Shaaron, *Discover Atlantis*, Hodder Mobius, 2006

Desmond, Lawrence, *A Dream of Maya: Augustus and Alice le Plongeon in nineteenth-century Yucatan*, University of New Mexico Press, 1988

Donnelly, Ignatius, *Atlantis: The Antediluvian World: A modern revised version* (ed. Egerton Sykes), Sidgwick & Jackson, 1999

Dunbavin, Paul, *Atlantis of the West: The case for Britain's drowned megalithic civilization*, Robinson, 2003

Erlingsson, Dr Ulf, *Atlantis from a Geographer's Perspective: Mapping the fairyland*, Lindorm Publishing, 2004

Flem-Ath, Rand and Rose, *When the Sky Fell: In search of Atlantis*, St Martin's Press, 1997

Flem-Ath, Rand and Wilson, Colin, *The Atlantis Blueprint*, Time Warner, 2001

Hancock, Graham, *Underworld: Flooded Kingdoms of the Ice Age*, Penguin, 2003

Hapgood, Charles, *Maps of the Ancient Sea Kings: Evidence of Advanced Civilization in the Ice Age*, Adventures Unlimited Press, 1996

Hilton, James, *Lost Horizon*, Summersdale, 2003

Hodge, Stephen, *Atlantis: A practical and inspirational guide*, Piatkus, 2000

James, Peter, *The Sunken Kingdom: The Atlantis Mystery Solved*, Pimlico, 1996

Johnson, Donald S., *Phantom Islands of the Atlantic: The Legends of Seven Lands that Never Were*, Quill, 1998

Joseph, Frank, *The Atlantis Encyclopaedia*, Career Press, 2005

Le Plongeon, Augustus, *Maya/Atlantis: Queen Moo and the Egyptian Sphinx*, Kessinger, 1998

More, Bacon and Neville, *Three Early Modern Utopias* (ed. Susan Bryce), OUP, Oxford's World Classics, 1999

Oppenheimer, Stephen, *Eden in the East: Drowned Continent of Southeast Asia*, Phoenix Press, 1999

Plato, *Timaeus & Critias*, Penguin, 1974

Ramaswamy, Sumathi, *The Lost Land of Lemuria: Fabulous Geographies, Catastrophic Histories*, University of California Press, 2004

Sarmast, Robert, *Discovery of Atlantis: The Startling Case for the Island of Cyprus*, Origin Press, 2005

Scott-Elliot, William, *The Lost Lemuria*, The Theosophical Publishing House Ltd, 1904

Spence, Lewis, *The Problem of Lemuria: The Sunken Continent of the Pacific*, Rider & Co., 1932

Zangger, Eberhard, *The Flood from Heaven: Deciphering the Atlantis Legend*, William Morrow & Co., 1992

Index

Page numbers in *italic* refer to the illustrations.

A

Aborigines *84*, 85
Achaea 28, 29
Achaean League 28
Acropolis, Atlantis 16, 44, 57, 124
Adam and Eve 23, 67, *163*
Adites 66
Aditya 67
Adon 67
Adonis 67
Aesop 38
Afghanistan 144
Africa 75, 80, 81, 85, 114, *114*, 121,
    159
Agartha 142, 146–7
Agassiz, Lake 121, 125
agriculture 21, 69, 124
Aguirre 154
Ahnenerbe 147, *147*
Aira 156
airships 10, 87, *87*, 106
Akashic Record 88–9
Akhenaten, Pharaoh *62*
Alexander the Great 150, 159
aliens 109
Allen, Jim 54, 56–9
alphabet 68–9
Altai mountains 145
Altiplano 54–9, *55*, *58–9*
Alveydre, Saint-Yves d' 146, 147
Amarna letters *32*
Amazing Stories 149
Amazon River 154–5
Ammurapi, King of Ugarit 32
Anatolia 38
Andes 54, 58
Andros 108

Andros Platform 108, 109
Anhuib 156
animals, Wallace Line 120–1
ankh symbol 67
Annwn 138
Ansalli 156
Ansesseli 156
Ansodi 156
Ansolli 156
Antarctica 113, 115, *115*, 116–17, 147
Anthroposophy 88
anti-Semitism 85, 153
Antilles *48*, 49
Antillia 49, 110, 156
Apollo 150–1
aqueducts 21
Arabian peninsula 66, 121
Arabs 114
architecture 69, 87
Arctic Circle 84, 149, 150, 152
Aristotle *15*, 36, 49
Arizona 157
Armed Knight *133*
army 21
Arthurian legends 132–3
Aryans 66, 84, 85, 126, 147, 151, 153
Asgard 67
Asia: early migrations 121
    Piri Reis map 114
    Wallace Line 120
Asia Minor 37, 39, 41
Association for Research and
    Enlightenment 102, 108, 111
Assyrians *68*
astral travel 106, 163
At-hothes 67
Athens 14, 16, 18, 19, *19*, 22, 24
Atlantean Halls of Records 103, 108
'Atlantes' (Toltec statues) *85*, 87
Atlantic Ocean 13
    Azores 70–1

Canary Islands 72–3
Donnelly's theories 62
Gibraltar 'plug' broken 45
Hy-Brasil 136–7
islands 49
Mid-Atlantic Ridge 25, 63, 70
Piri Reis map 114
plate tectonics 25
Spartel Island 74–5
trade between Mediterranean and
    South America 59, 99
Atlantis: daughter civilizations 62, 66
    destruction of 22–3
    and environmentalism 164–5
    evidence for 24–5
    and foundation of Egypt 14–15
    maps of *10*
    modern versions of 8
    as a parable for modern society 11,
        165
    in Plato's writings 8–9, 11, 13–16,
        18–25
    and reincarnation 163
    rulers 67
    and spiritual values 162–3
    technology 106
Atlantology, evolution of 10–11
Atlas 20, 38, 39, 66
atomic bombs 106
Aton *62*
Aurora Borealis 148
Australia 126
Austronesian languages 123
Avalon 138
Ayirangaal Mandapam, Madurai 128
Azaes 70
Azores 24, 25, *25*, 49, 63, 70–1, 136,
    156
Aztecs 15, 50–1, 59, 66, 69, 85, 86,
    110
Aztlan 51

B

Babylonians 9, *22*, 66, 67
Bacon, Sir Francis 64–5, 98–9, *98*
Bahamas 101, 108–9
Bailey, Alice 145, 161
Baltic 149
baths 16
'beach rock' formations 108–9, *109*
Belial 104, 105, *105*
Belize 52
Benalcásar, Captain Sebastian de 154, *154*
Bensalem 98, 99
Berbers 72, 110
Besant, Annie 88
Bible 30, 67, 80, 91, 104, 134, 152
Bimini 103, 105, 108–9
Bimini Road 108–9, *109*, 116
Black Pyramids, Guimar 73
Black Sea 37, 40, 69
Blavatsky, Madame 62, *82*, 86, 95, 161, 162, 163
    background 82
    and Hyperborea 151
    Isis Unveiled 82
    and Lemuria 81, 82–3, 84–5, 120
    Root Races theory 84–5
    The Secret Doctrine 83, 102
    and Shambhala 142, 145
    Theosophy 82, 88
Blessed Isle 137
Bogotá 155
Bolivia 59
Bolsheviks 144, 146
Boreas 150
Borneo 124
Bosporus Straits 37
Brahmatina 146
Brasseur de Bourbourg, Abbé Charles-Étienne 52–3
Brazil 114, 137
Breasal 137
Brendan the Navigator, St 137
Brennan, Herbie 56
Bristol 136
Britain 146, 150, 152
Brittany 133, 134–5
bronze *68*, 69

Bronze Age 91, 122
    eruption of Thera 42
    Helike 29
    Minoans 40–1
    Mycenae 36
    Plato's description of Atlantis 8–9, 16, 24, 76
    Sea Peoples 32–3
    Tartessos 30–1
    Troy 37
Buddhism 92, 142–5
buildings 21
bull cult 16, 41, *41*
Bulwer Lytton, Edward 146
Bushmen 85
Byzantine Empire 159

C

Cabot, John 136
Cadiz 30, 31
calendar, Egyptian 59
Cambay, Gulf of 127
canals: Altiplano 56–7
    Atlantis 20, 21
    Aztec 51
    Sundaland 124
    Toltecs 86
Canary Islands 15, 24, *24*, 25, 69, 72–3, 85
Cantre'r Gwaelod 135
Cardigan Bay 134, 135
Caribbean 49, 101, 103, 108–11, 114
Carthage 31, 34–5, *34*, *35*, 48, 49, 72, 110
Castleden, Rodney 41
Caucasus 121, 159
cave art *111*
Cayce, Edgar 62, 101, 102–6, *103*, 108, 109, 161, 162, 163, 165
Celts 131, 133, 134, 138–9
Central America 15, 52–3, 62, 66, 83, 110
Central Asia 144, 146, 158
Chaldeans 66
Chandragupta II Vikramaditya *95*
channelling 163
Chiapenese 66
Chichen Itza *63*

Children of the Law of One 104–5
China 120, 146
Christ 145, 159
Christianity 67, 91, 104, 134, 139, 144, 145, 158–9
Churchward, James 90–5, *94*, 97, 120
Cíbola 156–7
City of the Golden Gates 86
City of Lions 132, *133*
City of the Seven Pagodas 126–7
City of the Waters 86
city-states 28–9, 30–1
Classical Atlantology 10
Cleitas 16, 20
Cliff Palace, Mesa Verde National Park *157*
climate 124
coins *28*, *70*, 71
Collina-Girard, Jacques 74–5
Collins, Andrew 101, 110
Colombia 154, 155
Columbus, Christopher 49, 101, 110, 114, 136, 156
Con 156
continental drift 80, 81
Cook, Captain 148
Cooper, Diana 162–3
Copper Scroll (Dead Sea Scroll) *104*
Corinth, Gulf of 28
Cornwall 132–3, 152
Coronado, Francisco Vásquez de 157
Cortés, Hernán 51
Corvo 70, 71, *71*
'Cosmic Fire' 145
creation myths 9, 51, 59, 66, 91, 110
Crete 40–1, 42, 43
Critias II 14, 15
Critias III 15
Cro-Magnons 85
Croesus, King 38
cross symbol 66, 67, *67*
Crusades 158–9
crystal power 10, 106
Cuba 49, 101, 110–11, 114
culture heroes 9, 110
Cuzco 54
Cyprus 44–5, *45*
Cyprus Arc 44–5, *45*

D

Dahut 134
Dana 139
Darwin, Charles 80
David, King of India 159
Day, John 136
Dead Sea Scrolls *104*, 105
death rays 106, 165
Delhi, Pillar of 94–5, *95*
Delos 151
Deros 149
Deucalion 9, 23, *23*
Deutsche Arbeiterpartei (DAP) 153
Devil 134, 139
Diaz-Montexano, Georgeos 75
Dido 34
diffusionism 9
Diodorus Siculus 70
Dogger Bank 76–7
Dogger Hills 76
Dolphin Ridge 63
Donnelly, Ignatius 14, 64–7, *65*, 93, 95,
    103, 162, 164
   Atlantis: The Antediluvian World 61, 62–3,
     64, 66, 83, 102
   Atlantology 10
   and the Azores 70–1
   Caesar's Column 65
   and the Canary Islands 72
   *The Great Cryptogram: Francis Bacon's Cipher
     in Shakespeare's Plays* 64–5
   importance of the alphabet 68
   and the Lisbon tsunami 75
   on pyramids 15
   Ragnarok, the Age of Fire and Gravel 64
Douarnenez Bay 134
Doyle, Richard *139*
Dravidians 126, 128
Dropides 14
Drust, King of Lothian 133

E

earthquakes: in the Altiplano 58
   destruction of Helike 28, 29
   Gibraltar 'plug' broken 45
   Kumari Kandam 126
   Lisbon *75*

Spartel Island 75
   Tantalis 39
Easter Island 90
Echeyde 73
Eckart, Dietrich 153
Eden, Garden of 11, 23, 67, 122, 159,
   163
Egypt 92
   ankh symbol 67
   as Atlantan colony 62
   calendar 59
   and Crete 41
   and the eruption of Thera 42–3
   legend of Troy 36–7
   pyramids 14–15, 69, 105, 117, *117*
   and Queen Móo 53
   and the Sea Peoples 32–3
   Sphinx *116*, 117
   sun worship *62*, 66, 67, *90*
   and Sundaland 121
El Dorado 154–5
El Salvador 52
electricity 106
elephants 53, *53*, 76, 90, 120, 124, *125*
Elfhame 138
Elissar, Queen 34
Elizabeth I, Queen of England 98
Elysian Fields 48–9, 67, 138
Embarr 139
Empire of the Sun 90–1
energy: crystal power 106
   energy beings 103, 104
   Vril 87, 146, 147
Enlightenment 99
environmentalism 164–5
Epic of Gilgamesh 9
Erlingsson, Ulf 76–7
Estevanico (Esteban the Moor) 157
Etelenty 14
Ethiopia 66, 159
Etruscans 70
euhemerism 66
Euler, Leonard *148*
evolution, theory of 80
Ezekiel 30

F

fairies 138–9, *139*
Fairyland 138, 139
the Fall 11, 23
Faroes 152
fascism 82
Fiji 90
firestones 106
Fischer, Dr Heinz 148–9
floods and flood myths 9, *9, 22–3*, 23, 62, 66
   in the Altiplano 58
   Gibraltar 'plug' broken 45
   India 119
   Indo-Pacific region 120
   Mu 53
   Tartessos 31
Florida *48*, 156
Flying Saucer magazine *149*
Fortunate Isles 48, 137, 138
fossils 80, 81
France 134–5

G

Gadeiros 31
Gades 30, 31
Galanopoulos, Angelos 42, 43
Garden of Eden 11, 23, 67, 122, 159,
   163
gardens 16
Gardens of Alcinous 67
Gardens of the Hesperides 48, 67
Gardner, Marshall *148*
Genghis Khan 159
geology 10, 24–5, 80, 108–9
German nationalism 153
German Workers' Party 153
Gibraltar, Straits of 30, 44, 45, 74–5, *74*
Gilgamesh 9
Giza 113, 117, *117*
Gnosticism 162–3
goats, sacrifices 73
Gobi Desert 145
Goethe, Johann Wolfgang von 88
Golden Age 11, 22, 163
Golden Lotus Pond, Madurai 128
gopurams (towers) 128
Graciosa Island *24*

Gradlon, King of Armorica 134, *135*
Grail legend 99, 142, 144–5
Grand Canyon 157
Great Game 146
Great Pyramid, Tenochtitlan 50
Great US Exploring Expedition (1838–42) 148
Greater Atlantis 21
Greece: alphabet 68–9
  Dark Age 37
  flood myths 9, 23, *23*
  gods 67
  Helike 28–9
  Hyperborea 150
  knowledge of the Americas 48
  mythical islands in the west 48–9
  Sea Peoples 33
Greenland 152
Gresham College, London *99*
Guanches 72–3
Guatavitá, Lake 155, *155*
Guatemala 52
Guenuole, St 134
Guimar, pyramids 72, 73, *73*
Gutscher, Marc-André 75
Guyana 154
Gwyddno Garanhir, King 134, 135

H

Hades 38, 148
Haeckel, Ernst *80*, 81
Hall, Manly *8*
Halley, Edmund 148
Halls of Records 103, 108
Hancock, Graham 10, 113, 115, 116–17
Hannibal 34
Hapgood, Charles 115
Haunebu 32
Hawaii 90, 97, 123
healing 106
Hebrew alphabet 68
Hebrews 66, 67
Hecataeus 48
Helike 28–9
Hell 148
Hemis 92, *93*
Hendrich, Hermann *9*

Hennig, Richard 31
Herodotus *49*
heroes 9, 110
Herzog, Werner 154
Hesperides 48, 67
Hess, Rudolf *152*, 153
Heyerdahl, Thor 72
Hilton, James 142, *145*
Himachal Pradesh 145
Himalayas 82, 95, 142–3, 145, 146
Himmler, Heinrich 147
Hinduism 9, 66, 67, 84, 85, 119, 142
Hiram of Tyre 30, 59
Hissarlik 37, *37*
Hitler, Adolf 147, 153
Hittites 32, 39
Hodge, Stephen 25, 56
Hollow Earth theories 142, 146, 147, 148–9, *148*, *149*, 153
Holocaust 147
Holy Grail 99, 142, 144–5
Holy Land 158
Homer 36, 38, 67
Honduras 52
Horn of Africa 158, *158*
Huffstickler, Carol 109
hunter-gatherers 122
Hutton, Shaaron 162–3
Hy-Brasil 136–7, 138
'hybrid races' 85
Hyperborea 84, 150–1, *150*, *151*, 153

I

Iberia 31, 33, 110, 114, *114*, 156
Ice Age 74, 76, 110, 116, 119, 121, 124
Iceland 152, *153*
Idaii Sangam 128
The Iliad 36
Incas 9, 15, 54–5, 66, 69, 91, 155
India 62, 92, 94
  early migrations 121
  flood myths 9, 119
  geology 80
  Indo-Europeans 66, 123
  land bridges 81
  languages 123
  legend of Kumari Kandam 126–7

  St Thomas travels to 158
  submerged megalithic structures 116
Indian Ocean 83, 119, 125, *158*
Indo-China 125
Indonesia 124, 125
Ireland 49, 67, 77, 132, 136, 137, 139
Iron Age *77*
irrigation 21, 124
Isaiah 30
Isis 53
Islam 144
Island of the Saints 137
islands: palaeo-islands 74
  phantom islands 136, 137
Isle of Cranes 51
Isle of Delight 137
Isle of Man 152
Isle of the Seven Cities 156
Isle of Youth 110
Isles of the Blessed 48, 49, 156
Ismaili Shiites 144
Isolde 132
Istanbul 114
Italy 33
Izmir 39

J

James I, King of England 98
James, Peter 38, 39
Jansen, Olaf 146
Japan 96, 114, 144
Jerusalem 159
Jews 162
John the Presbyter 159
Jomon culture 97
Jonah 30
Joy, Barbara 71
Judaeo-Christianity 144
Justus van Gent *15*

K

Kalachakra tantra 142, 144, 145
Kalahari Bushmen 85
Kalapa 142, 143, *144*
Kansas 157
Kara-Khitan Khanate 159

Kazakhstan 145
Kent 152
Khafra, Pharaoh *116*
Kircher, Athanasius *10*
Kizilkum Desert 145
Knights Templar 99
Knossos 40, *40*, 41
Kogutski, Felix 88
Koreshanity 148
Körös, Csoma de 145
Krakatoa, Mount 42, *124*, 125
Kühne, Dr Rainer 31, 32, 33, 37
Kulasekhara Pandy, King 128
Kulika king 142, 143, *144*
Kumari Kandam 126–7, 128

L

Ladakh 92, *93*
Lady of Elx 31, *31*
land bridges 80–1, 84, 120–1
Land of the Young 138–9
Landa, Bishop Diego de 52–3, 68, 69, *69*,
    93
Land's End 132
language 68–9, 123
lasers 106
Law of One 104
Le Plongeon, Augustus 53, 62, 68, 93, 95
Lemuria 10, 79, 80–5, 88–9, 97, 120, 145
lemurs 81, *81*
Leo, constellation of 117
Leonais 133
Lethowstow 133
Letter of Prester John 159
Levant 34, 121
Libya 32, 37, 41
Linear B script 41
linguistics 68–9, 123
Lisbon earthquake (1755) 75, *75*
literature, Mayan 52–3, *52*
Little Sole Bank 133
López de Gómara, Francisco 50
Lost Horizon (film) 142, *145*
Low Countries 152
Lowland Hundreds 135
Lydia 38–9
Lyonesse 132–3, 138

M

Madagascar 80, 81, 123
Madhurapuri 128
Madinat Habu *33*
Madurai 126, *127*, 128, *129*
Mag Mell 138
Magi 159
Mahabalipuram 126–7
Mahedra, Mount 126
Malagasy language 123
Malay Archipelago 120
Malay language 123
Malaysia 80, 81, 124, 125
Maldives 126
Mannsperger, Dietrich 37
Manoa 155
Manu, King 119
Maori language 123
maps: phantom islands 136, 137
    Piri Reis map 114–15, *114*, 116
    world maps *49*
Marcellus 49
Mark, King 132
Marseilles 152
Massalia 152
Matsya 9, 119
Maya 52–3, *52–3*, 62, 110
    language 68–9, *69*
    pyramids 15, 52, 53, *63*, 69
    sun worship 66
    Troano Codex 52, 53, *92*, 93
Mediterranean: Cyprus Arc 44–5
    Gibraltar 'plug' broken 45
    Sea Peoples 32–3
    trade with South America 59, 99
    see also individual city-states and countries
Meenakshi 128
megalithic culture 77
Melanesians *122*
Merenptah, Pharaoh 32
Mérida, Bishop of 156
Mesa Verde National Park *157*
Meso-American civilizations 50–3, 59,
    110
Mesopotamia 66, 69, 92
Messiah 145
metallurgy 69, 94–5, 125
Mexico 66, 86, 105, 110, 156–7

Mexico, Valley of 50
Mexico City *50*, 51
Mid-Atlantic Ridge 25, 63, 70
mineral wealth 21
Minoan civilization 40–1, 42–3
Minos, King 40
Miocene 45
Mongolia 144, 145
Mongols 85, 144
Móo, Queen 53
Moors 110, 156
Mordred 132
Morvac'h 134, *135*
Mount's Bay 133
Mu 10, 53, 79, 90–3, 95, 97, 120
Muisca 155
Multan 144
Muslims 156, 159
Muthal Sangam 128
Muvians 90–1
Mycenae 33, 36, 40
Mystical Atlantology 10
myths: creation myths 9, 51, 59, 66, 91,
    110
    culture heroes 9, 110
    euhemerism 66
    the Fall 11, 23
    see also flood myths

N

Naacal 92, 93
Naga 92
Nahua people 51
Nahuatl language 86
nanotechnology 165
Native Americans 110, 154, 156
Natuna Besar 124
navigation 69, 125
Nazi Party 82, 85, 147, 149, 153
NCV Steel 95
Neolithic *123*
Nestorian Christians 159
New Age philosophy 82, 88, 95, 142, 145,
    161, 162–3
New Mexico 157
Newfoundland 136
Newgrange *76*, 77
Niamh 139

Nile Valley 62
Nininger City 64, *64*, 65
Niobe 38
Noah's Ark 9, 23
Norse myths 66, 67, 138
North Africa 72, 110
North America: Cabot reaches 136
   Lake Agassiz 121, 125
   Seven Cities of Gold 156
North Pole 148, *149*
North Sea 76, 149
Norway 76
Nova Scotia 99
nuclear weapons 165

O

Oak Island 99
O'Brien, Christian 71
Oceanus 48, 49
Odin 66
The Odyssey 36
Ogygia 70
Oisín 139
Okinawa 96
Old Testament 104
Olympus 67
Omagua 155
Oppenheimer, Dr Stephen 121, 122,
   123
Orellana, Francisco de 154–5
orichalcum 21, 54–5
Orion's Belt 117
Ossendowski, Ferdynand 146, *146*
Otto of Freising 158
Ottoman empire 114

P

Pacific Ocean 15, 79–99
   flood myths 120
   Lemuria 83
   Mu 90–1
   Sunda peoples 125
   Yonaguni 96–7
Pakistan 144
palaeo-islands 74
Palaeolithic Era 74, 75

Palenque 67
Pampa Aullagus 54, 56–7
Panchen Lama, Third 145
Paradise 11, 49, 136, 139, 162
Parthenon, Athens *19*
Parvati 128
Patagonia 114
Patrick, St 139
Pausanias 29
Peloponnese 28
Persia 48, 66, 85, 159, 162
Peru 54
petroglyphs, Mayan *53*
Phoenicians 48, 110
   alphabet 68
   and the Azores 70
   Carthage 34–5
   coins *70*, 71
   gods 67
   sun worship 66
   and Tartessos 30–1
Pico, Mount 70
Pico Island 70
pictograms, Mayan *52*
Picts 133
Pillar of Delhi 94–5, *95*
Pillar of Poseidon 16
Pillars of Hercules 22, 30, 31, 37, 41, 45,
   74, 75, 85
Pindar 150
Piri Reis map 114–15, *114*, 116
plants, Wallace Line 120–1
Plate, River 59
plate tectonics 24–5
Plato 8–9, 13–16, 18–25, 122
   and Carthage 34–5
   and the Cyprus Arc 44, 45
   dating of Atlantis legend 76
   describes elephants in Atlantis 53, 124
   descriptions of canals 56–7
   on destruction of Atlantis 22–3
   and destruction of Helike 28
   Dialogue of Critias 8, 13, 15, 18–19, 22–3,
     25, 28
   Dialogue of Timaeus 8, 13, 14, 15, 18–19,
     22, 28, 37, 47, 49
   evidence for Atlantis 24–5
   locates Atlantis in Atlantic Ocean 62, 63

   and Minoan civilization 41
   in *New Atlantis* 98
   The Republic 18–19, 99
   Revisionist Atlantology and 10, 30
   and the Sea Peoples 32
   sources 14, 36
   and Tartessos 30, 31
   and Thera 43
   topographical descriptions 8, 54, 71, 75,
     110, 124
Pleiades 109
Pliny the Elder 72, 150
Plutarch 49
pollution 165
Polo, Marco 159
Polynesia 97
Poopó, Lake 54, 56–9, *58, 59*
Porto, Archbishop of 156
Portugal 49, 70, 114, 156
Poseidia 108
Poseidon 16, 20, 28–9, *29*, 49, 55
Poseidonis 85
pottery 69, 122
power station 106
Prasann, Dr Sunil 124
pre-Columbian civilizations 110
Prester John 158–9
Proclus 49
Proto-scientific Atlantology 10
Psonchis 14, 15, 37
psychic energy 87, 106
Ptolemaic maps 114
Pueblo Indians 157, *157*
Punic Wars 34
Punta del Este 110, *111*
Puranas 9
pyramids 14–15, 69
   Aztecs 50, 51, 69
   Canary Islands 72, 73, *73*
   Egypt 14–15, 69, 105, 117, *117*
   Inca 55, 69
   Maya 15, 52, 53, *63*, 69
   Mesopotamia 69
Pyrrha *23*
Pytheas of Massalia 152–3

Q

Quechua language 54
Quetzlcóatl 51, *51*, 55, *85*
Quillacas *55*
Quimper 134

R

Ra 67, *90*, 91
Ra-Mu 91
race, Root Races theory 84–5, 88, 151
Raleigh, Sir Walter 155
Rama 67
Rameses III, Pharaoh 32, 33, *33*
Ray-mi festival 66
reincarnation 102, 163
religion: Mu 91
    Theosophy 82
    see also Christianity; Hinduism; Islam; sun
        worship
remote viewing 163
Revisionist Atlantology 10, 30
rice paddies 124
rivers, Sundaland 125
Rmoahals 85
Rock, Joseph *145*
Roerich, Nicholas 144–5
Romans 70, 81
Rome 34
Root Races theory 84–5, 88, 151
Rosenberg, Alfred 153
Royal Society 99, *99*
Rudbeck, Olof 151, *151*
rulers 20
Russia 146
Russian Revolution 144, 146

S

Saaremaa 152
Sahara Desert 117
St Brendan's Isle 137
St Michael's Mount 133
St Patrick's Causeway 135
Sais 14, 15
Salomon's House, Bensalem 99
Samarkand 159
San Miguel 156

Sangams 126, 128
Sanskrit language 66, 68
Santorini 40, 42–3
Saracens 158–9
Sargasso Sea 106
Sarmast, Robert 44–5, *44*
Sarn Badrig 135
Scandinavia 62, 66, 150, 151, 152
Schäfer, Ernst *147*
Schliemann, Heinrich *36*, 95
Schliemann, Paul 95
Schulten, Adolf 31
Scilly Isles 132, 133, *133*
Sclater, Philip 81
Scotland 133, 152
Scott-Elliot, William 83, 86, 89, 95
sea levels 74, 116, 126
Sea Peoples 32–3, *32*, *33*, 59
Second Coming 105, 145
Seithenyn, Prince 135
Seljuk Turks 159
Semites 85
Septe Cidades 156
Seven Caves myth 110
Seven Cities of Gold 110, 156–7
Seven Stones, Cornwall 132
Shakespeare, William 64–5, 99
Shambhala 142–5, *144*, 146
Shangri-La 142–3
Shaver, Richard 149
Shetlands 152
Shiites 144
Shiva 128
Siberia 150
Sicily 18, 35
Sipylus, Mount 38, 39
Socrates 15, 18
Sodom and Gomorrah 134
solar cross 66, 67, *67*
solar power 106
Solomon, King 30, 59
Solon 14, 15, *15*, 36, 38–9, 77
solstice, summer 73
Sons of Belial 104–5, 106
South Africa 80
South America 62
    Altiplano 54–9
    El Dorado 154–5

Incas 54–5
    Piri Reis map 114
    pyramids 15
South-East Asia 92, 121, 123, 126
South Pole 115, 148
Spain 59, 75, 156
Spanish conquistadors 50, 51, 52, 54, 154–5,
    156–7
Spartel Island 74–5
Sphinx 14, 105, 113, *116*, 117
spiritual values 162–3
Spitsbergen 152
Sri Lanka 126
Sri Meenakshi Temple, Madurai *127*,
    128
statues, Toltec *85*, 87
Steiner, Rudolf 62, 88–9, *88*, *89*, 95, 145,
    161
Stewart, Andrew C. *11*
Stone Age 9, 119
    Dogger deluge 76–7
    Guanches 72
    Jomon culture 97
    Maya 52
    palaeo-islands 74
    Spartel Island 75
    Sundaland 121, 122, 124–5
Storegga continental slope 76
Strabo 36, 133, 152–3
submarines 106
Suchandra, King of Shambhala 142
sun worship 66, 67
    Egypt *62*, 66, 67, *90*
    Guanches 73
    Mu 91
    pyramids of Guimar 73
Sunda Shelf 121, 124, 125
Sundaland 120–1, 122–5
Sundareswar 128
Suppiluliuma II, King of the Hittites 32
Sutlej Valley 145
Symmes, John Cleves, Jr. 148
Syria 159

T

tablets, Naacal 92, 93
Tagalog language 123

Taiwan 97
Tambora 42
Tamil Nadu 128
Tamils 126
Tantalis 38–9
Tantalus 38–9
Tara 77, *77*
Tarshish 30, 59
Tartessos 30–1, *30*, 33, 59
Tasmania *84*, 85
Tauca, Lake 59
technology 106, 124–5
Teed, Cyrus 148
Teide, Mount 73
telepathy 10, 89
Temple of Apollo, Delos 151
Temple of Poseidon, Atlantis 16, *17*, 20, 21, 77
Tenerife 72
Tennyson, Alfred, Lord 132
Tenochtitlan 50, 51
Teotihuacan 67
Terra Australis Incognito 114
Tesla, Nikola 106
Texcoco, Lake *50*, 51
Thailand 120
Theosophy 81, 82–6, 88, 102–3, 142, 144, 145
Thera 40, 41, 42–3, *42*, *43*
Thirteen Treasures of Britain 135
Thomas, St 158
Thomas the Rhymer 138
Thoth 67
Thrace 150
Thule 151, 152–3
Thule Society 152, 153
Tibet 142–3, 147, *147*
Tibetan Buddhism 142, 143
Tierra del Fuego 114
Tigris, River 159
Tir Nan Og 138–9
Titans 38
Titicaca, Lake 54, 55, 58
Tiwanaku 56
Toltecs 83, 85, *85*, 86–7
Topkapi Palace, Istanbul 114
trade, between Mediterranean and South America 59, 99

Trevelyan 132
Tristan 132–3
Troano Codex 52, 53, *92*, 93
Troy 36–7, *36*, *37*
tsunamis: Boxing Day tsunami (2004) 126–7, *165*
   destruction of Helike 28, 29
   Dogger Island 76–7
   eruption of Thera 42
   Gibraltar 'plug' broken 45
   Kumari Kandam 126
   Lisbon 75, *75*
   Spartel Island 75
Tuatha de Danaan 139
Tula *85*, 87
Tunapa 55
Turanians 85
turbidite 75
Turkey 37, 38
Tyre 34

U

UFOs 109, 147, 153
Ugarit 32
Ultima Thule 152
underworlds 148
Ungern-Sternberg, Baron von (Mad Baron) 146
United States of America 103
Ussher, Bishop 80
Utnapishtim 9, *22*

V

Valentine, Dr Manson 108
Valhalla 138
Venus 85
Vikings 136
Viracocha 9, 55
volcanoes: Azores 71, *71*
   Canary Islands 73
   Sundaland 125
   Thera 40, 41, 42–3, *43*
Votun 66
Vril 87, 146, 147

W

Waldorf Schools 88
Wales 134, 135
Wallace, Alfred 120–1, *121*
Wallace Line 120–1, *120*
The War of the Sons of Light Against the Sons of Darkness (Dead Sea Scroll) 105
West Africa 114, *114*
West Indies 101, 108–9, 114, 156
White Island 51
White Russians 144, 146
Whitehead, A.N. 18
Wickboldt, Werner 31
Winwaloe, St 134
Wotan 66
writing, Mayan 52–3, *52*

Y

Yelü Dashi 159
Yonaguni 96–7, *96*, *97*, 108, 116
Ys 134
Yucatán peninsula 52, 105
Yugas 84

Z

Zangger, Eberhard 36–7
Zelitsky, Paulina 110–11
Zeus 22–3, 38
Zhang Zhung texts 145
Zippsala 39
Zodiac 67
Zuni 157

Acknowledgements

AUTHOR ACKNOWLEGEMENTS
Thanks to Sandra, Clare and the rest of the team at Godsfield.

PICTURE ACKNOWLEGEMENTS
akg-images 10, 36, 39, 49, 50, 80, 89, 98, 105, 152, 163; /Bildarchiv Monheim/Rainer Kiedrowski 35; /Hervé Champollion 116; /Columbia Pictures/Album 145; /Peter Connolly 34; /IMF 3/ILM/Album 164; /Erich Lessing 15, 18, 29, 33, 41, 62, 68, 70; /Jean-Louis Nou 95, 104; /ullstein bild 147. **Alamy**/Carmo Correia 71; /Rick Frehsee 109; /Mary Evans Picture Library 9, 22, 23, 52, 91, 103; /Melba Photo Agency 111; /Nature Picture Library 24; /North Wind Picture Archives 124; /The Print Collector 43; /Robert Harding Picture Library Ltd 155; /Anders Ryman 59; /SAS 122; /Westend61 25. **The Art Archive**/Archaeological Museum, Tikal, Guatemala/Dagli Orti 53; /Dagli Orti 42, 51; /Musée du Louvre, Paris 32. **Art Directors & Trip**/Tibor Bognar 157. **bpk/Münzkabinett, Staatliche Museen zu Berlin** 28. **The Bridgeman Art Library**/British Library, London, UK 158; /Giraudon, Min. Défense - Service Historique de l'armée de Terre, France 48; /Musée Guimet, Paris, France 144; /National Library of Australia, Canberra, Australia 84; /Private Collection/The Stapleton Collection 139. **Christie's Images Ltd. 2002**/Norman Alfred William Lindsay 150. **Corbis UK Ltd**/Archivo Iconografico, S.A. 31; /Yann Arthus-Bertrand 37; /Bettmann 75; /Danny Lehman 85; /Chris Lisle 127; /Ric Ergenbright 93; /NASA 58; /Enzo & Paolo Ragazzini 125; Reuters 44, 55. **Santha Faiia** 96. **Fortean Picture Library** 8, 82, 83, 88, 94, 114, 148, 149; /Janet & Coin Bord 133; /Matthew Henry Brock 138; /Andrew C Stewart 11. **Getty Images**/AFP 165; /Daryl Benson 117; /Jean du Boisberranger 123; /Kim Heacox 115; /Hulton Archive 99; /Robert Harding World Imagery 19, 40, 76; /Stone 63; /Stone/Art Wolfe 81; /Roger Viollet 146. **Irish Image Collection**/QP 77. **Masahiro Kaji** 97. **Dr Rainer W Kühne/EUROMAP/ESA** 30. **Minnesota Historical Society**/Photograph by Shepherd 64, 65. **NASA**/Image courtesy Jacques Descloitres, MODIS Land Team 45 left; /Provided by the SeaWiFS project, NASA/Goddard Space Flight Center, and ORBIMAGE 74. **The Natural History Museum, London** 121. **Photo12.com**/Hachédé151; /Oronoz 92, 154. **Robert Sarmast, Author and Explorer** 45 right. **TopFoto.co.uk**/Roger-Viollet 135; /Werner Forman 153.

Executive Editor Sandra Rigby
Managing Editor Clare Churly
Executive Art Editor Sally Bond
Designers Annika Skoog & Claire Oldman (for Cobalt ID)
Illustrator Lee Gibbons
Picture Researcher Emma O'Neil
Production Controller Simone Nauerth